Art As Consciousness

The Call of the Invisible One

by

Mary Saint-Marie/Sheoekah

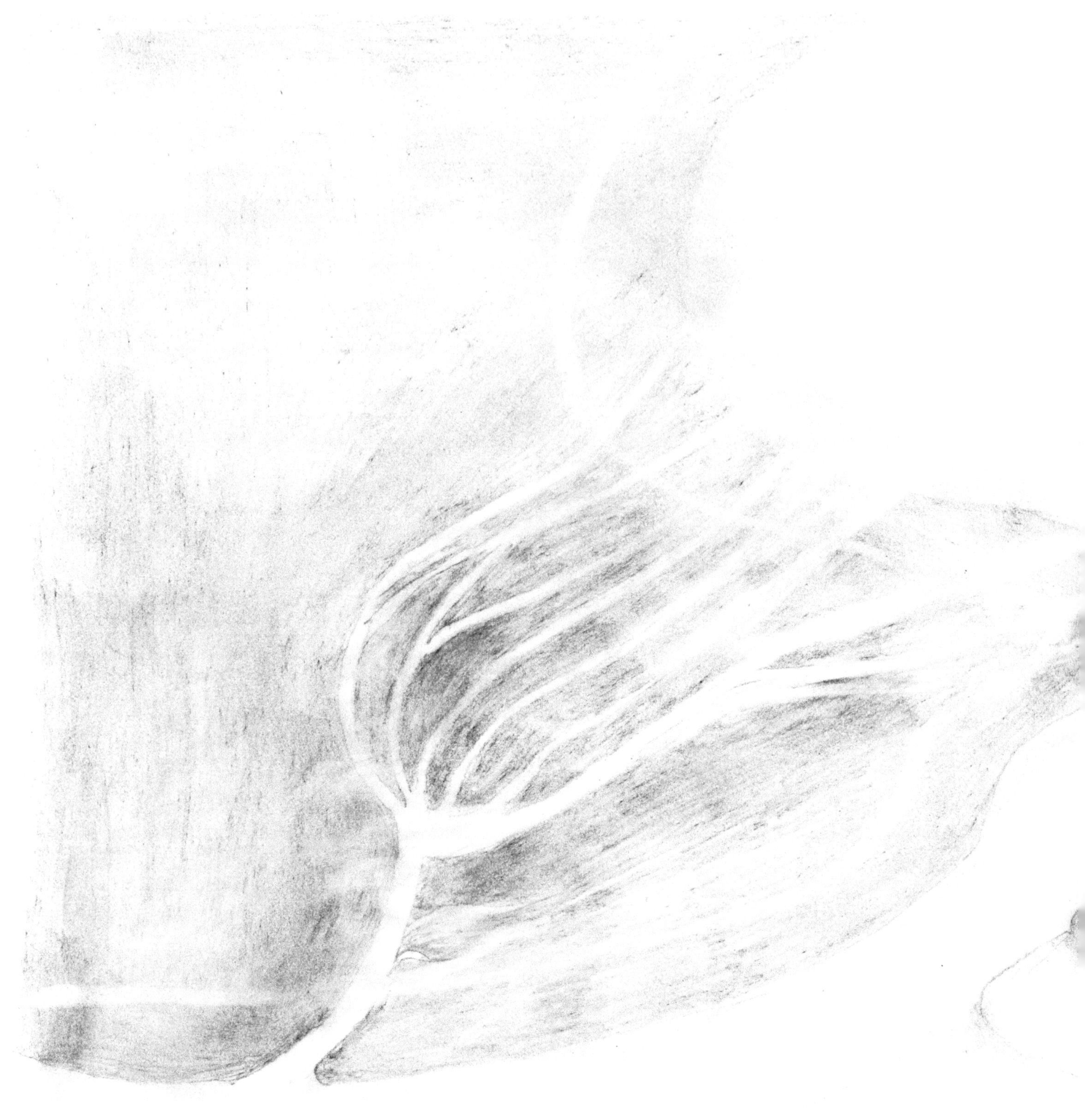

...a visual prayer of childlike wonder and innocence...
...a visual prayer of The formless One AS form...
...a visual prayer of the Unmanifest...as manifest...
...a visual of the personal as the Impersonal...
...a visual dedication and devotion to the Infinite...

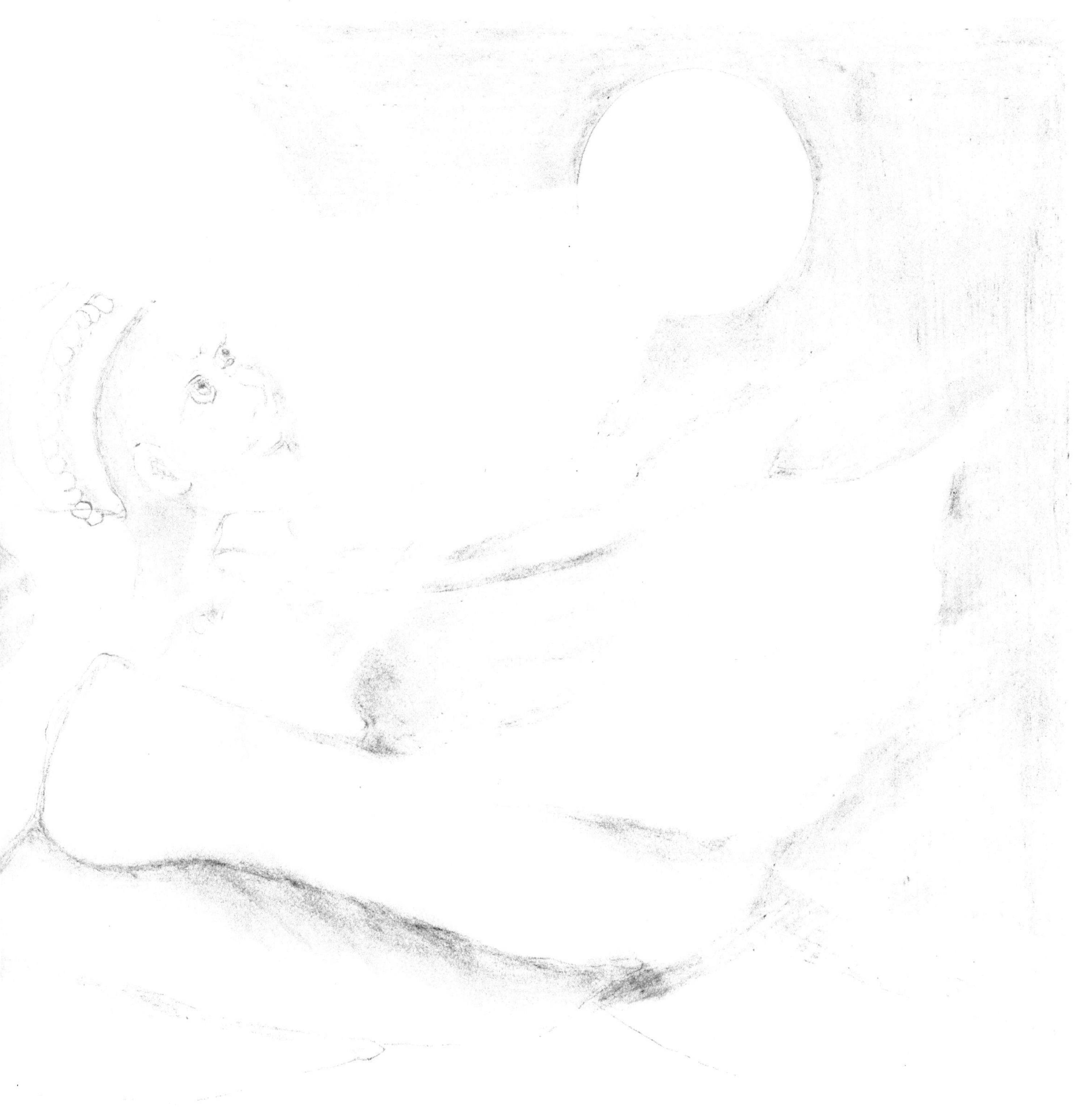

Art As Consciousness

The Call of the Invisible One

Published by Ancient Beauty Studio, www.marysaintmarie.com

ISBN: 978-0-9646572-2-9 (sc)

All artwork by Mary Saint-Marie

Front Cover Art: *Universes Within*

Back Cover Art: *The Image of Infinity*

Credit for NASA Public Domain Image of M35: Atlas Image obtained as part of the Two Micron All Sky Survey (2MASS), a joint project of the University of Massachusetts and the Infrared Processing and Analysis Center/California Institute of Technology, funded by the National Aeronautics and Space Administration and the National Science Foundation.

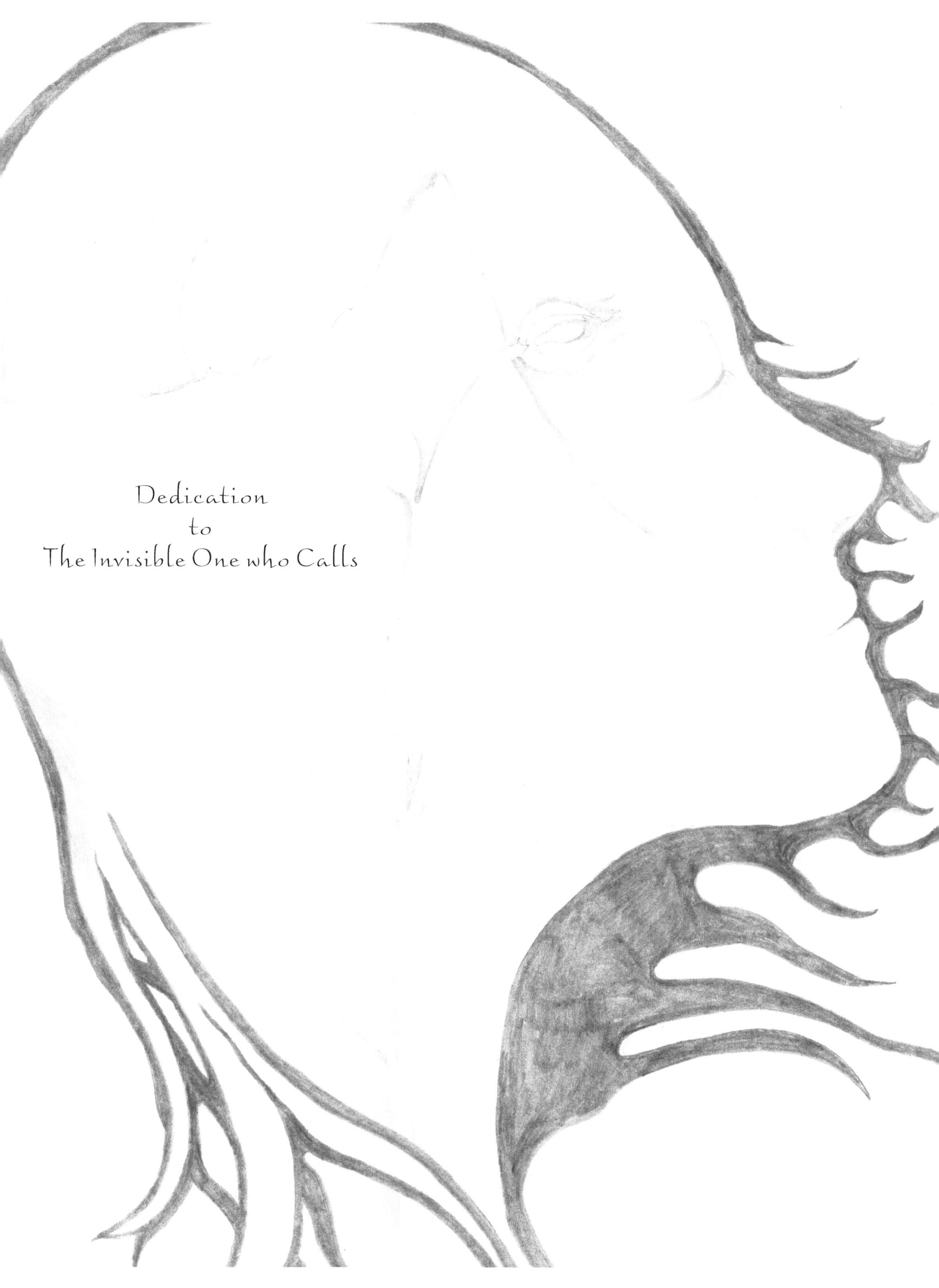

Dedication
to
The Invisible One who Calls

Contents

Acknowledgments

The Art-of-the-Soul for *ART AS CONSCIOUSNESS* came to me mainly in the mid to late seventies and the early to mid eighties, while I was raising my two beautiful daughters as a single mother.

I would like to thank Kimberly and Rebecca for being a strong spiritual presence in my life during their early years. While they were young, I created a huge art table from a door for them with supplies to create. As I expanded my life and consciousness, through the expression of aware visionary drawing, I was able to do it in the field of light where they, too, were creating pieces of such love in form.

During much of this time I was listening to sacred chants, especially those by Paramahansa Yogananda. And I listened to Gregorian chants, as well.

I deeply thank all the mothers and many friends from that period of my soul growth; you supported me in many ways as I moved into creative expressions attuned to the Spirit.

I thank the many teachers, such as Hazrat Inayat Khan, Paramahansa Yogananda, Muktananda, Walter and Lao Russell, Nicholas and Helena Roerich and mystic Joel Goldsmith. They inspired me with their luminous words, alive with Spirit, which inspired me often with images of Being that entered me, from the art paper, to be expressed as art.

Art as Consciousness became a passion.
A way to be devoted, dedicated and consecrated to the One.
A way to "feel" and realize The Call of the Invisible One.
A way to grow in intuition and awareness of co-incidents.
A personal, creative way of spiritual practice of the ever present Presence of the One!

I am grateful for the inspired images that came to me during these years. They became my friends and companions and spoke deeply to me of a reality beyond the belief of separation, i.e. human sense of good and bad. They spoke from the Realm of the Real. I learned to listen inwardly.

I am ever in love with the Earth and the Sky! They reveal themselves in life and in artistic expression as the One, unceasingly.

I am ever in love with Beauty and her role in our lives.

Appreciation fills me for the muse role of Laura Daen who shouts play!

Louis Mitchell has given me great technical and aesthetic support.

Aaron Rose has offered the gift of ease in the art form of designing a book. He has taken the "it's hard" out of it. And he is constantly listening to the soul of the book and bringing it into manifestation.

The technical support for this book has been magical:

Art Scanning by Louis Mitchell, LightSource Creations, Medford, Oregon

Design and Layout by Aaron Rose, Mount Shasta, California

Edited by Mary Saint-Marie and Aaron Rose

Photography by Rebecca Allen, Mount Shasta, California

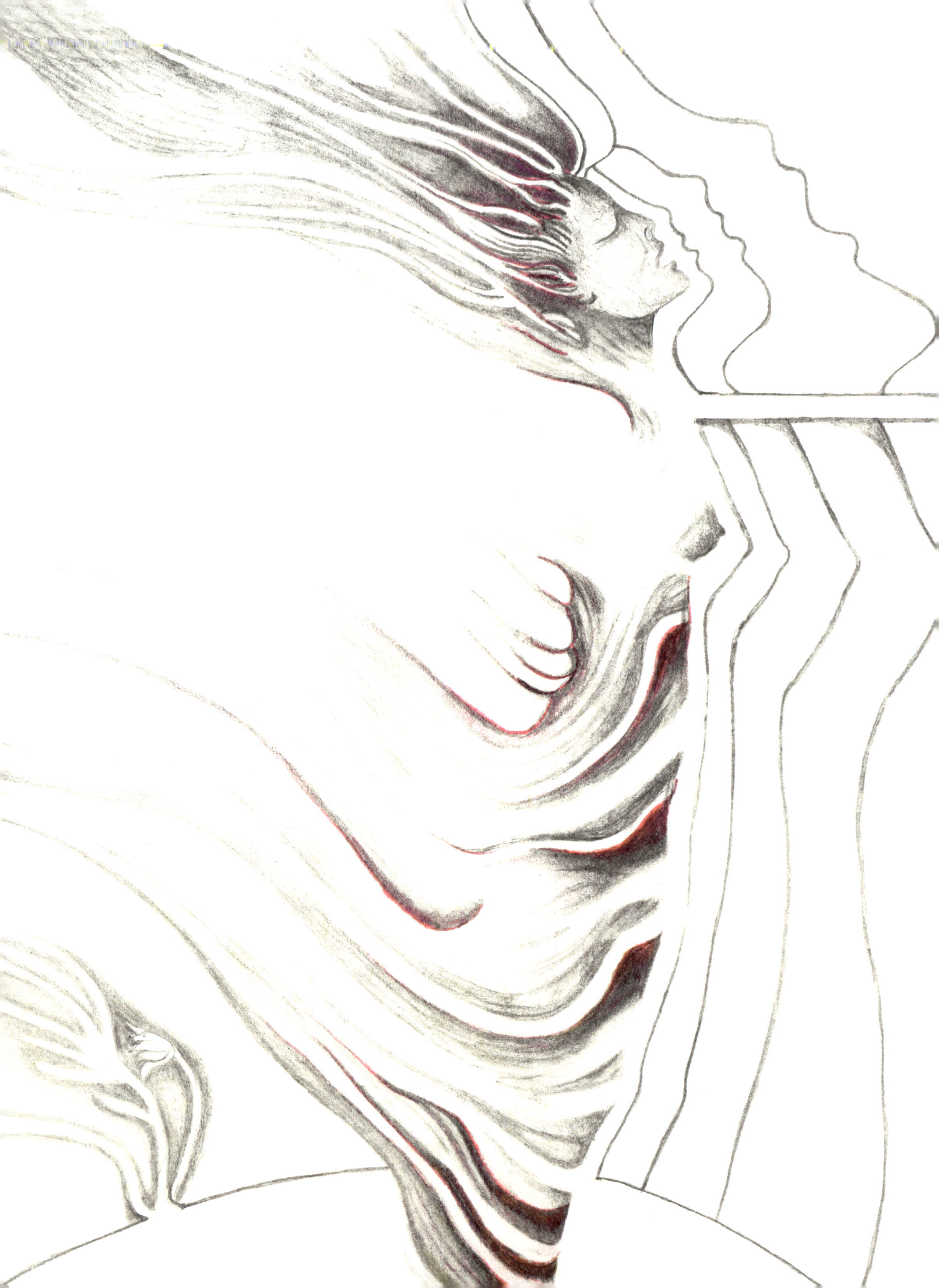

Introduction

The Sacred Call of the Invisible One

Ok. How does one write an introduction to a book whose art started 42 years ago and seemed to have its own life for 12 years?

A body of work began due to an immense inner impulse that was strong and relentless. It seemed that it was a matter of life or death. That impulse inspires me to create with endless mediums. Multi-media. That impulse also inspires the use of many techniques. Multi-technique. And the impulse inspires me to share of the "inner awakening" that ensued after a near-death experience in 1971, in a head on car collision, unveiling Soul Joy and Life as a Spirit, a Consciousness, the One. Multi-dimensional. And non-dimensional.

Chronicled in this book is mainly a "black and white" body of work. Simple pen and pencil drawings. Its stark simplicity and childlike nature invite the viewer inward. It is a carrier for innocence and purity. It invites an experience of the One Self. It invites one to exalt in consciousness and in the very cells. Embodied. The Infinite embodied!

In 1970, after my first daughter was born, I awoke to the beauty of light and dark. Black and white. I was unceasingly pointing out to her the play of shadows of the sun on the floor, walls, and surroundings. She loved it. And I loved it.

This art is a call. It is a call to feel within. It is a call to know from within. It is a call to express from within. The Self-expression is the current call to humanity.

This sacred art is a Call from the Invisible One. It called me. Now perhaps it will either call you or reflect or mirror that which you have already experienced and realized.

For about a 12 year period, this art style of mainly pen & ink and pencil held me. It embraced me. It taught me. It literally assisted in my awakening and in my ability to just Be in the ineffable joy of creation and of the awareness reflected to me.

Art as Consciousness and Art as Spiritual Practice

Art as Elevated Consciousness, no matter what the form, has the distinct and wondrous role of bypassing the human thinking and left brain analyzing. It may touch a much deeper place. The Soul. It may catalyze one to feel with the Soul faculty. Hours may pass and one is feeling the sacred presence. It does not come and go. It is sustained.

When one does feel with the Soul faculty, there is Joy. There is exaltation. And life changes. There is a sustained relationship with the Infinite and the relationship with the so-called outer world changes. The world is within and now love can flow freely...in whatever form.

It is an amazing sacred practice for staying in the here and now. It is a relentless teacher. For while one focuses and concentrates, one equally and simultaneously begins to decentrate and expand. One is one's own yin and yang. It is a foundation for epiphanies and realizations and revelations of unconditioned love.

This felt Essence may elevate one out of the denser human beliefs and conditions. They seem to melt away as the illusions that they are. A thought in time and space, ever creating dramas and discords.

This felt Essence may elevate one into pure Consciousness. There are no beliefs in separation and beliefs in duality in this pristine awareness. It is a luminous state that pervades space and time and is neither. It is beyond the realm of problems.

Art as Consciousness or I Am Awareness is mystical art. It may open visions and realizations and revelations, though there is nothing new. It may open the heart and even the mind. When the heart and mind do open, there is a sacred beholding....

Art as Consciousness unveils the synapse point between the formed and The Formless. The visible and The Invisible. One becomes aware of The Unmanifest as manifest. The sense of separation from the sacred does disappear.

Mystical art is an inner attunement. It speaks of the beauty of the Essence world that is everywhere present, in everyone and everything. It is a both a reflection and a revelation of world beyond the material. The Eternal.

Mystical art speaks about the Undivided One.

It speaks of Life as Awareness.

We are that I Am Awareness.
We are that…Alone.
There is no other.
Together…we are that.
The One.

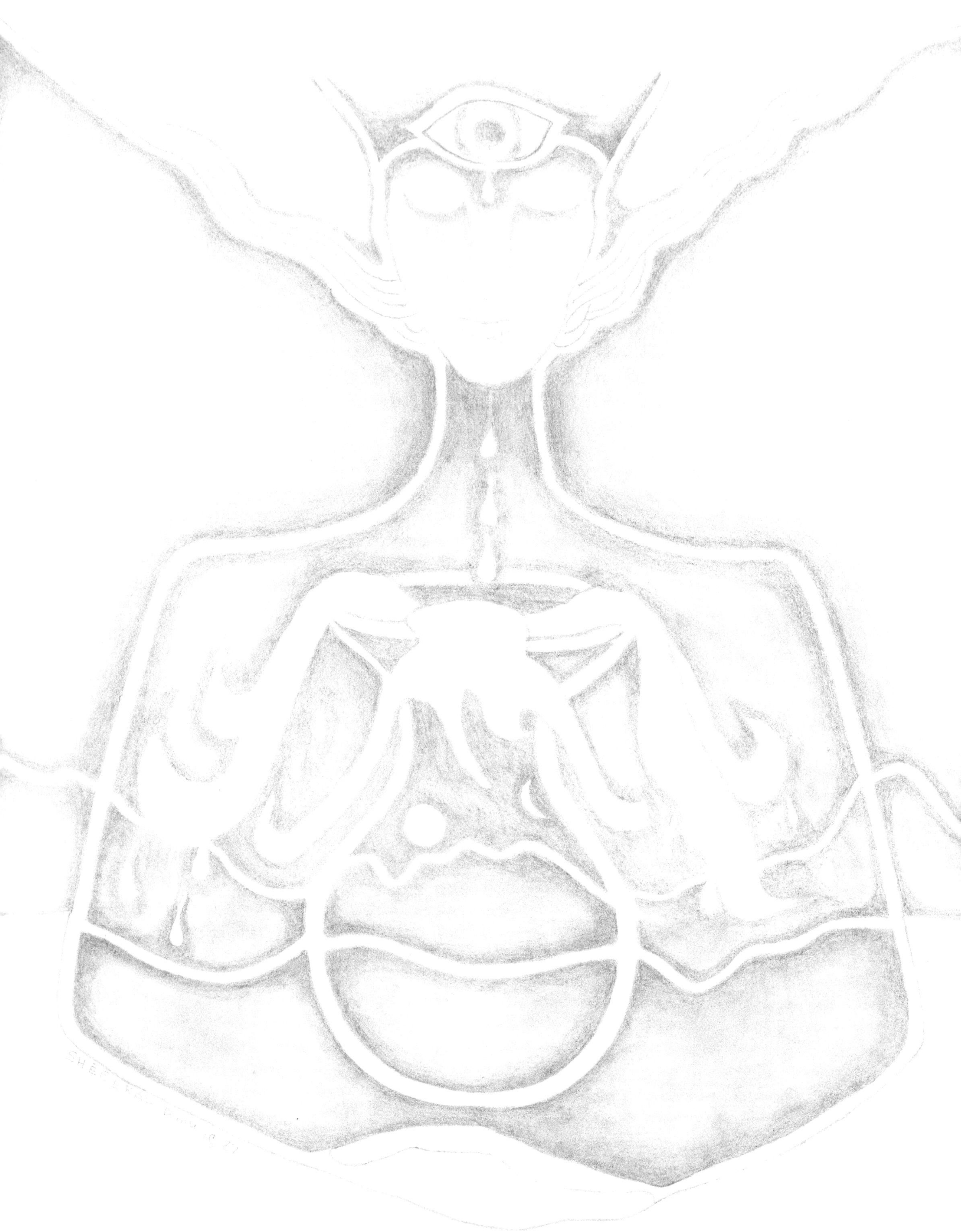

Preface

Birthing Art from the Withinness

Art as Consciousness. This book is a natural and organic response to the many art collectors and friends over the years who asked to know more about my multi-media, multi-technique, multi-layer and multi-dimensional art. I have been asked many questions and done many art consultations on this subject. What unfolded for me was art expression from Spirit. Soul Expression. All of us now...learning to BE the non-dimensional. Spirit. The very presence.

It started in the 60's when I was studying fine Art at the University of Wisconsin. It was the time of the counterculture revolution with Vietnam protests on campus. It was the time of pop art artists, such as Alexander Calder, Claes Oldenburg and Andy Warhol. It was a time of huge plastic installations and psychedelic art.

I was both a high school English teacher and a fine Arts student. It was a strange double life. The University of Wisconsin is very progressive and liberal and I was being introduced to vast new ways of seeing almost everything. I loved it.

I will give one small example of how one art student turned my life around. In class, we were given an art assignment. I struggled over this for weeks. When we were showing our project in class, this young man held up a most beautiful branch that he had found while walking in the woods. That branch fully demonstrated the point of the project. I was astounded. In one moment I was in an assignment box; in the next moment, there was no box.

In art classes, after that experience, I was drawn only to my own intuitive expressions, much to the dismay of my professors, who were caught up in that which was in vogue. I seemed to be flowing down a different river. And there was no box.

I found my self always putting white bands around most of my figures. I did not call them auras. They were just powerful light fields around many figures. I had one professor who said I seemed to be painting angels. Little did I know that I was in the very early stage of pioneering visionary art. It was around 1967.

I continued to create and express and began to find a deeper and unfiltered Awareness that was a guiding light. And it has gone from drawing to multimedia painting to multi-media presentations to writing and educating. Most recently it has been orchestrating sacred theater and an animation meditation.

In the sections of the book that follow, one will be able to read details of the processes which I used in this very simple 12 year phase. There will then follow art that represents these phases.

There comes a time where we cannot separate the practical aspect of the process and the Consciousness of that which is expressed. Like the clay of a sculpture being one with the image being created.

Art As Consciousness is Devotion and Dedication to the Infinite

Art as Consciousness represents more than a mental commitment to painting. It represents a devotion, a dedication to the Infinite One. The Timeless One. The Eternal. Soul is infused into the art expression.

I learned from Lao Russell in 1981 how to infuse Soul into art. And from Walter Russell I learned to enter the art studio as if entering a sacred sanctuary. Although it appears that I was serious, the results are a "lightness" that is joy!

I began to learn how to be at one with the medium, the paper, the instruments used. We became the sweetest soul community, all creating the image that was landing upon the paper. Always with a candle burning. Reminding me of the Light, Spirit, Source, if my mind started to dwell in a region I did not want to be. It began to break my "habits" of engaging and indulging in thoughts that did not serve. It began to reveal freedom.

The idea of a sacred sanctuary for creating, with no interference or distractions, grew in importance. I thirsted for the holy solitude.

And the 12 years unfolded revealing ever a deepened experience of being present in Presence. Then there are the presents, the gifts, the grace of that inner flow.

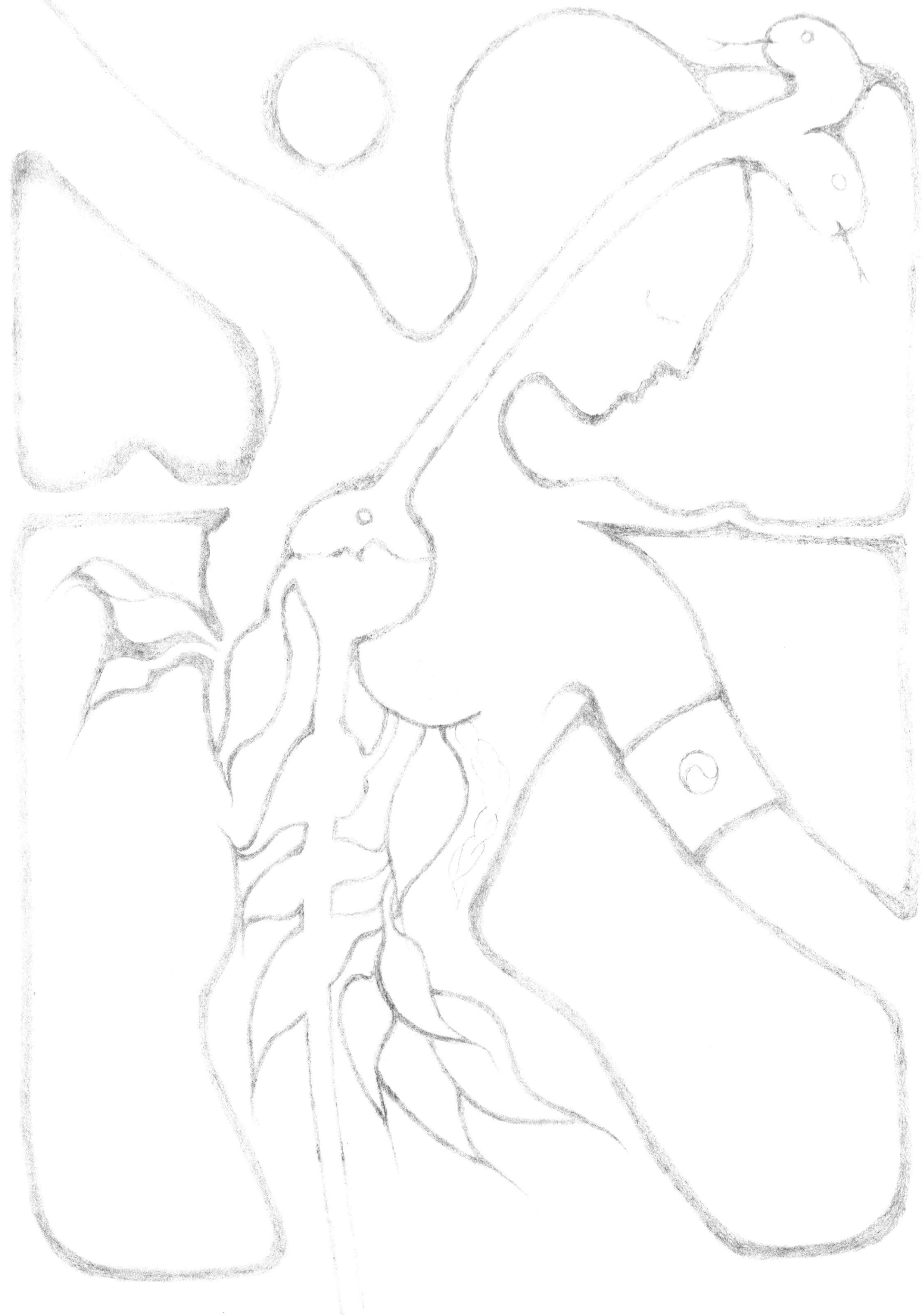

Art as a Spiritual Practice

Devotion and Dedication to the Infinite Presence

This book embraces the awareness of what I describe as Art as Consciousness. Or one could even say Consciousness as Art. Or expanded is...Art as Life Itself.

Many people over the past 45 years have wondered at what they described as my intense discipline. I would never have thought to describe it as such. It is a deep inner impulse to Express. Expression for all of us is Life Itself, coming forth as our Life. Thus the Inner Being comes forth as Divine Animation on this Earth.

Instead of suppression, oppression, impression, compression, depression, we now reverse the flow to EXPRESSION of the Divine Life that resides within as our very Being. This idea of Expression from the within outward is the reverse of all of those worldly pressures that are from the outside in, sometimes seeming to push the very Life from us. Certainly they can smother the inner Creativity and create suffering.

Many people have also described my life as a hermit or recluse. My version is this. Many people in the world, especially those in the arts, love the solitude. That aloneness is not lonely. It is the alignment with the Oneness. This type of solitude carries the frequency of ecstasy.

In this solitude is borne a devotion and dedication to the Infinite Presence. In this solitude is borne a one-pointed focus. In this solitude is borne concentration that becomes a decentration. Being.

And one begins to see what is a distraction and what enhances one's Life Expression. Art is revealed as a teacher. Emotional issues were being revealed as the belief in "separation from the divine" that they are. This sense of separation creates fear and all its off-springs of suffering. I had to learn to welcome each surfacing "problem" as a gift. I had to begin to learn to "rise above the problems." As I learned not to engage, indulge and feed these problems, they began to starve with lack of attention. They begin to disappear. The world tempts us into the belief in the duality, the battles, and if we say yes, that is our world.

Expression in the Arts allows one to practice. It allows one to practice seeing Holy Relationships with everyone, everything and every place.

Thus, each image in this book allows for individual viewers to see as an allegory. The image may then be interpreted by each viewer for its meaning in their own life. The images are as visual parables. I never intended the art to be didactic, but as I continued to draw, I found that I was attuning myself to higher frequencies. The drawings became a mirror and a reflection for the Awareness that was upon me.

When that Inner Authority comes forth, there is an outer sanctity in our lives. Our lives do change. The Changeless One does bring the change.

Awakening in the Sixties

It was the sixties and I was studying Fine Arts at the University of Wisconsin. I was simultaneously teaching high school English and later working as an assistant coordinator at WHA-TV in public educational television, also at the University of Wisconsin. At WHA-TV, we piloted the newly created Sesame Street program. I was married and had a very progressive mainstream life. Action and intellect!

I had been taking art classes at the University of Wisconsin, because it moved and touched me more than the teacher position that I had. I was not a full-time student, so I did not have first choice of the art classes available. Many times I would find myself choosing multi-media art classes simply because they were available that semester. Little did I realize that I would later on totally fall in love with multi-media art mediums, forms, processes, techniques. Nor did I ever imagine that I would "create" a new type of original multi-media that I had never heard of anywhere. (That is a later story of learning to go within and receive. And of learning to communicate with the so-called other side. In this case it was William Blake. And of learning to be one with everything I was using in my art studio.)

One day I walked into the art counselor's office. I remember feeling that something was missing in my art classes. I did my best to explain. I told him that I went to amazing art exhibits and saw art that I loved. It deeply moved me. He told me to drop out of art school for a while and just "pursue" life. He said I would find the "it" that I was looking for. I did and I never returned to the classes.

The Unmanifest Unveils Itself

In 1971, I found myself living in Oregon, divorced and finding another life that was buried inside of me. For a time, during this transition period, I worked in a shoe department at a department store. I was so bored that I reorganized all of the shoes in the back. They loved it. Later I was an English Instructor at a college.

In that year came a head on car collision to awaken me profoundly. (Although I do not believe that we need to awaken with disaster and suffering.) At the moment of the impact, I said, "God, I'm yours." At that moment, I saw my life through my Soul and through a divine Joy and I saw my life past, present and future all rolled into One Life. I remember knowing that the book, *Finnegan's Wake*, was the structural framework, from my life in literature, through which this experience could come to me. It would be very difficult to put in words a description of that. Somehow I simply understood. It made my mind fertile, open and receptive. I was aware of this when the collision (not an accident) occurred. It was a seeming portal in my world to a higher and clearer world. Beliefs fell away. I was now aware of Consciousness that is usually blocked, tainted, distorted and/or diluted with the belief in separation. I was now aware of Pure Consciousness. The ecstasy of this experience was beyond mental and earthly imaginings. The so-called human thinking mind cannot travel to these rarified regions. After the experience I could see light (aura) around all living things, especially the trees. I could see a little of the illumined life.

Emanations of light were apparent.

I knew with crystal clarity that I had agreed to live the life that others wanted me to live and that I believed I had to live. It was smothering me. It was not my life.

I had now left behind my teaching career, academic art, marriage. Soon after that I left the second teaching position at a college and all of the safety, security and stability that enticed me, even lured me.

I could not deny the Realm of the Real that had been realized during this brief and potent glimpse that was a momentary near death experience. I had the growing desire to live from this new Awareness. But how?

This Realm of the Real was "more real" than our seeming physical plane of existence. A deep commitment and devotion to this presence arose.

I began to live a life of great simplicity. I let go of media of 40 years. I gave away my television. I did not use a radio. I let my magazine and newspaper subscriptions go. I found inspiration in new ways. First it was listening to sacred chants and songs. Later I began to hear the inner music. I discovered how much I loved the stillness. Just empty.

And during all of this I made many mistakes.

Inspired to Travel and the Move to the Mountain

Before the car crash/near death experience, the only alternative or spiritual book I had read was *Be Here Now*. I read it eight times in a row in 1971. On the eighth time, I simply had an experience of merging and being One with everything around me. No drugs, no meditation.

Just reading. I was not expecting it. So there was some earthly fear associated with it. It was all so new. I had no understanding. I had no idea of thousands of years of sacred texts and present day experiences that were filled with such accounts.

Soon after, I had a close call with a psychiatrist who had no experiential understanding of the mystical experience. He wanted to label it something else from an unenlightened state and give me drugs. I tried to help him understand. That is another story. It ended well.

I bought a Kelty pack, a sleeping bag, one change of clothes, some clogs. I packed a hair brush, a toothbrush, my passport and some money. I bought a Rapidograph pen, some magic markers and art quality drawing pad. And I was off to something that was calling to me. I had a yearning in my soul, but no destination.

I am telling this story, for it reveals the simplicity of my life. I had a few thousand dollars and the inspiration arising in my soul. I had touched a place in my soul beyond human success and failure. I did not look back. I could not look back.

This particular part of the journey carried me on a drive across America. Then the flight to Spain, along with hitchhiking, took me to Morocco, Greece, Italy and across Turkey, Afghanistan, Iran, Pakistan and into India and Kashmir. I was an ex-teacher from Iowa, an out of the box traveler, a single woman and add to that...one recently awakened through a near death experience where the Unmanifest unveiled a glimpse of Itself.

The mention of this part of my story is important. Here is what the University of Wisconsin art counselor was speaking of. He said to "pursue" life. This is where the experiences continued to arise that shaped and sculpted the formative years of my life as artist.

I was from the heart land of America; I was naïve; I was right-brain dominant.

In Iowa schools in the 40's and 50's, they did not teach about the male dominant society of most of the world. Especially the Middle East. I will tell a story that helps to generate a feeling for the experience. In Afghanistan, I would step up the high step into this tiny café type of place. I ordered chai. I wondered where the women were. I was 29 and alone in one of the hookah bars. The men would stare at me like I had just landed from Venus or somewhere alien. They served me. I was totally oblivious. O how innocence serves! I was marveling at how they sat squat, at their clothing that allowed them to do that and at the simplicity of life. I even had a local seamster make me two outfits. Very loose and wide bottomed pants, almost skirt-like in bright traditional colors. Then I could join in and squat also. Now I had more to pack into the Kelty pack.

I had a further awakening moment to the human condition when some children of an Afghani village invited me (now life was pursuing me) into one of the homes where I was fed by the women of the village who could not speak English, nor did I have anything other than my language translation book. Together we learned the enchanting world of gestures. Children danced and sang for me. They fed me from a platter from dishes brought in by many village women, when they heard, through the children, that there was a white woman roaming the village with her face showing. I was transformed by the time I left. More education about the imbalance of man/woman situations on the planet in that one afternoon than my entire high school and college education. The woman of the home asked to go with me in the travel bus (that was being repaired again). She would leave children, husband, town, country for the freedom that she was witnessing. I was stunned. As we drove away from that village, I realized that she probably was not alone, in longing for freedom.

This and many more experiences showed me the imbalance between man and woman in this culture and others. I had seen a realm beyond these imbalances, these human conflicts. I was clear that we could rise above this realm of unequal yin and yang.

Questions about life began to come to me. And a few answers.

The Phases and Creative Process of Early Visionary Drawings of the Seventies and into the Eighties

Rapidograph and Magic Marker Mixed Media Art

On the early part of this six month journey, Rapidograph drawings began to flow through me. They eliminated everything that I had ever learned about art. Without lifting my pen from the paper, these mystical figures, that seemed hauntingly beautiful, would emerge. One single and solitary line. The figures seemed to be walking right out of a Lawrence of Arabia scene. They appeared to be Christed beings, walking out of the desert landscapes. They had a mysterious tone. An essence that touched me. A horizon line and/or a sun would emerge. It felt like I could feel the very soul of that part of the world. And this was many years before I knew of mystic poet seers, such has Rumi and Hafiz.

As I continued to be open and empty, the solitary figures kept coming. They were like living and visual prayers of just Being. So utterly simple. I was satisfied. Something very deep was being expressed. I had no words or stories and explanations for any of it. Just raw. Original. Simple. Childlike.

I will not tell the many adventures here of the 6 months in these countries, but it was this awakening mixed with emotions, questions and sexuality surfacing. The near death experience let me know that there were Realms of the Real, in Awareness, beyond all this world teeming around me and in me. I did not get yet that the world is within.

In Venice, home of much art, I bought small gold frames and had them mailed to Oregon. And they made it. They were just the perfect size for these mystical drawings that now had color on the suns and sometimes on these robed and caped emerging figures.

On my return to Oregon, in 1972, I created my first visionary art exhibits in three galleries, including the college where I had taught. The art sold. From that moment, I bypassed juried shows, chose myself and to this day have done over 150 exhibits at many types of venues and I have collectors around the world and nation. Little did I realize then that I was one of the early artists pioneering visionary art. Most galleries at that time did not even know the word.

Once I returned to the West Coast of the U.S., I needed to find a place to land. I had two goals. Find the perfect place to realize the withinness more deeply and a beautiful place to raise my beautiful and creative daughter. That prayer brought my answer through a dream. I moved to Mount Shasta. We rented a simple room in a large and very old home.

Air Brush as a Tool of Expression

Soon after I moved to Mount Shasta, I met the now famed Gilbert Williams, a visionary artist just beginning. He was in the process of buying some new airbrush equipment, so I received his old equipment in exchange for helping to hostess his wedding. I had no idea how to use a compressor and an airbrush, so I asked if he would teach me. He answered that he did not have time; he had a wife and needed to paint. So he came to me in a dream and taught me some basics. I began.

The entire awareness of Art as Consciousness began to dawn on me at this time. I also saw art as a way to devotion and dedication to this Realm of Light I had experienced. It was love with no conditions. It was an ineffable presence. People from around the world call it many names. I knew that it was the Infinite, partially unveiled.

By this time, I had a second beautiful daughter and for two years I air brushed the mother principle. Having two young daughters filled me with the identity of this universal energy of mothering. Madonna and Child. I painted this theme in many forms. I was immersed in it. It allowed me to express how I felt about being a mother. The concept of the immaculate conception (pure ideal) came to me at that time. Sacred Vision. Holy Sight.

One day I realized I could feel that the air brush method was affecting my lungs. I simply quit. I sold all of the equipment and again, I never looked back.

Pencil, Reverse and Eraser Drawing as My Teacher

Then arrived a long eight plus years of pencil drawing. I fell in love with HB pencils. Not too hard. Not too soft. And I fell in love with what I learned much later was being called Layering in the art world. Many of the pencil drawings in this book are from that period. Others sold before they were ever photographed. I learned early that art comes through us not to us. Like children.

I deepened in my realization that art, in this case drawing, was a powerful spiritual practice. Not only was it a simple way to feel and experience the Power of the One, it began to reveal to me that this Power, this Ecstasy was the Only Power. The One Power. I could feel the Universal Force live through me as the drawings birthed. I spent as many hours in the days as I could in my studio. I certainly had not learned how to keep this going all the time or as strongly, during the other parts of my life.

It was a beginning.

One has to realize that I was waking out of being raised in a family that did not go to church of any nature. I seemed to have found my own inner sanctuary early. My mother told me, several years before her departure, that my first three years were spent "sitting on a little stool in the middle of the living room staring and smiling into space with no talking." That was not acceptable in that era. She told no one. She said that I was very joyful! She could feel it. By age four I had found nature and running off and it was my sanctuary. I was in an alcoholic family, so no one really knew where I was. Shortly after that I became adept at climbing into trees and just Being. I was joyful there. Eating fruit and nuts. Fresh mulberries. And I was joyful by the lakes, ocean and with the animals. And the sand. And the freedom that nature does offer.

Many types of nature experiences arose as our air force military family moved from town to town to various air bases in Mississippi and Texas. And I was not accustomed to a home mom baking cookies and such. I had a flying mom. A pioneering mom. She was one of early female pilots, complete in goggles, aviator hat and one piece zippered flight suits flying open cockpit, doing triple loops, all while she was pregnant with me. She was part of the Ninety Nines, right after the Amelia

Earhart period and she flew Powder Puff Derby over the ocean. The nature experiences and the adventure life caused me to be flexible and open to life. It also awakened me to deep experiences of earth and sky. Ground school and flight school awareness. Earth and sky.

It was during the seventies that I discovered, through experience, what I mentioned as layered drawing and reverse drawing. Sometimes I call it "drawing from the background, that is, the negative." Being extremely agile in the right brain, intuitive capacity, these were heaven-borne techniques for me.

Layered and reverse drawing allowed me to develop my intuition. I loved it. I did not have to analyze, report, memorize or even explain. I just allowed. Learning the Art of Allowing was like flying to another planet for me. I did not have to think. I did not even have to imagine. I just had to open and allow. Peace arises. And The Ineffable. Presence.

This is essentially how it worked. I would lay in a pencil background very slowly and carefully on the paper. Often it would be six to eight layers. I would attune to the higher frequencies of the Christ Presence (or whatever one wants to call this It or Isness) and was aware that a Force was this so-called process. The Unseen. In effect, it could be called an art prayer, art meditation or art contemplation. Or just being empty. Emptiness Itself.

Clearly it was an act of devotion and simple dedication to this presence. I loved it. I could feel the peace, the calm as I drew. And it certainly served as a contrast for the times that emotions were arising and I did not feel the peace and the calm and had not yet learned what to do about it.) Drawing as my teacher had arrived. Gratitude filled me for the opportunity to know the power of unbridled artistic expression.

I was continuing to read spiritual books from around the world during this time. I remember reading things that said that the awakening ones were too self-absorbed. Well they were and they are. They are busy realizing the so-called human self as the One Self. The Only Self. It is something that each person will need to awaken to.

As my Awareness grew, I realized there was no separation to my personal life, my inner art expressions and the universe. All was moving together as one whole. And it was sacred.

As the many layers of pencil began to be put on the paper, I was attuning inwardly. So the layers were being put in with a Oneness Consciousness. I would also begin to "turn the paper" and look at the drawing from all four directions. That also was a meditation. My inner vision (third eye) had opened during the near death car collision. The pencil drawings became the practice for that to continue to open.

It was during this time that I developed Soul Sight or spiritual sight at a new level. Some call it second sight or shamanic seeing. I could see clearly the image in the pencil layerings that wanted to surface and be brought into focus. The image was already laid into the layerings as I drew.

Then through intuition and inner guidance, I began to also use what

I called "reverse drawing." So now between the layerings, I would "draw from the background or the negative" by using kneaded erasers or fabric as a positive instrument to "bring out the image" that was evidenced. As I would work with the layers with pencil and eraser instruments, the revealed image continued to emerge and come more into focus with details.

The car crash/near death experience was not the end of the upliftment into the Realms of the Real. I began, in meditation, to be uplifted many times in inner vision to what I named the Archetypal Realms of the Real. There would have to be another book to describe these revelations and epiphanies. They seem more real than this plane of existence. And joyfilled. For there is no duality. No wars, no battles, no conflicts. Simply never-ending ecstatic exploration of the art of creation. Galactic Shamanism. Ability to merge into and from any form!

For a while I called this "seeing the future," for it is available to us. Finally I realized it was available now. Another state of consciousness now. A realization.

Why have I mentioned these experiences and not gone into the details of them? I simply have mentioned them, for they were a large part of the experience and revelation that then became a part of my drawings and later my multi-media paintings.

Also during this time, around 1978, my inner hearing opened. Sometimes I heard angelic music, sometimes celestial and sometimes music of the spheres. My favorite is music of the spheres.

I will mention how the inner hearing opened the first time. I was with a man friend who just announced that he was also with another woman. I realized how attached I was. I was in pain. I prayed for help and restated my dedication to the infinite. I began to listen within. And the music began to come. That was my release from the attachment to the relationship. I was done. I did not look back. The music comes and goes. It is exalted in nature and is there for us all.

Hearing this music profoundly affected me and it affected my art, supporting me in learning how to identify with the Unseen.

There was always a soul sense of knowing when the drawing was complete. There simply was no more inspiration to continue. The Energy was no longer there. Complete.

During this pencil phase, I continued reading many spiritual books from all over the globe. I had an appetite to hear how various religions, traditions, paths, ways, groups and tribes experienced The One. They all talked about the Wordless, Nameless One with many words and names. It was easy to see that the Isness is celebrated in so many different forms. Seeing the parallel stories of the Infinite served to underline the underlying fact of Oneness.

During this period, I would often fall fully in love with a sentence, a short quote or an affirmation that was alive. The words felt infused and pregnant with Spirit. They allowed me to "feel" presence deeply. My heart was open. The words went from my mind to my heart.

I would contemplate those words, as I put in the pencil layers. Or just

Be empty. The image would continue to appear. The image seemed to be a portal that continued to allow the feelings of the Arising Presence. It was a period of very refined Beingness for me.

I spent much time with my daughters out in nature. Nature, from childhood on, continued to inspire! This was all side by side with the emotions, beliefs and human sense of separation that all had their "things to say"! I was only beginning to be aware of how I allowed those things to live. Through indulging and engaging and believing in them.

During this time, I studied for three years with Lao Russell. She began to share with me how to Soul infuse all my art. She shared that only soul awake people can see and understand the deeper aspects of soul inspired art. It was a blessed time.

Pencil and Colored Pencil Mixed Media Art

Toward the end of the pencil phase, color began to call. I continued with the same techniques, but added colored pencil to the paper.

Later I did some drawings in all colored pencil. And following that I began to add in the water soluble colored pencil and crayons. I brought in pastels. Ink. Sometimes charcoal. And I brought in the sacred element, water.

The use of water and watercolor pencils, charcoal, inks, pastels combined with these pen, pencil and colored pencils marks the beginning of yet another of the phases in my ever changing art forms and expressions.

In my first art book, *The Sacred Two*, can be seen the mixed media painting series that is quite a complicated process of printmaking, painting and drawing all on the same piece. And there is the use of brushes, brayers, glass, fabric, erasers, sponge, cotton, tape and on. Which of the processes and which of the mediums or tools to be used at any given time was all done with intuition. I learned to intuit and "read" the communications from the water and the color tones. The process became more of a dance of the infinite, not knowing what was next, but being a ready lover.

In all of the art phases, I was learning how to be aware of time while practicing the Non-Time. The Timeless Realm. Clearly...the present moment. Now.

In the second art book, *The Star-Stone Essence*, I began to work very subtly. This series, called "whispers on the desert wind," is also mixed media with watercolor painting and pencil and water soluble colored pencil drawing...married. These paintings look so simple yet they took so much more time than the previous multi-media series. I was becoming more and more aware of the Animating Presence that works through us and AS us in our lives, as we step aside. The One Self animating the seeming human self. Painting allows the awareness.

During this time another phase of artistic creation birthed. I began to create Sacred Enactments of Ancient Remembering. They were multi-media presentations, called *SHE...it is...who Remembers.* They were created with my art slide shows, poetic odyssey, narration, dancing. And through the use of excellent lighting, my dance shadow became a part of the creation, bringing the stark drama of the simplicity of "feeling." Always I had a wonderful musician bringing music to the event. For a while the music of Ainu tribe native, Oki Kano, was an integral and important part, creating the felt sense of the One. He plays the healing instrument of his tribe. The Tonkori. Also, harmonium, didgeridoo, drums and other voices were to become part of the traveling "sacred enactment." It continued to shape shift and change.

During the first multi-media phase of art, I also began to sculpt altar art. They were as 3-D art inspirations to go within. They were revealing Life itself as a Living Ceremony. All sacred. Already Whole.

And during this phase of art, the creative flow was strong and began to open writing. Poetry. Poetic Odysseys. Passages. The first book, *Galactic Shamanism* came during this time. Later even a sacred play flowed through during a two day retreat.

I am taking the time to share how all this came through, for the drawing opened the painting and that opened the sculpting and the presentations and finally into the writing, including the play, *The Monitor and Laughter of the Gods.* One seems to beget the next and the next. Birth after birth. Creativity is not ours. It flows through us, not really to us. We are empty and open. A vessel. An awaiting lover. The dance of yin and yang as our very life.

Art As Consciousness

I began to have the inspiration to create an art book with my pen and ink and pencil drawings that had been stored away for years. They were stored for I found that art collectors and buyers preferred my next series of bold, colored multi-media paintings.

I asked myself why I would create the book. The answer came to me that the drawings were transmissions of the universal energy that I had opened to. They represented and conveyed a state of consciousness that many are now opening to.

Because they are so simple and subtle, they offer a silent, gossamer invitation to go within, to open, to experience, to be. They invite one to feel and realize this arising presence that is everywhere present. They invite one to allow this animating presence in their own life. There is but one life and we are that.

I also had been aware that there was value to the simplicity of both ink and pencil. The black and white is, in itself, an experience, as there are no colors to grab the attention and the senses.

One is invited to see the value of simplicity.

One is invited, by the medium, to see and feel essence prior to color.

Mystic Art-of-the-Soul

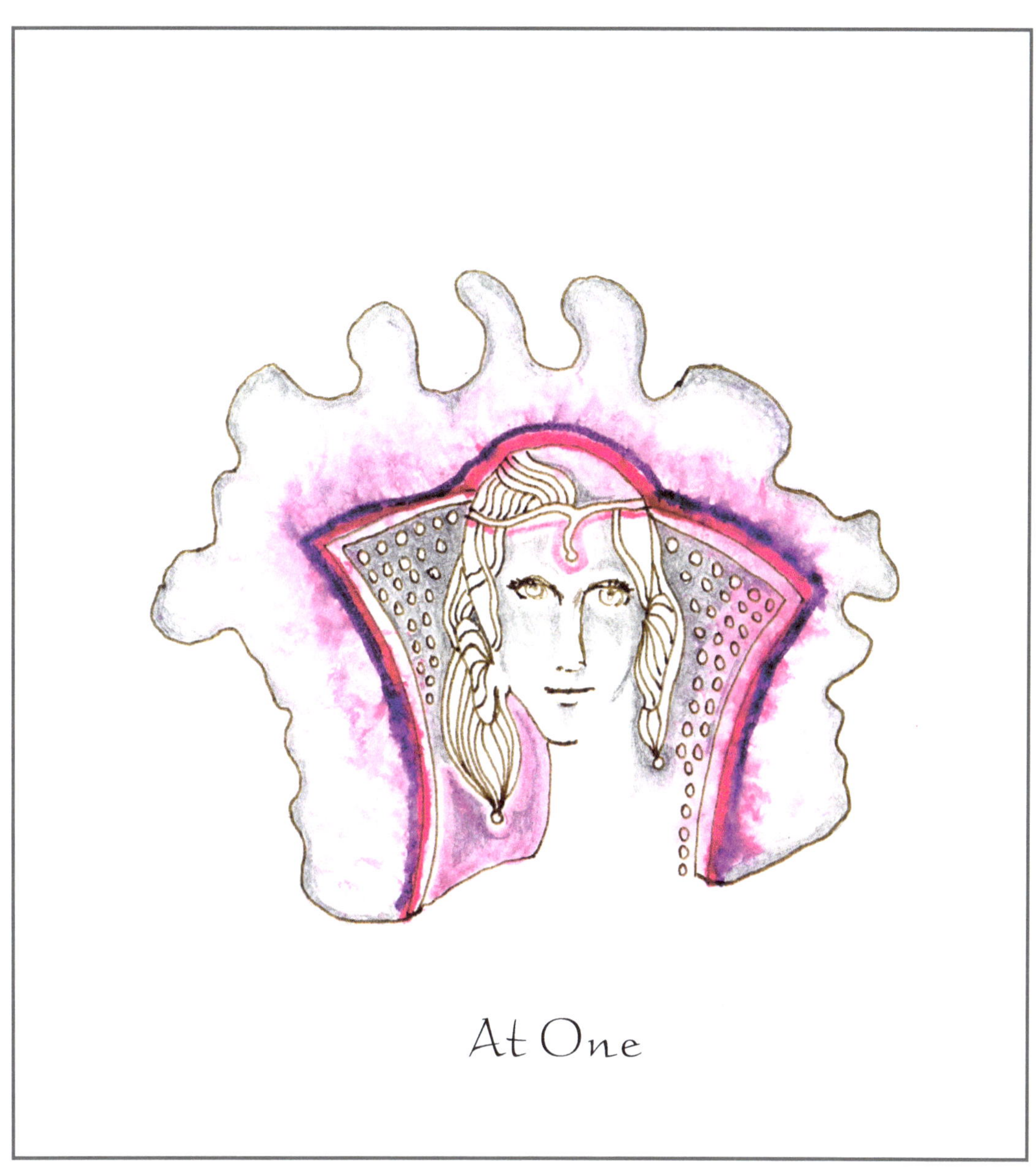

At One

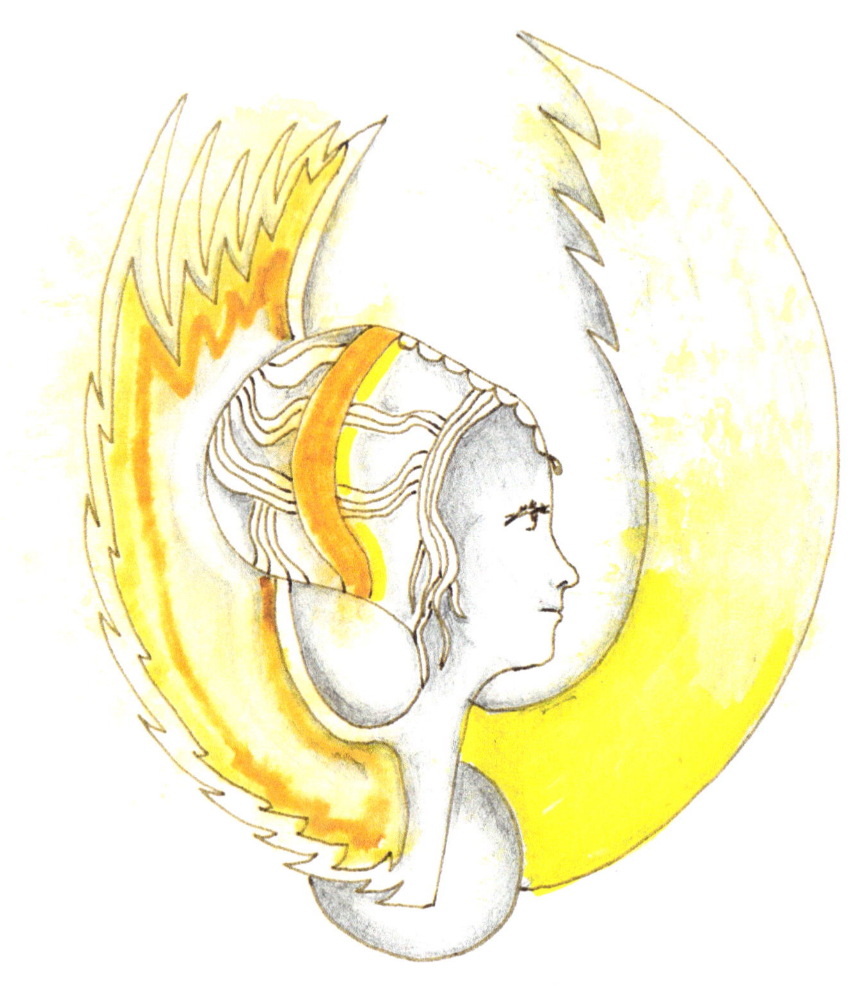

Winged One

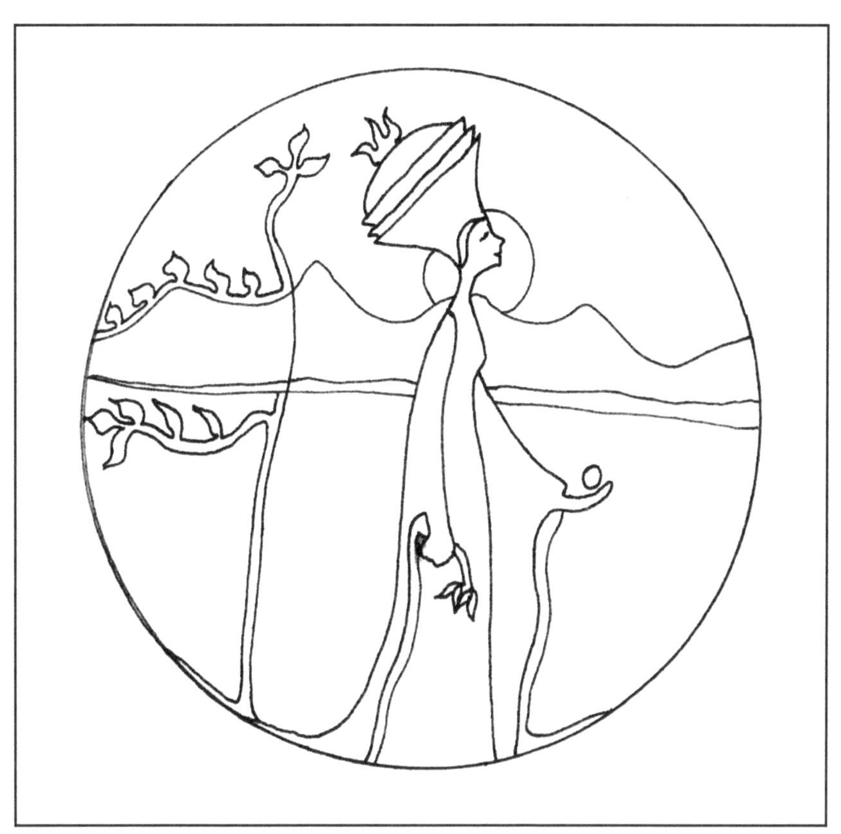

I bring a gift...

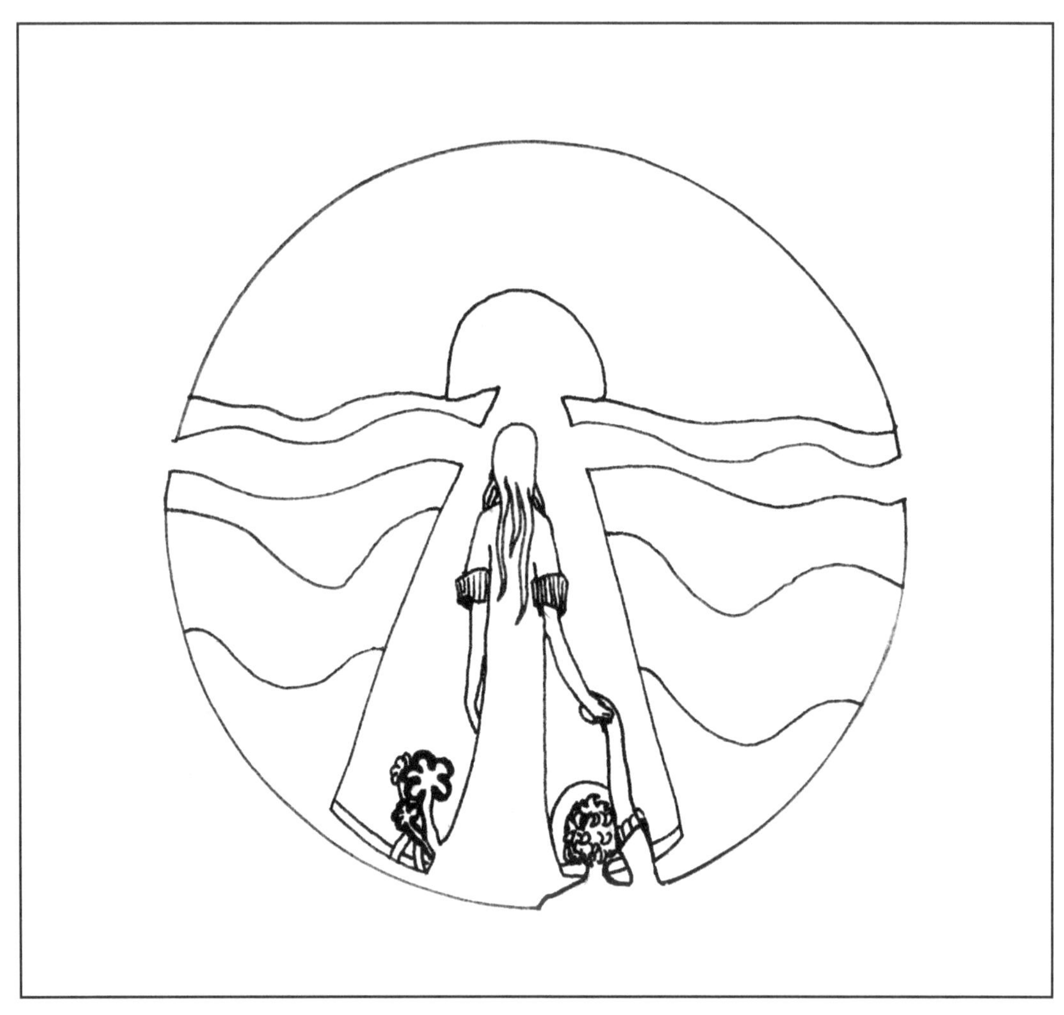

into the sun we move...

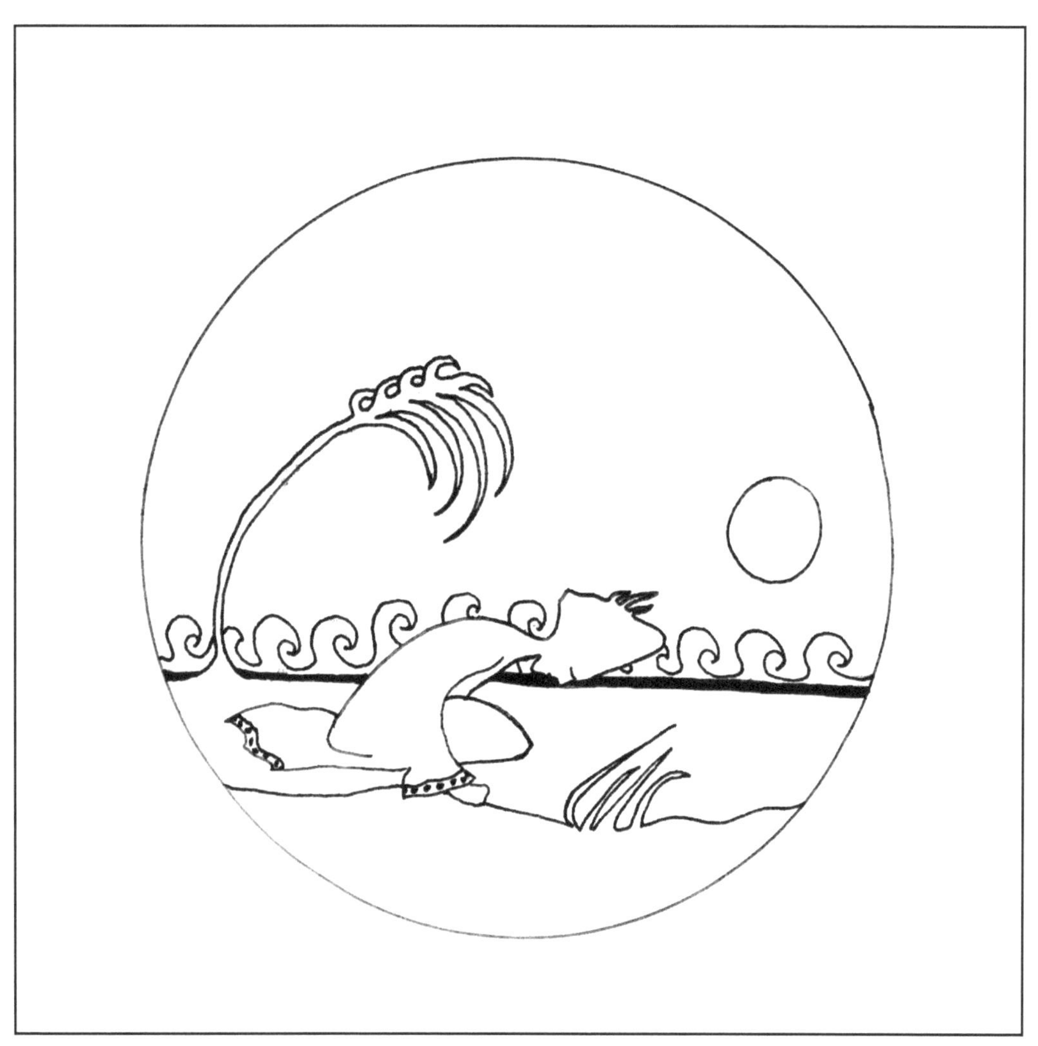

I Am Grateful

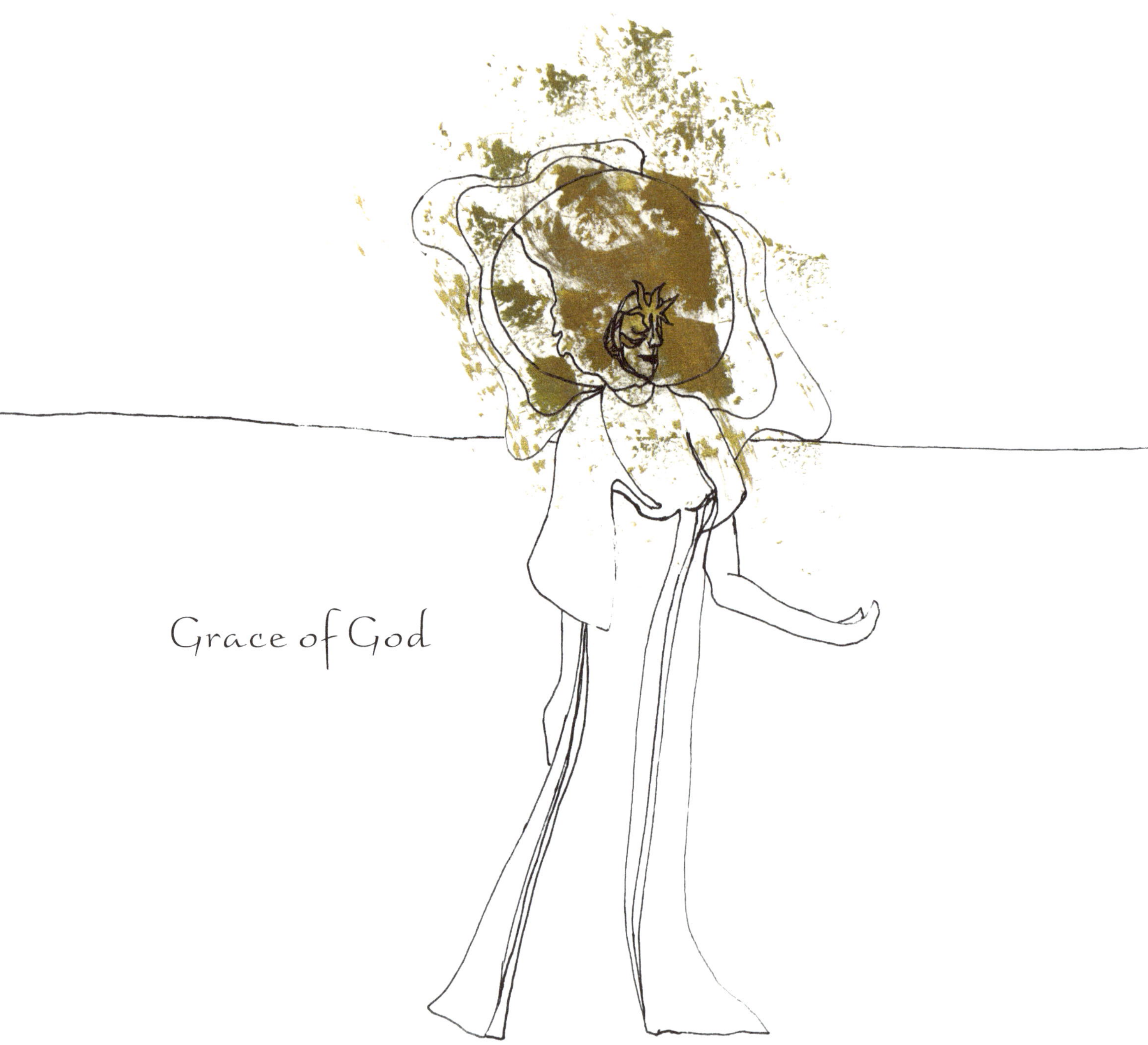

Grace of God

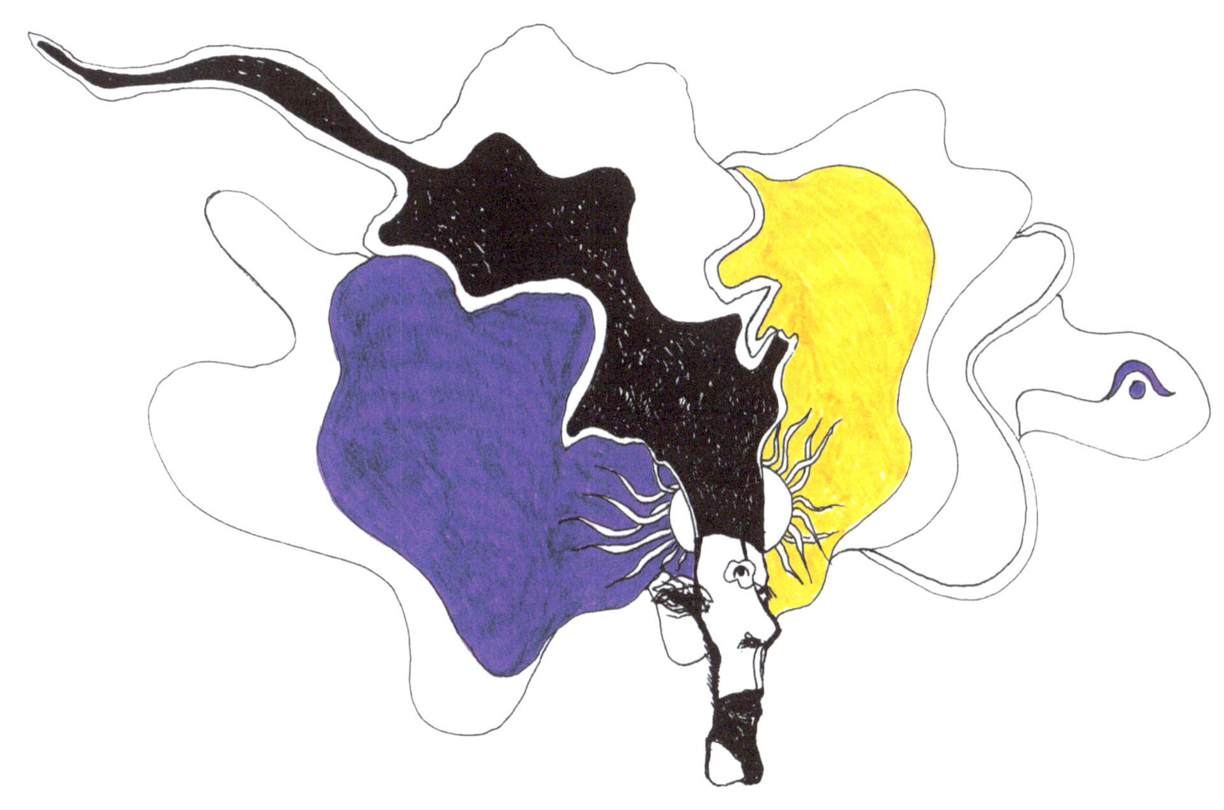

Radiant Sun

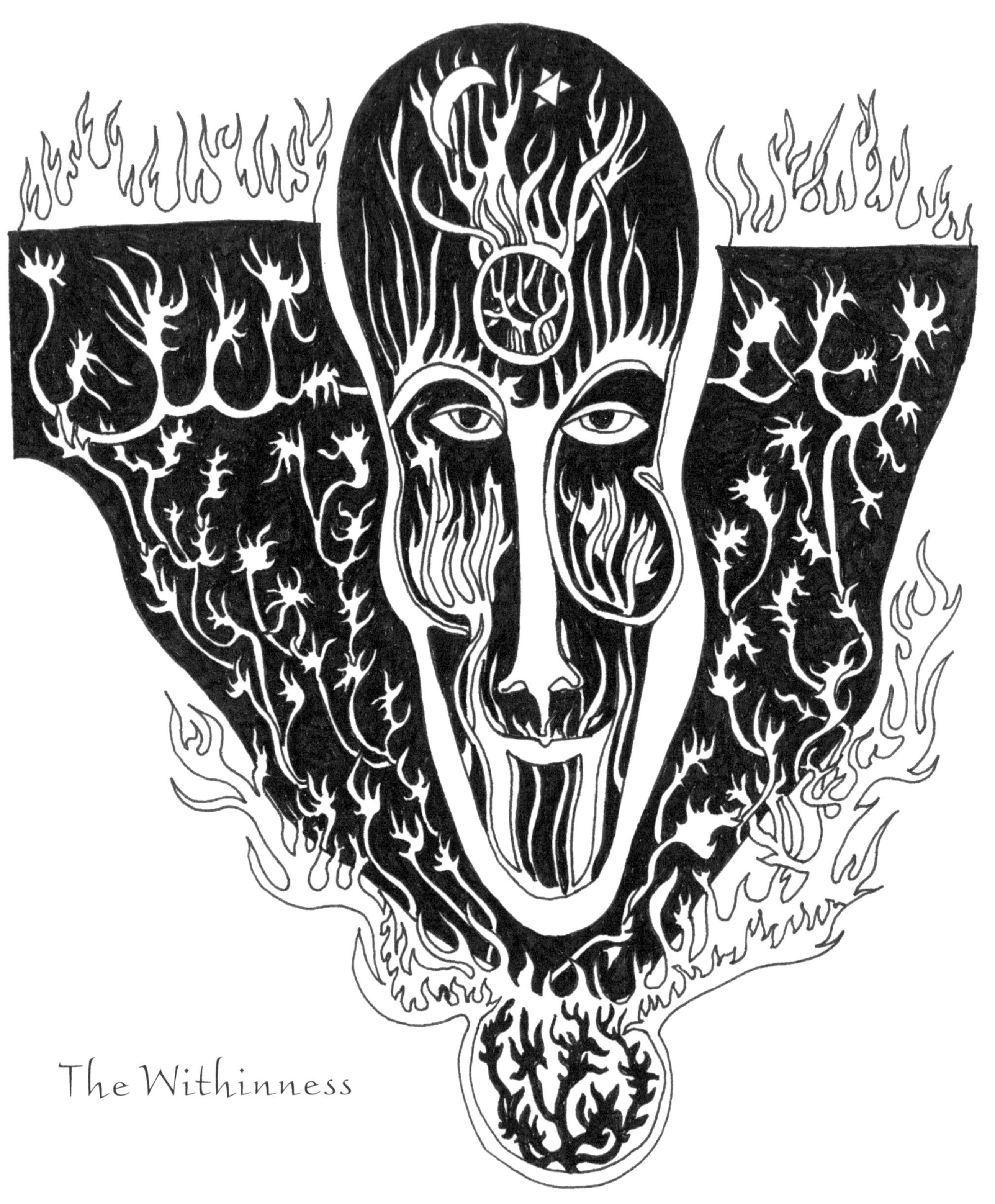

The Withinness

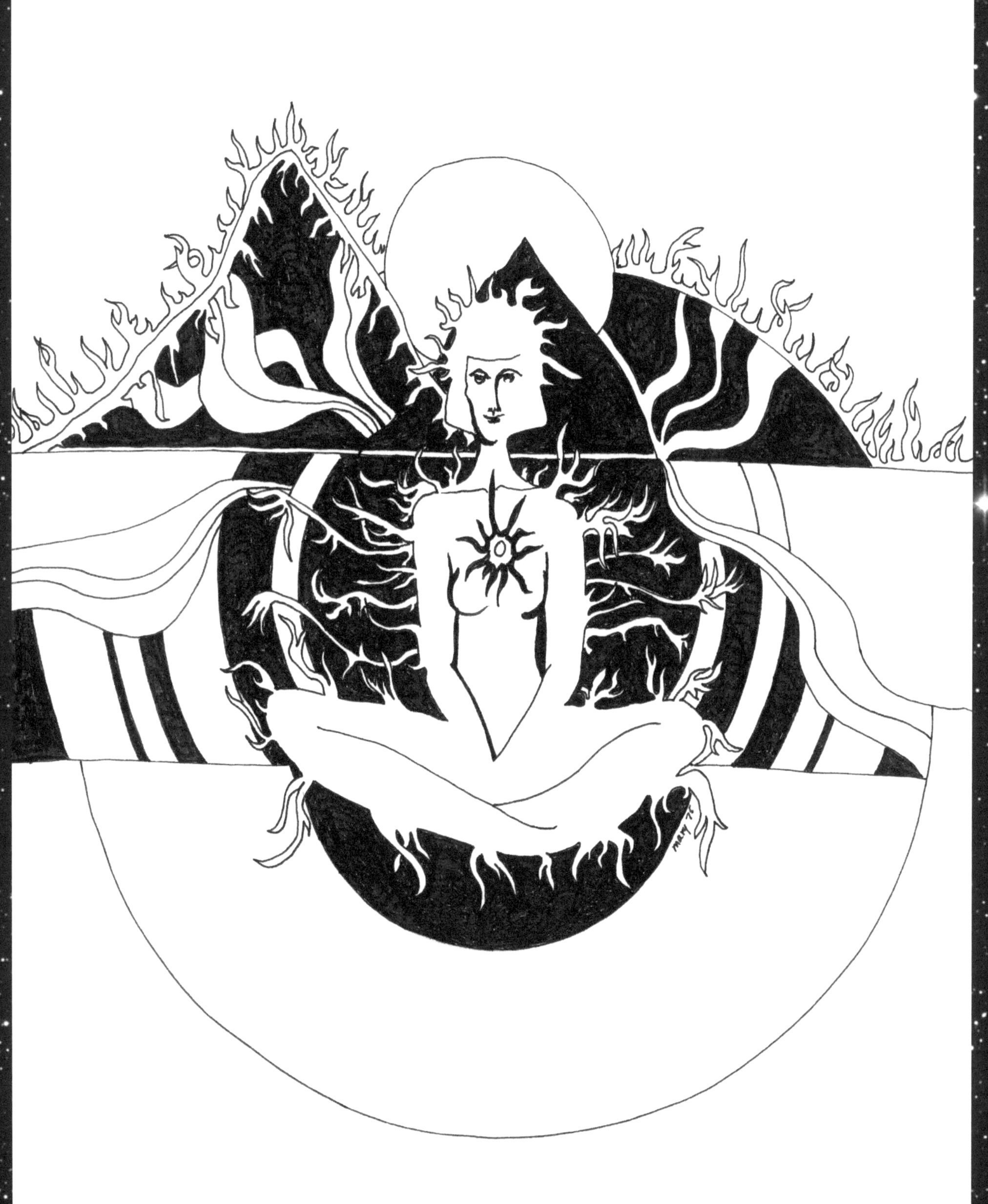

peace manifest...as everywhere present

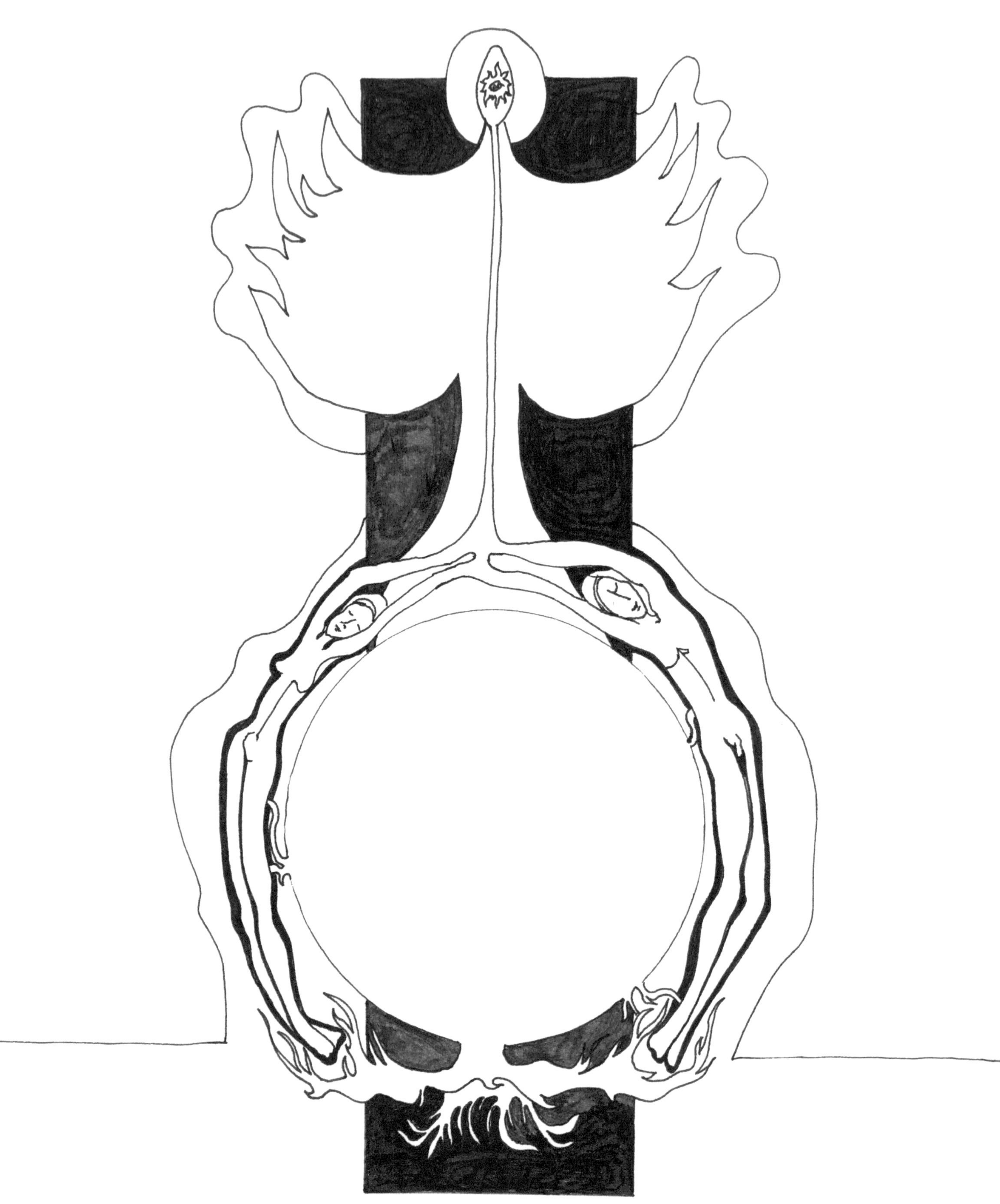

Flight to Oneness

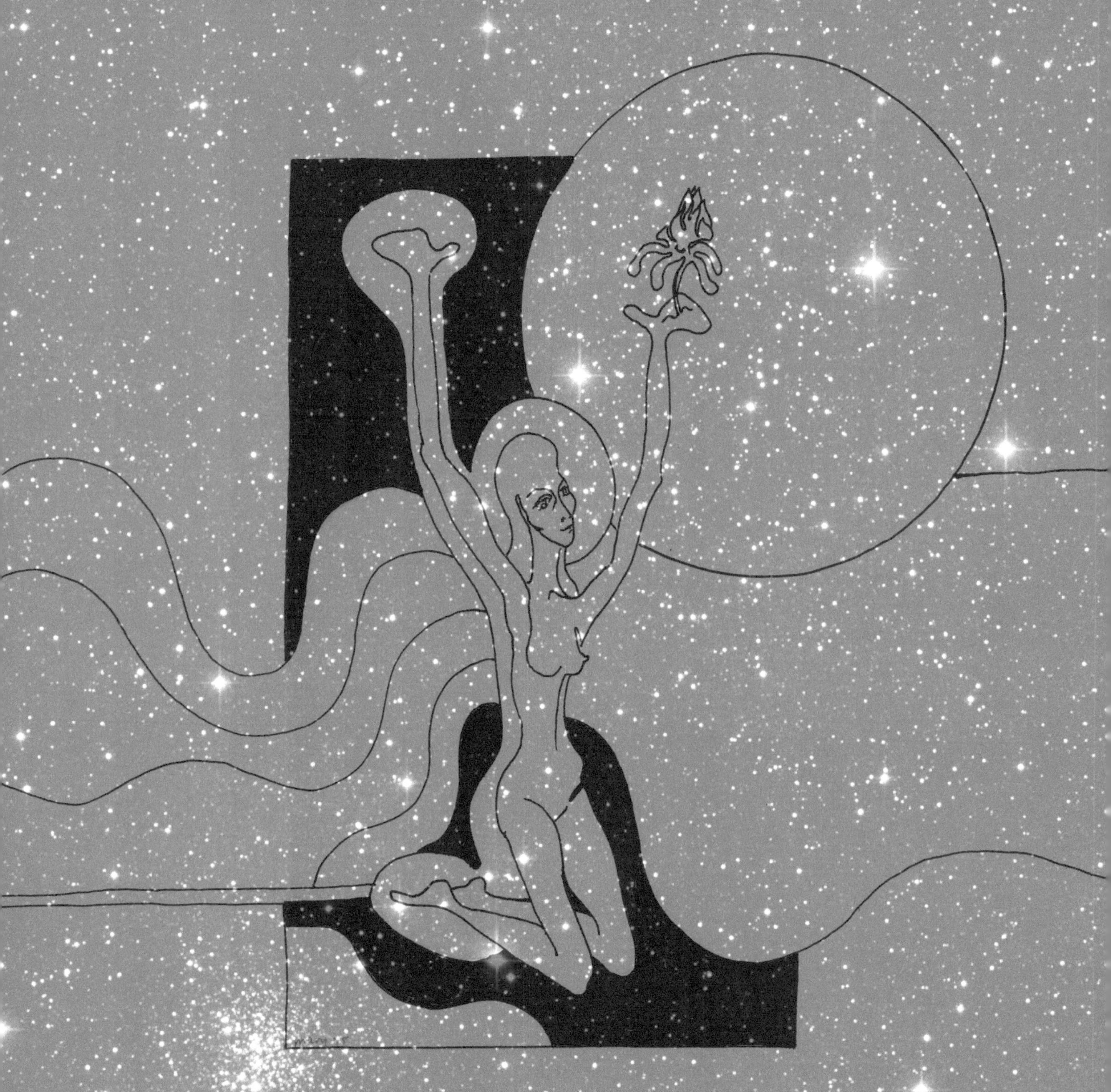

feeling the embodied presence...

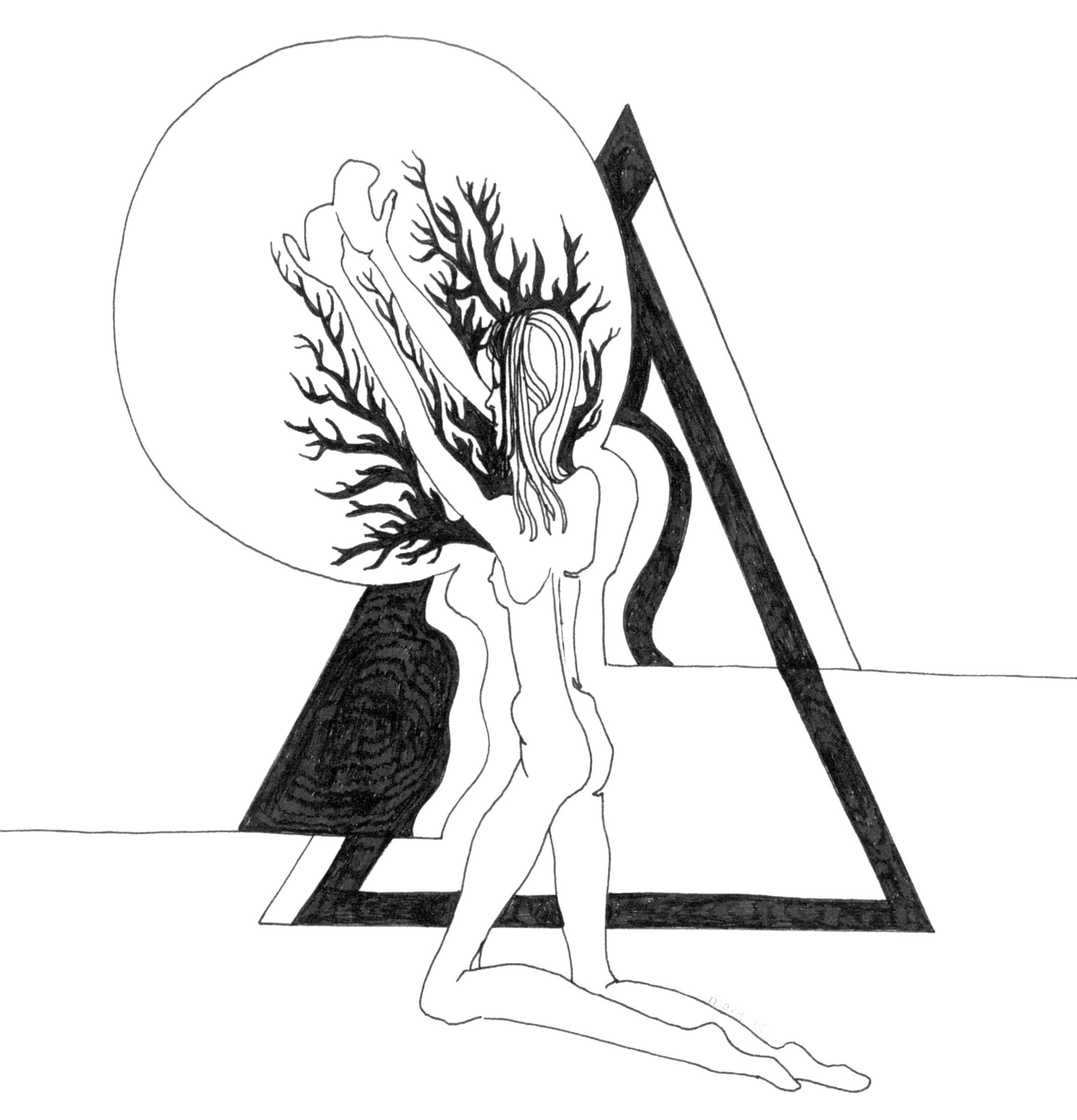

Prayer for Guidance

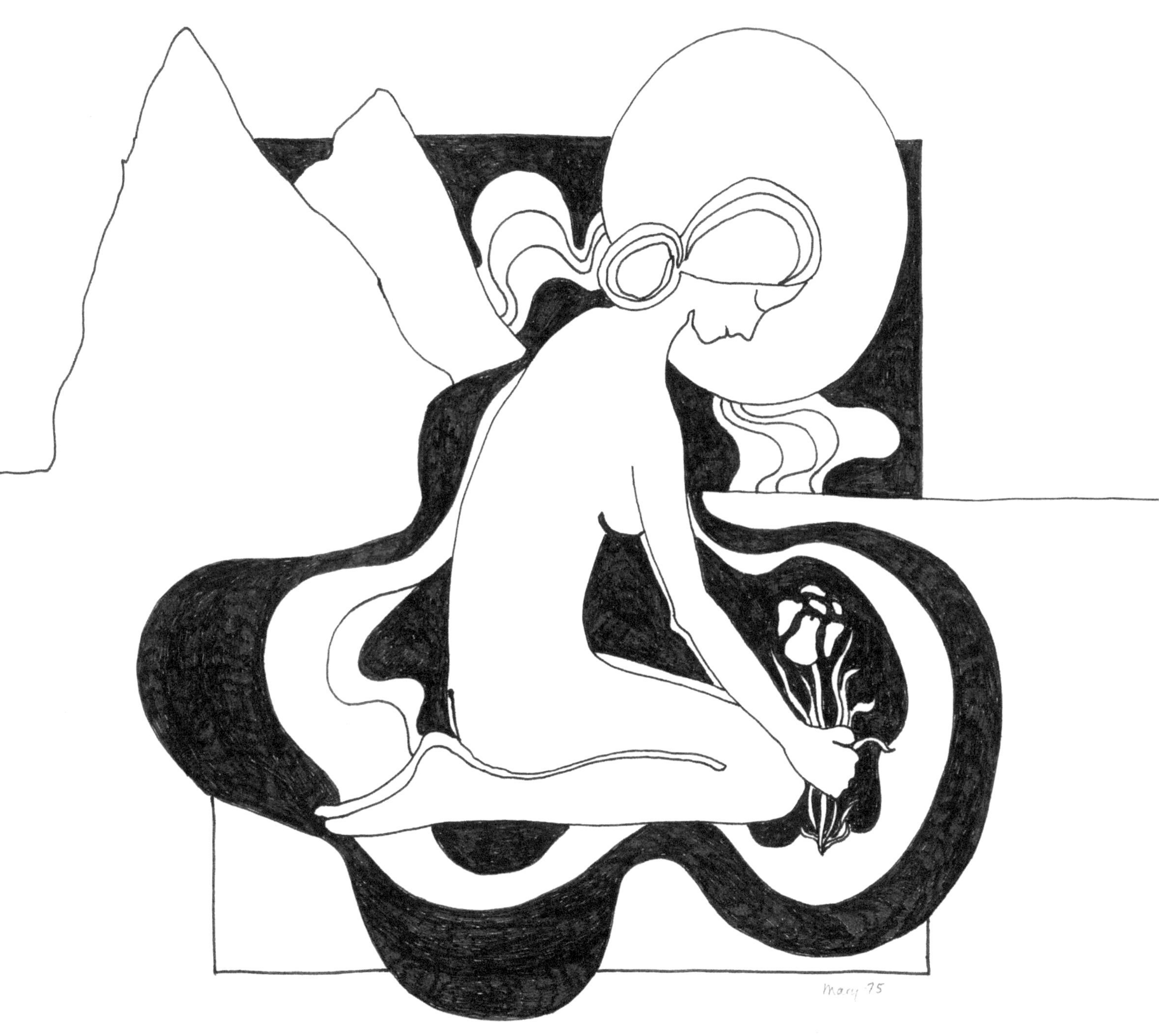

Open to Life's Mystery

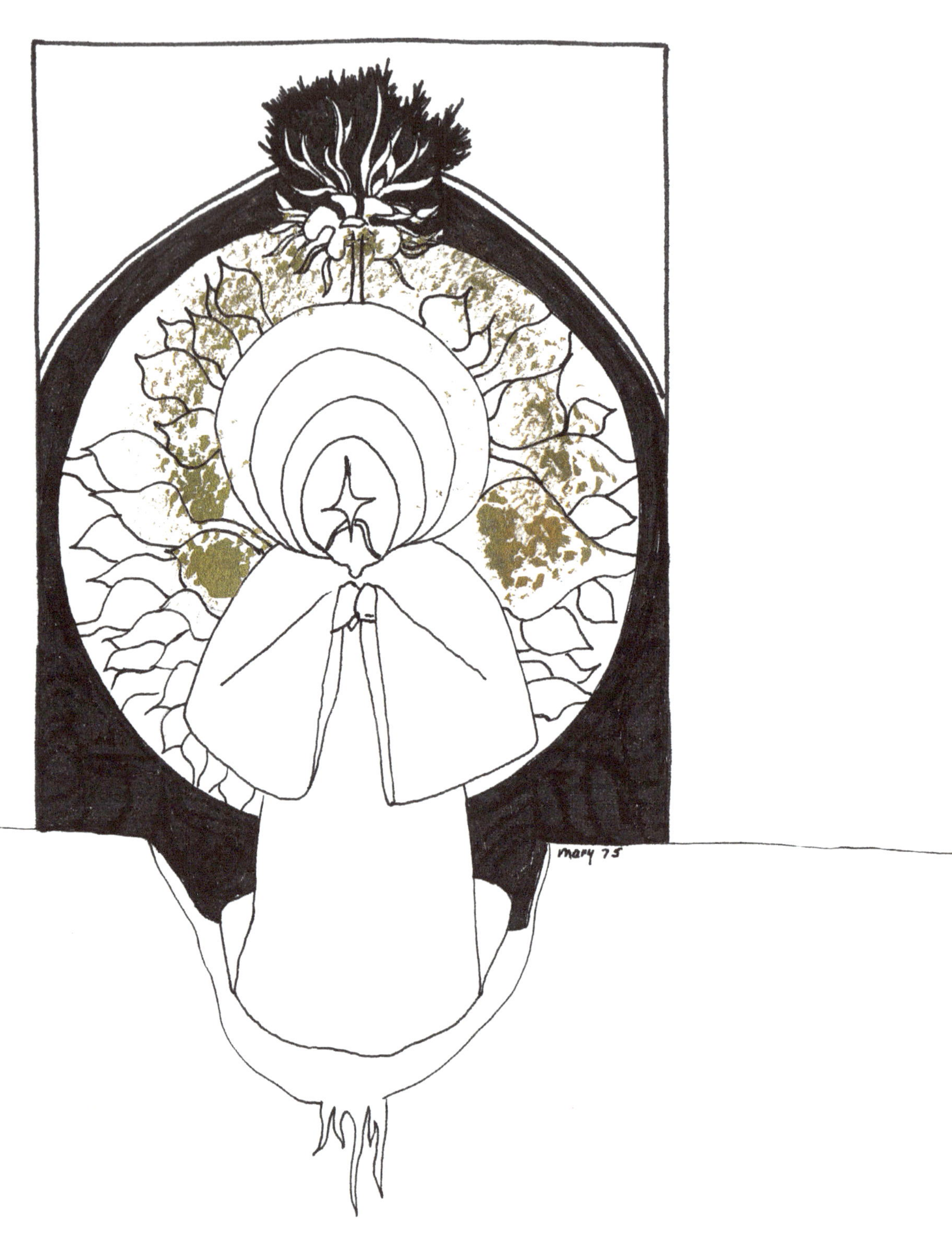

Devotion to the Stillness

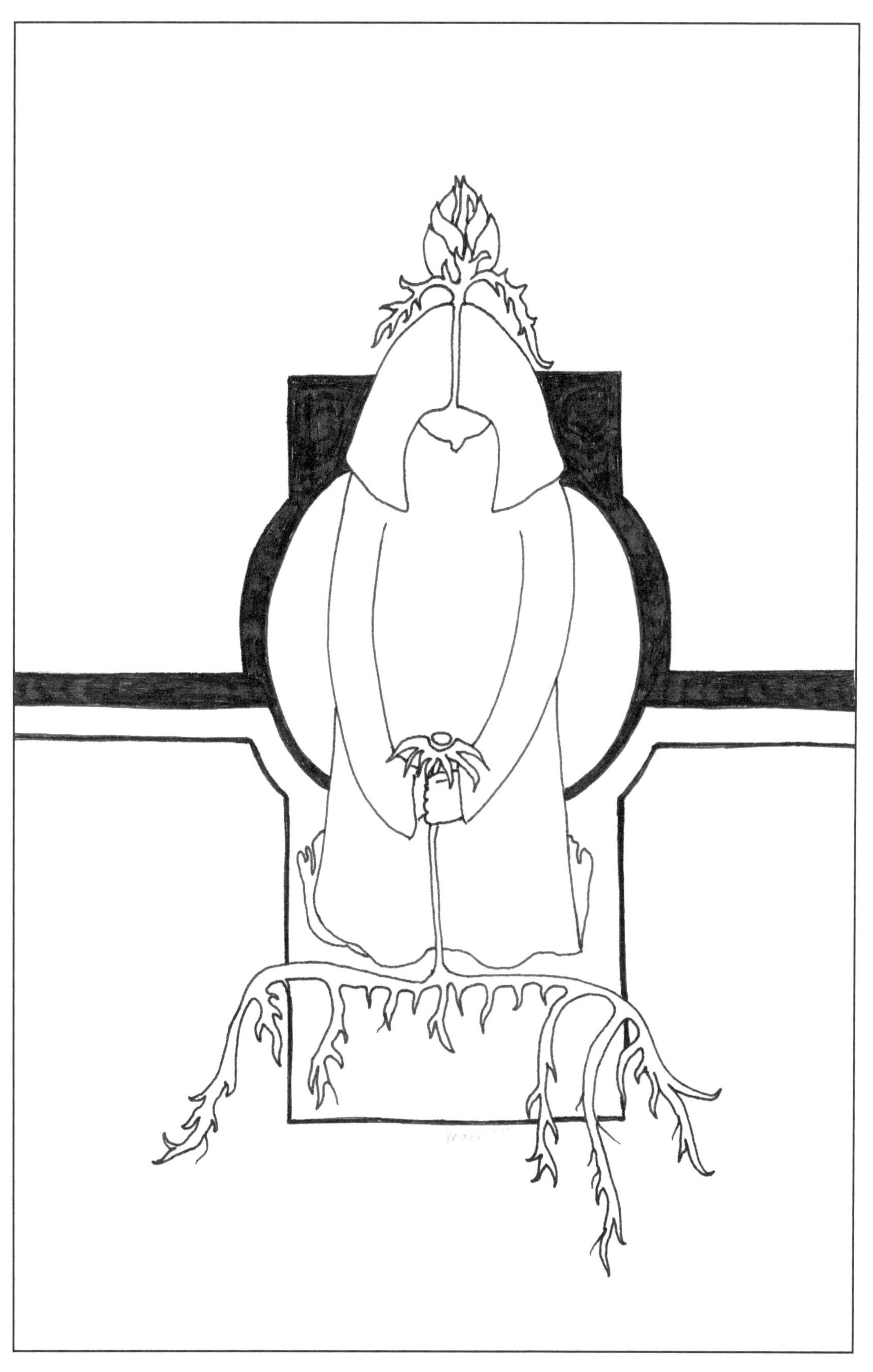

The Soul's Joy

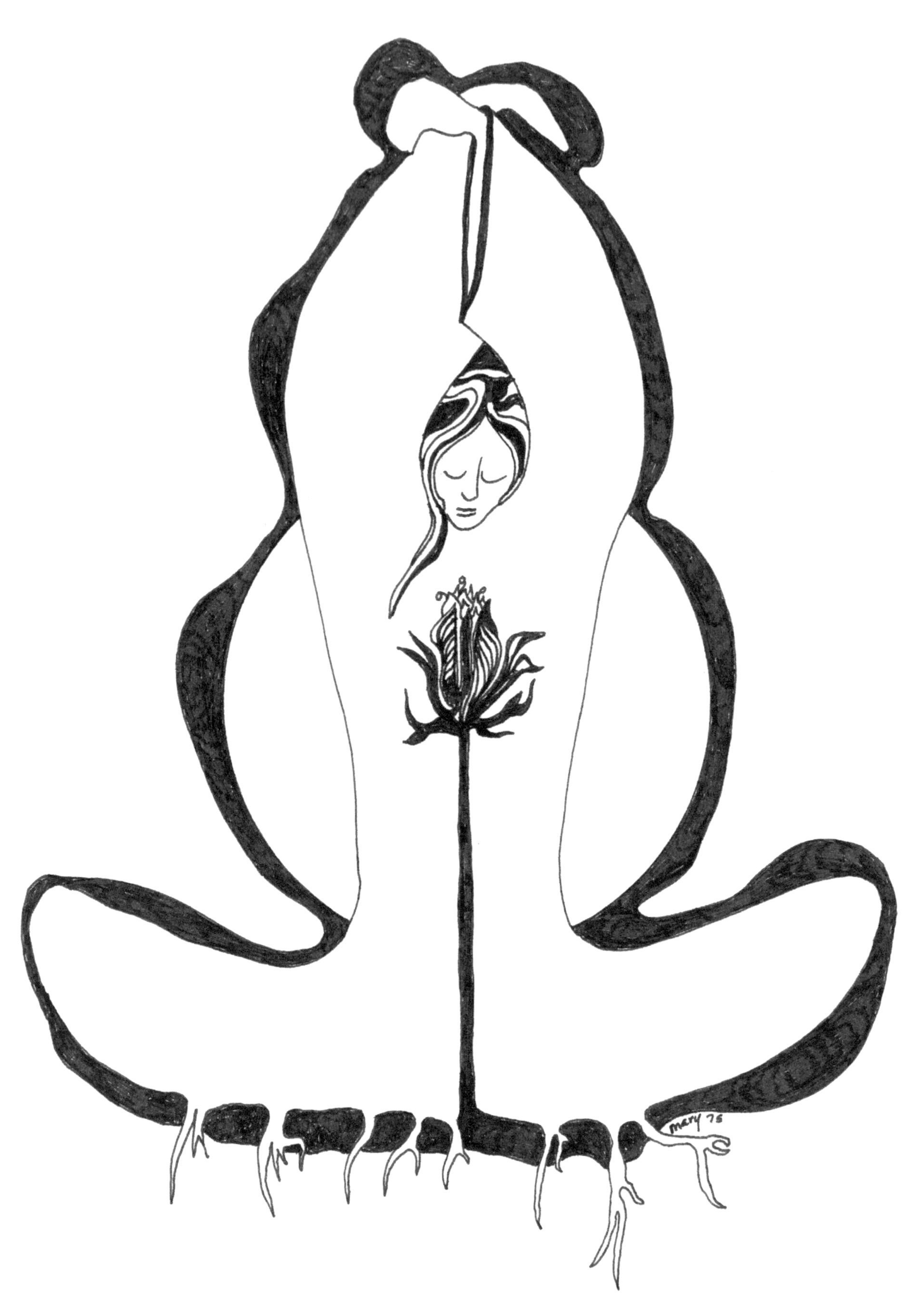

Dedication to the Heart

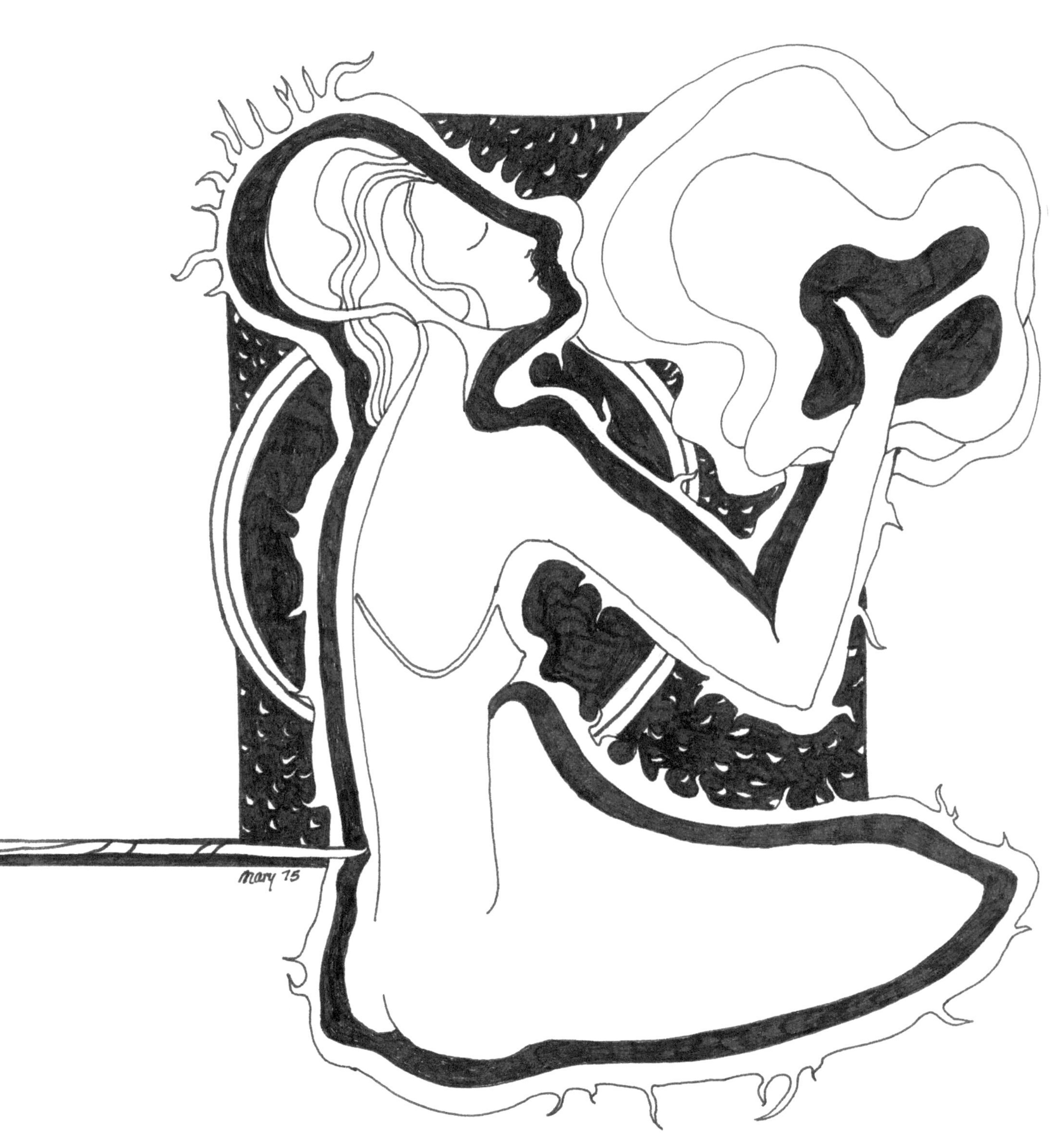

Devoted to the Way

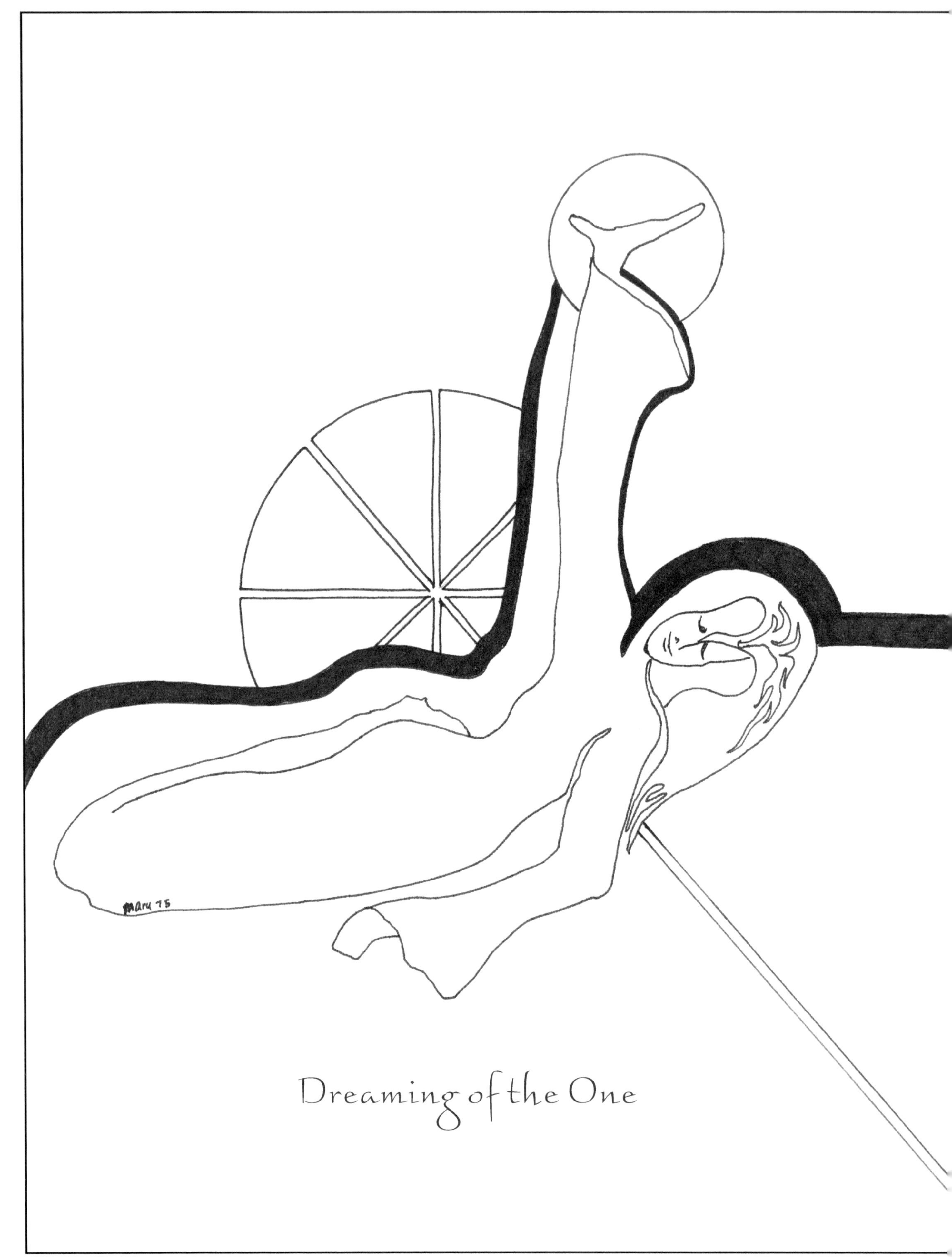

Dreaming of the One

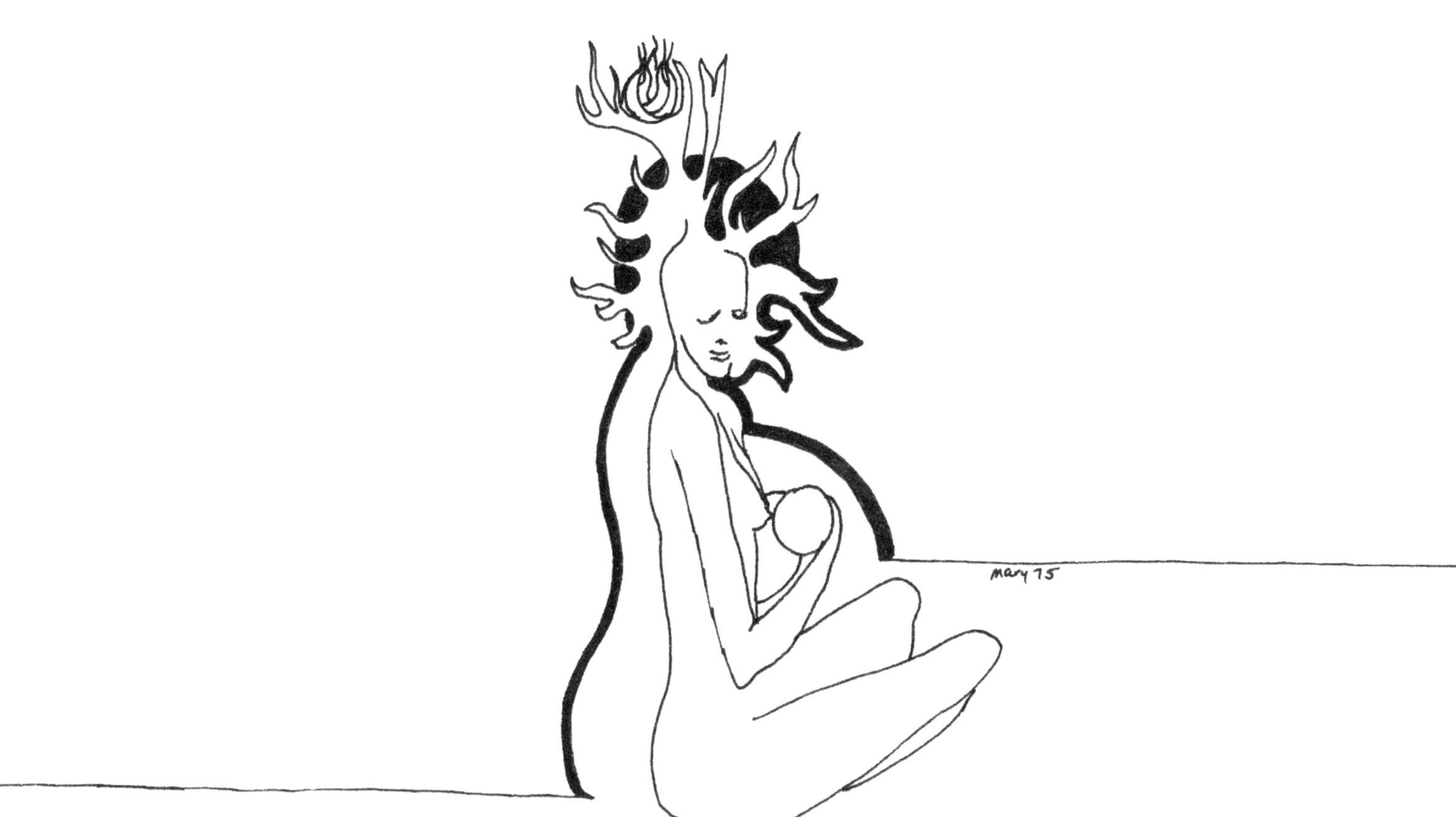

I AM the Spirit…

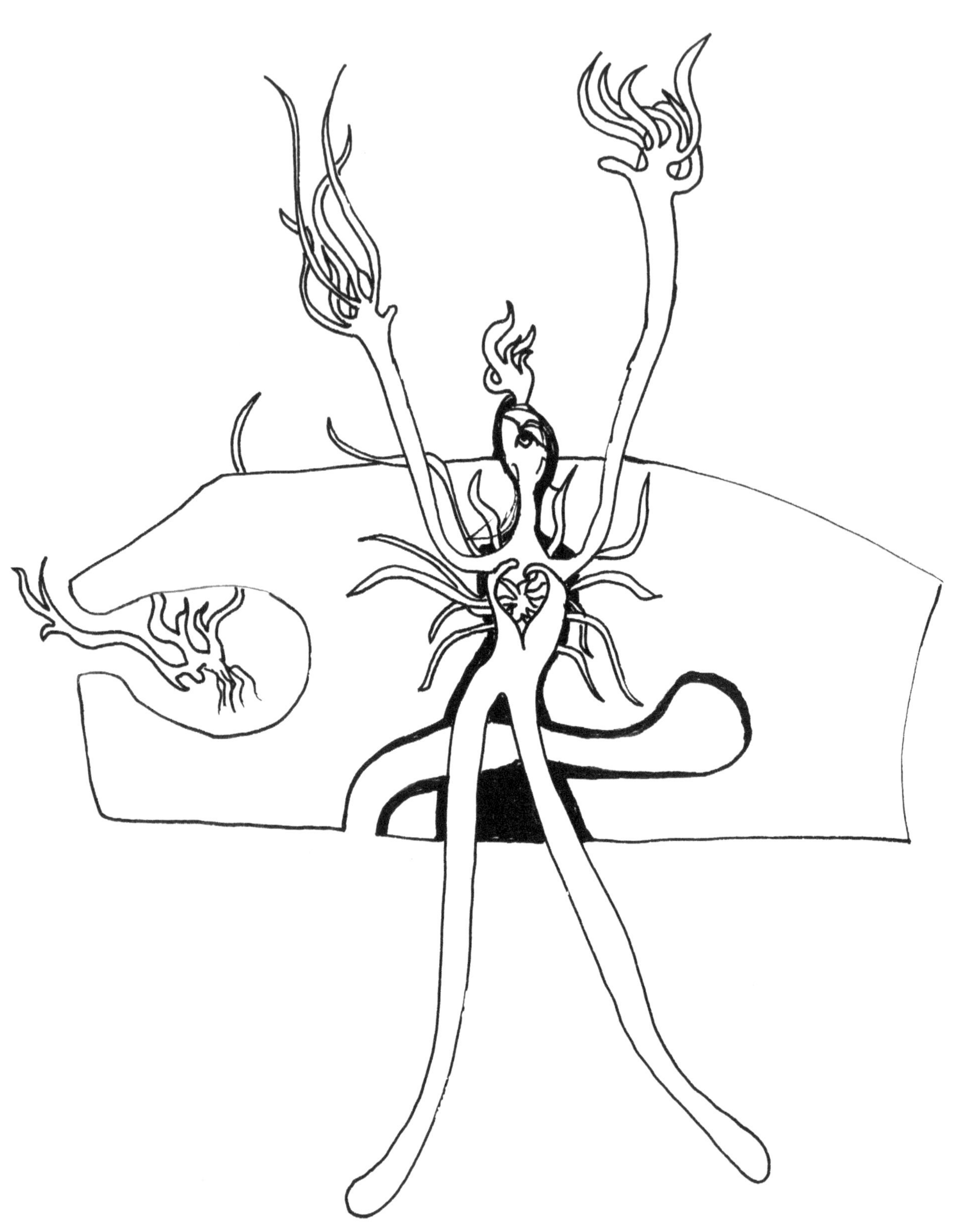

Love in Animation

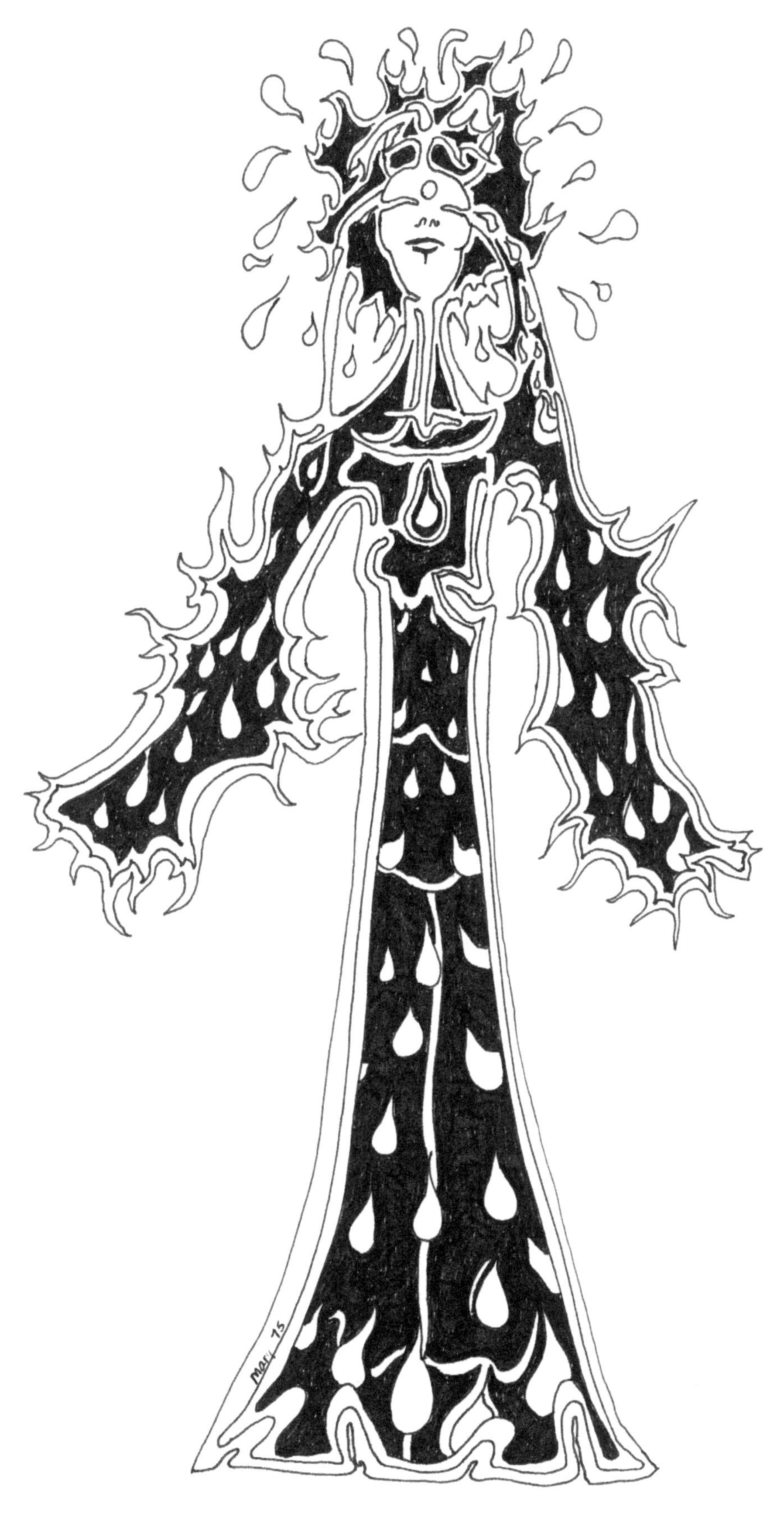

Tears Borne of Love

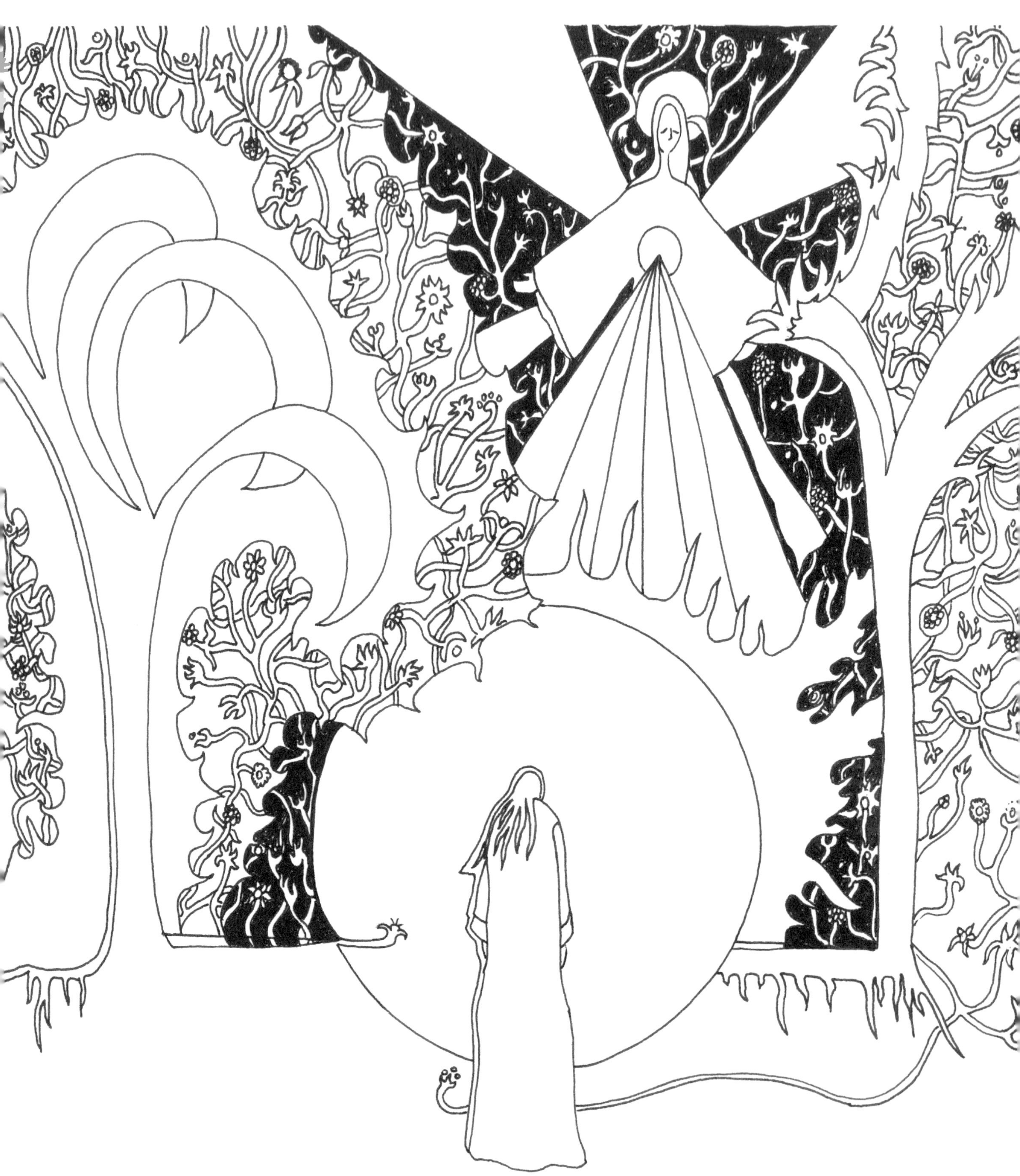

Nature Come As Beauty

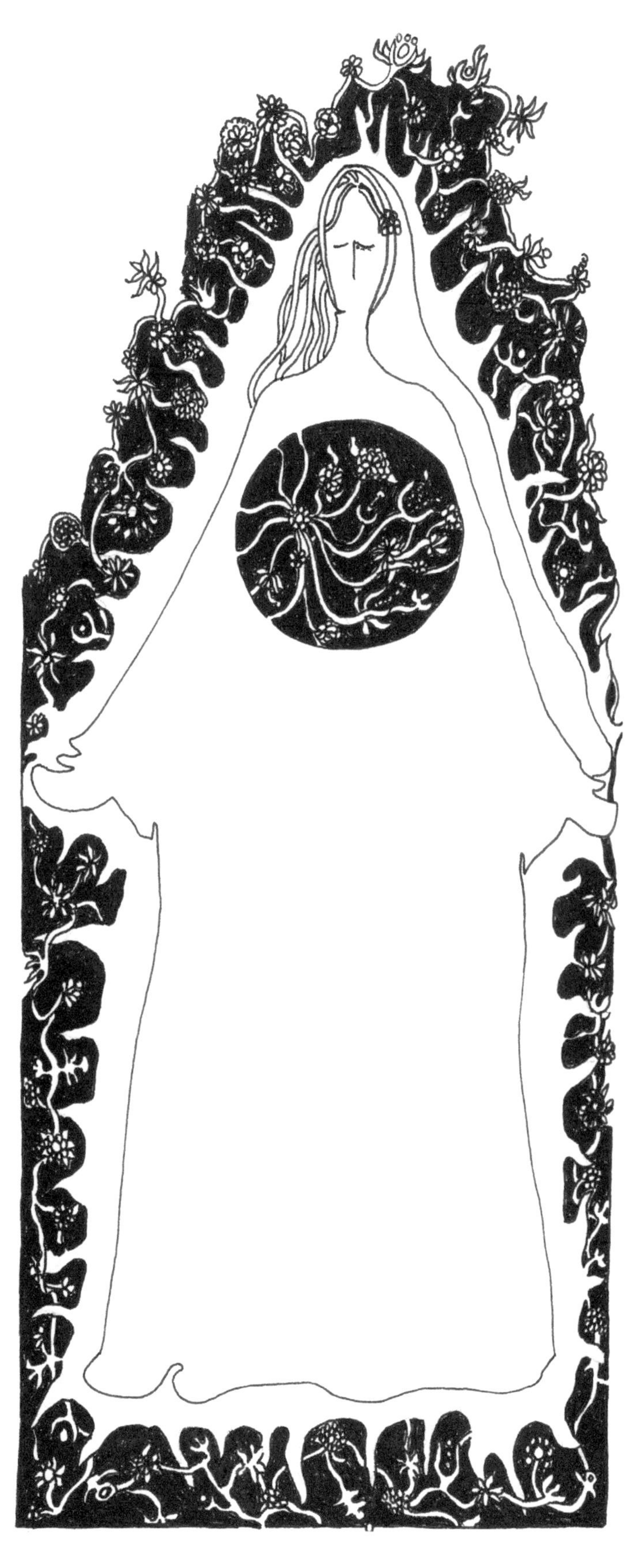

Blossoms of Devotion

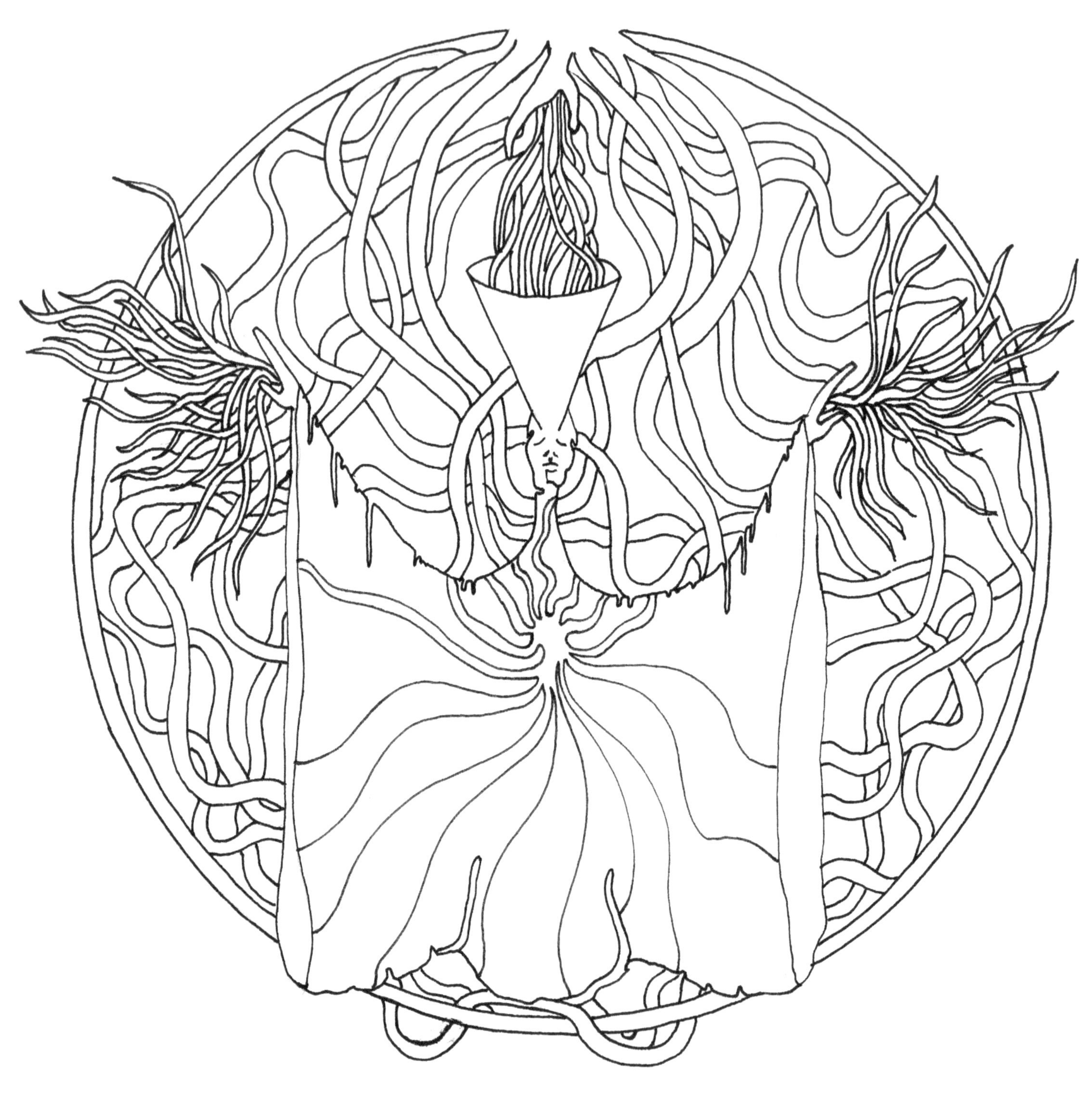

The Call for Divine Energy

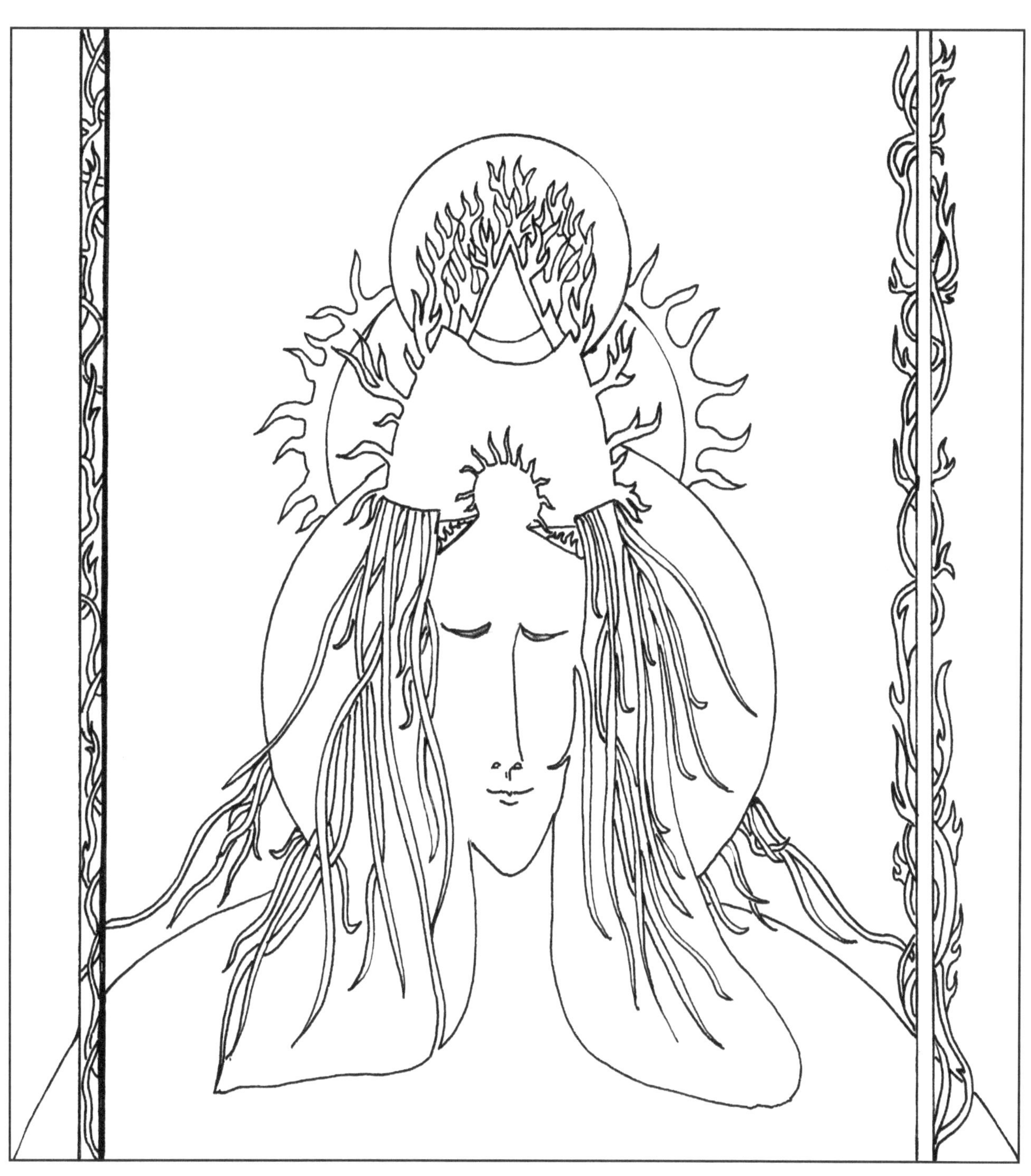

Freedom's Call

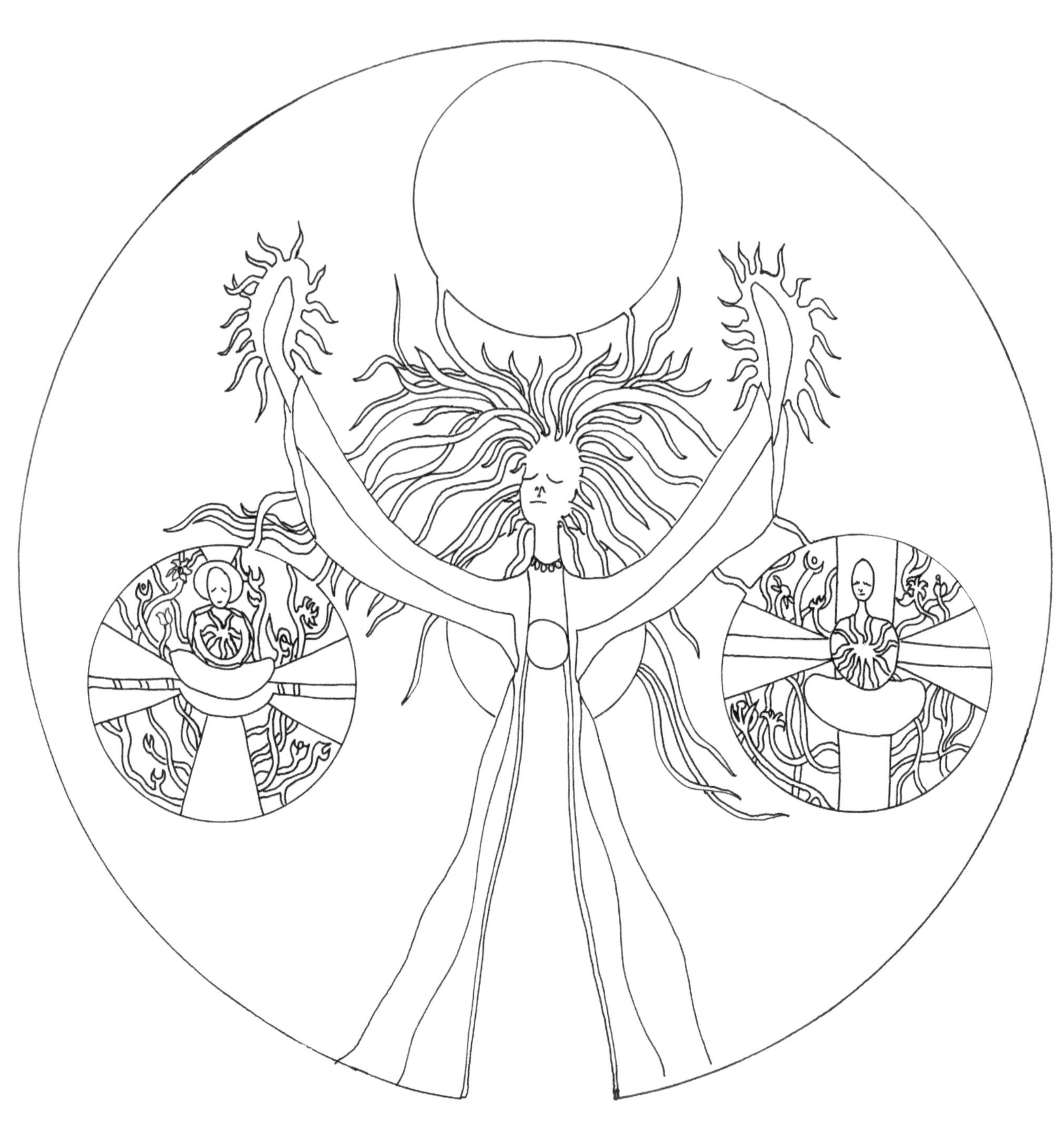

Dedication to the One

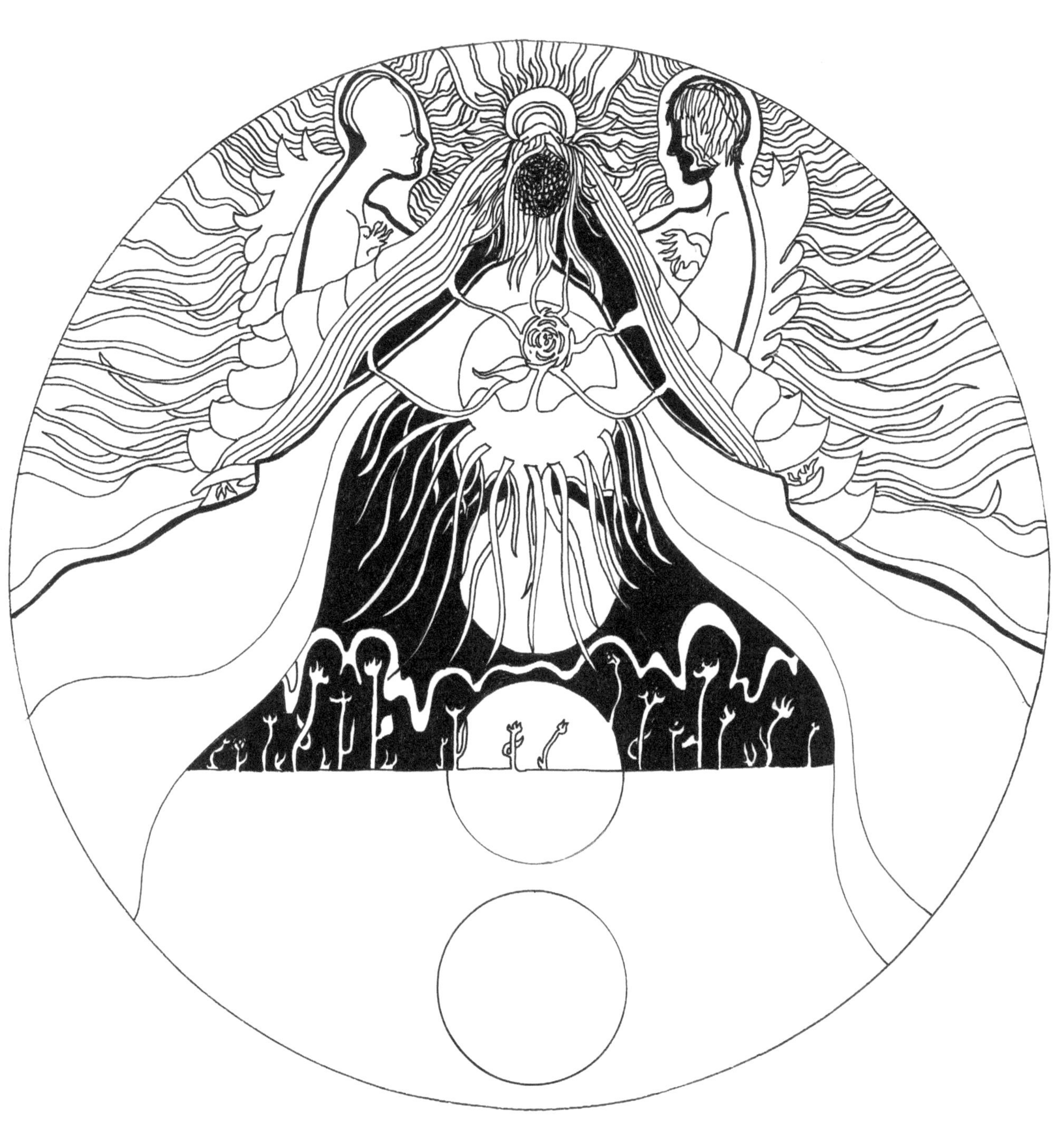

The Scent of Devotion

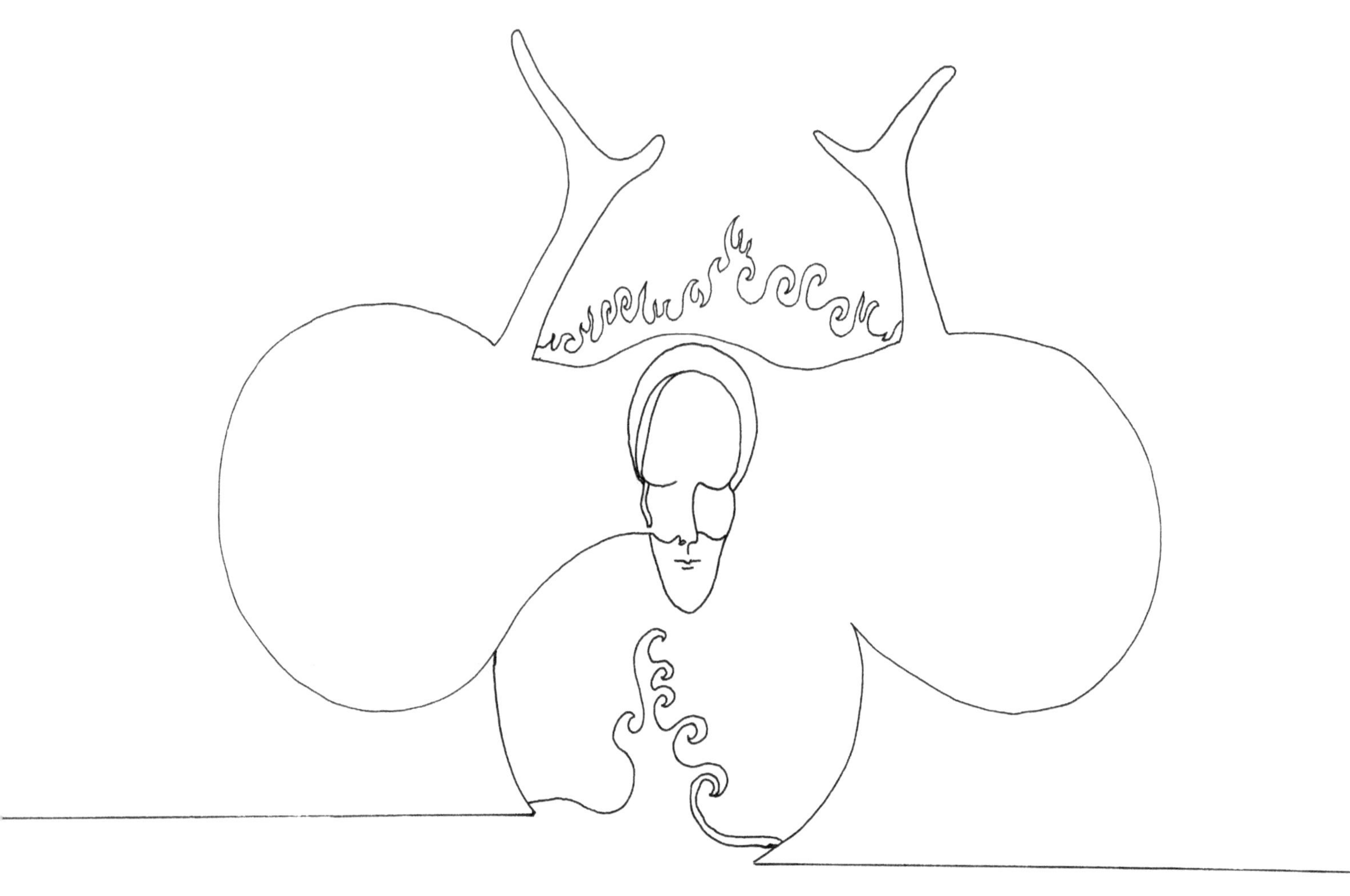

Purification

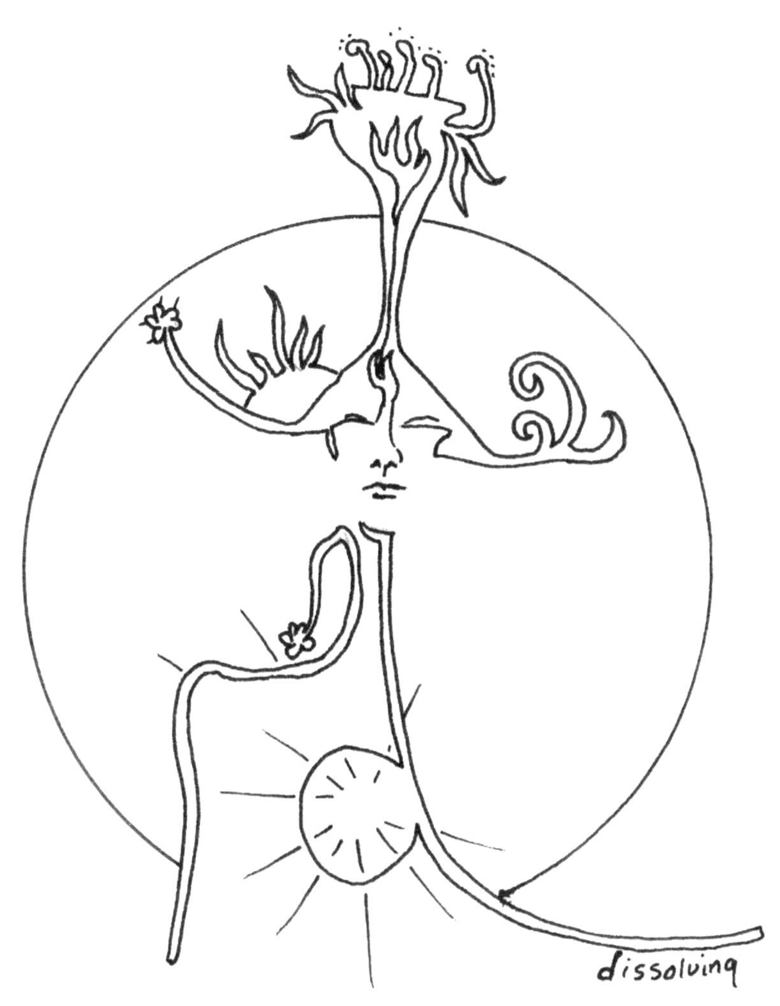

Dissolving in the Light

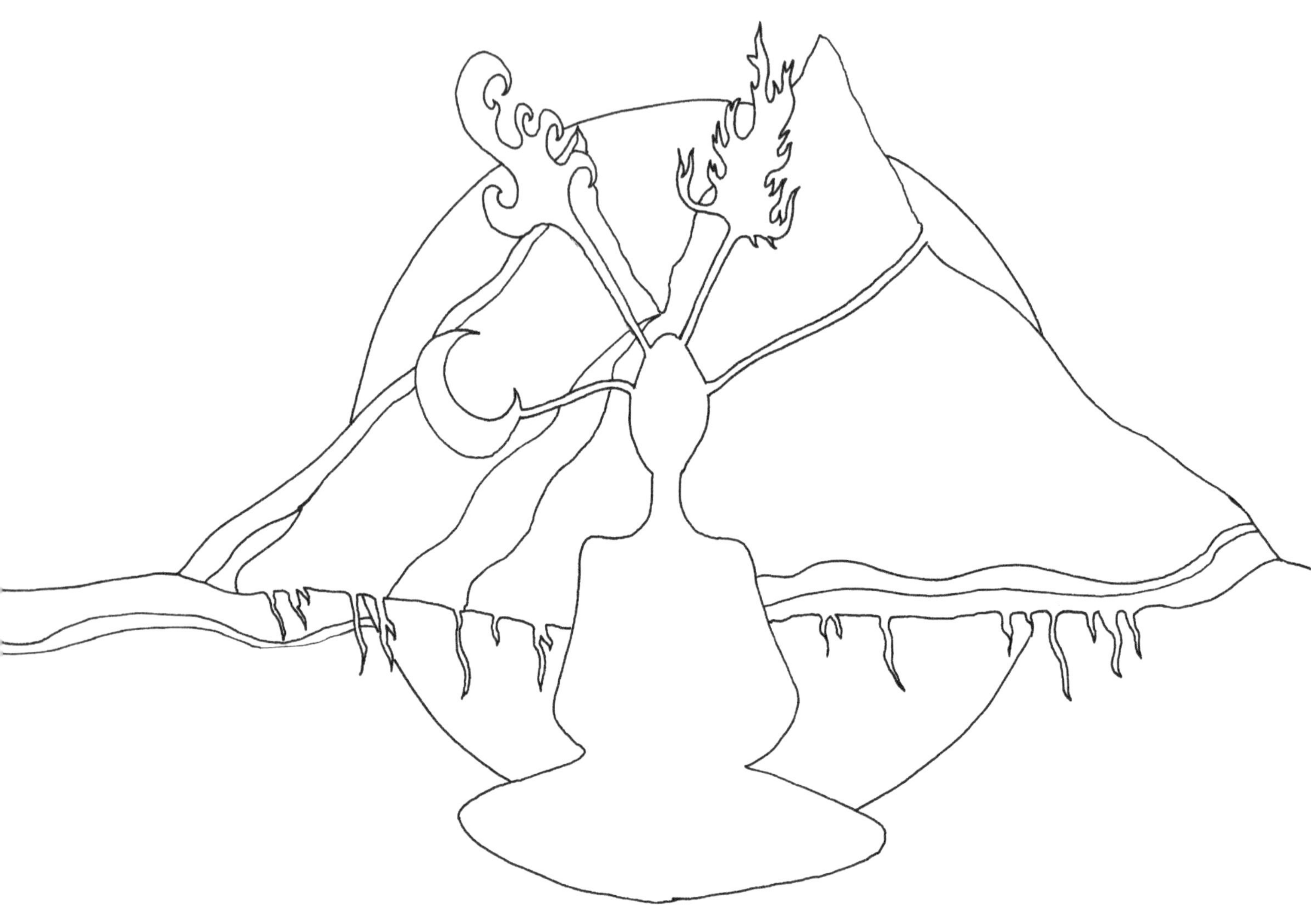

Feeling the Stillness

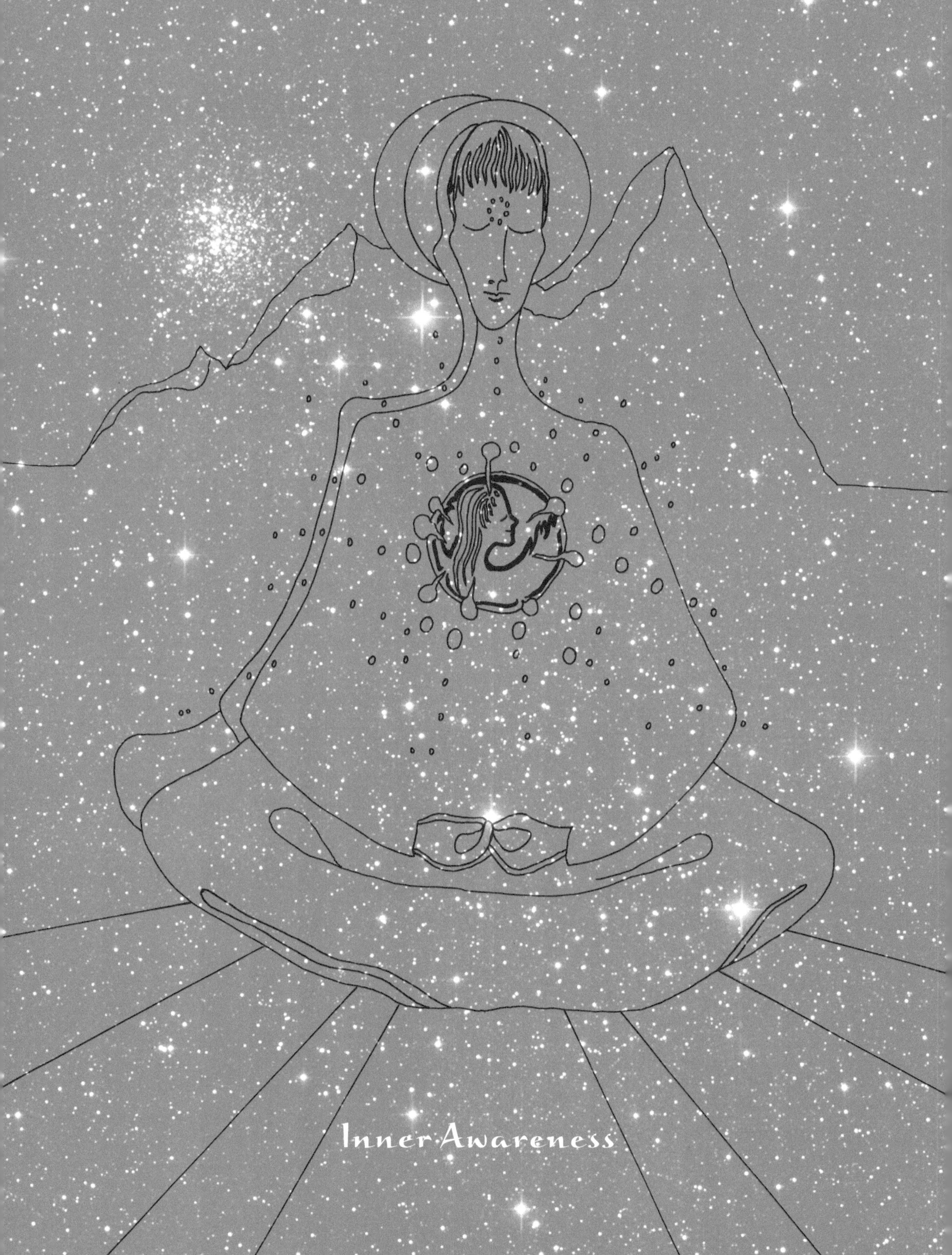
Inner Awareness

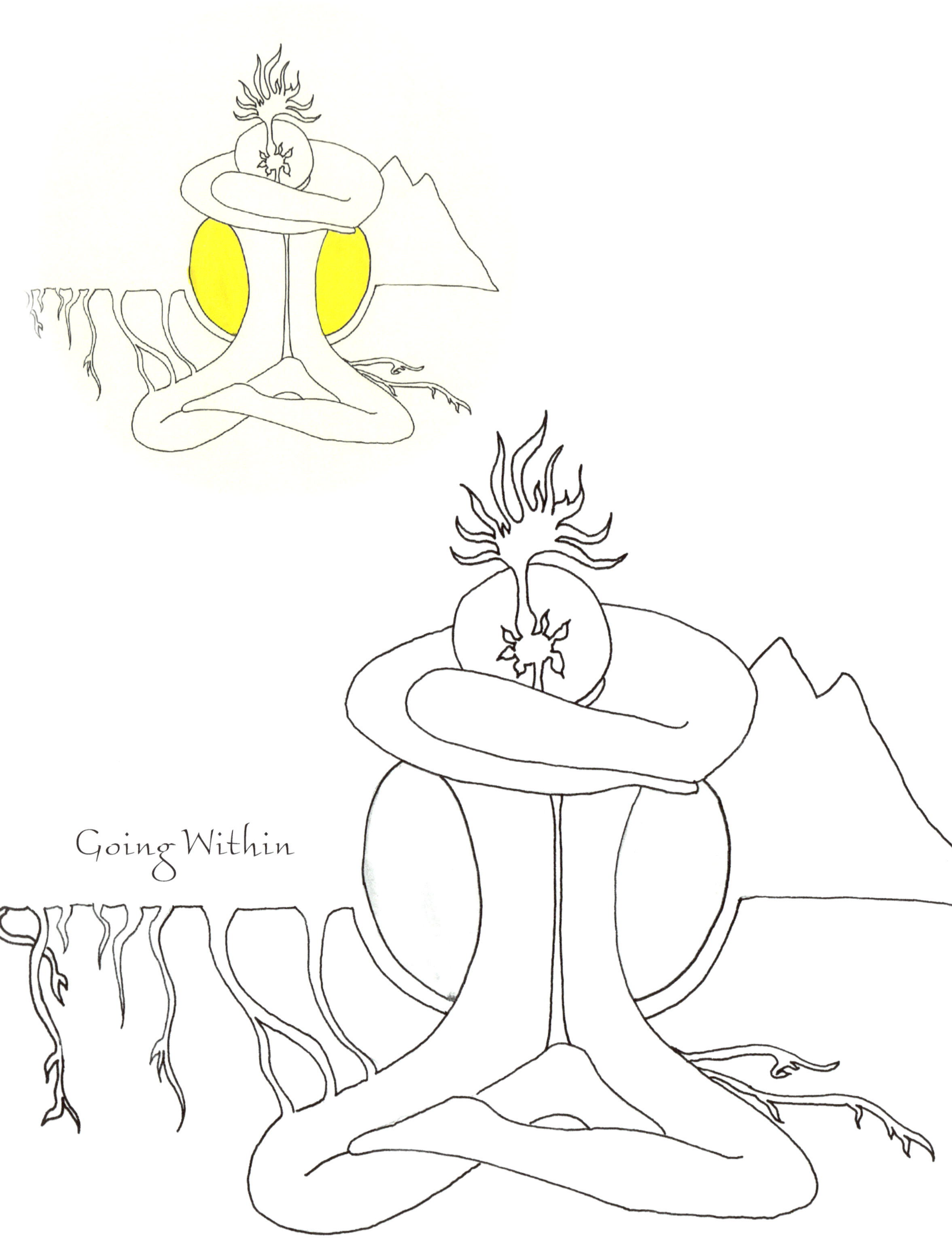
Going Within

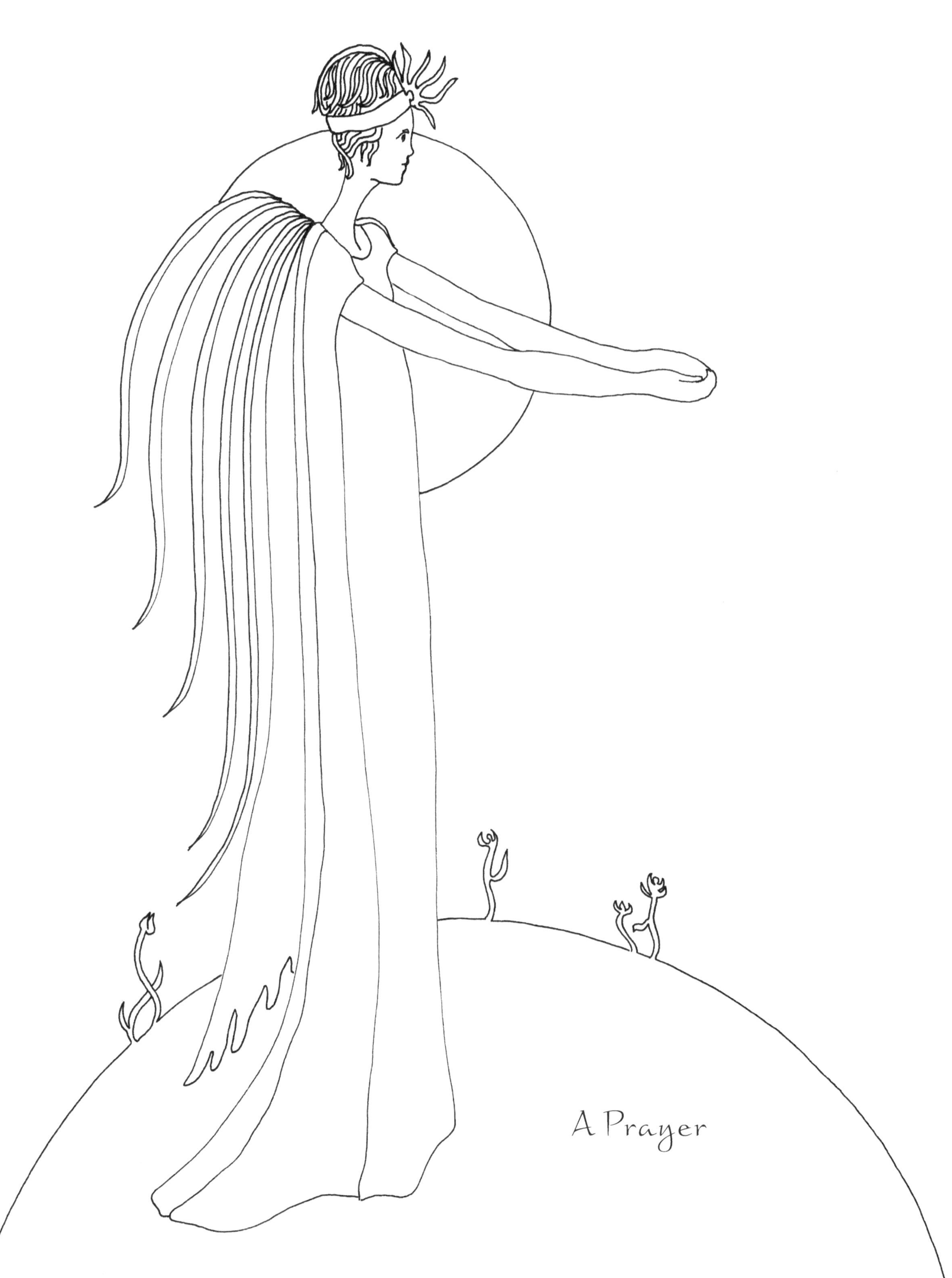
A Prayer

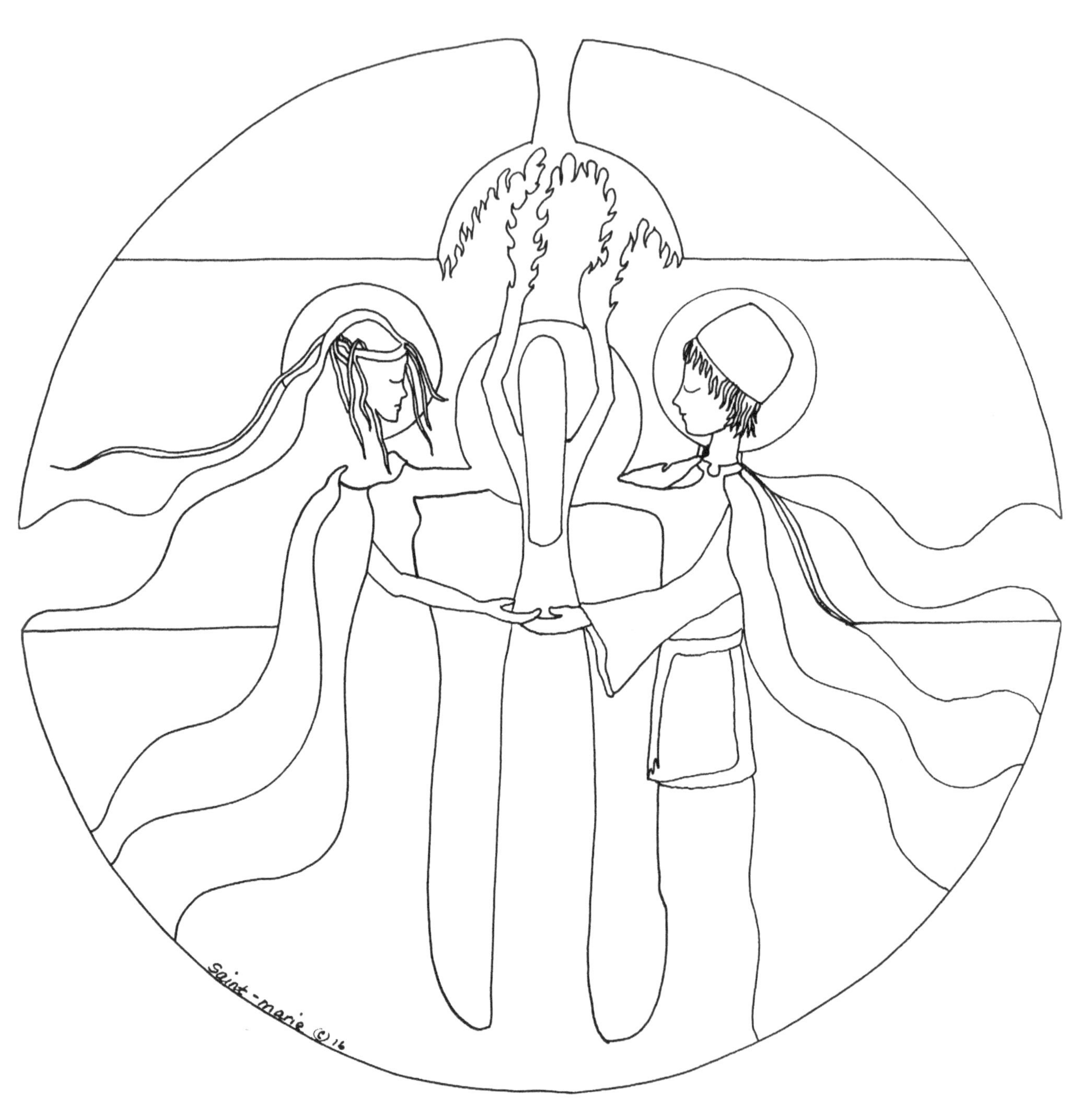

The Sanctuary of the One

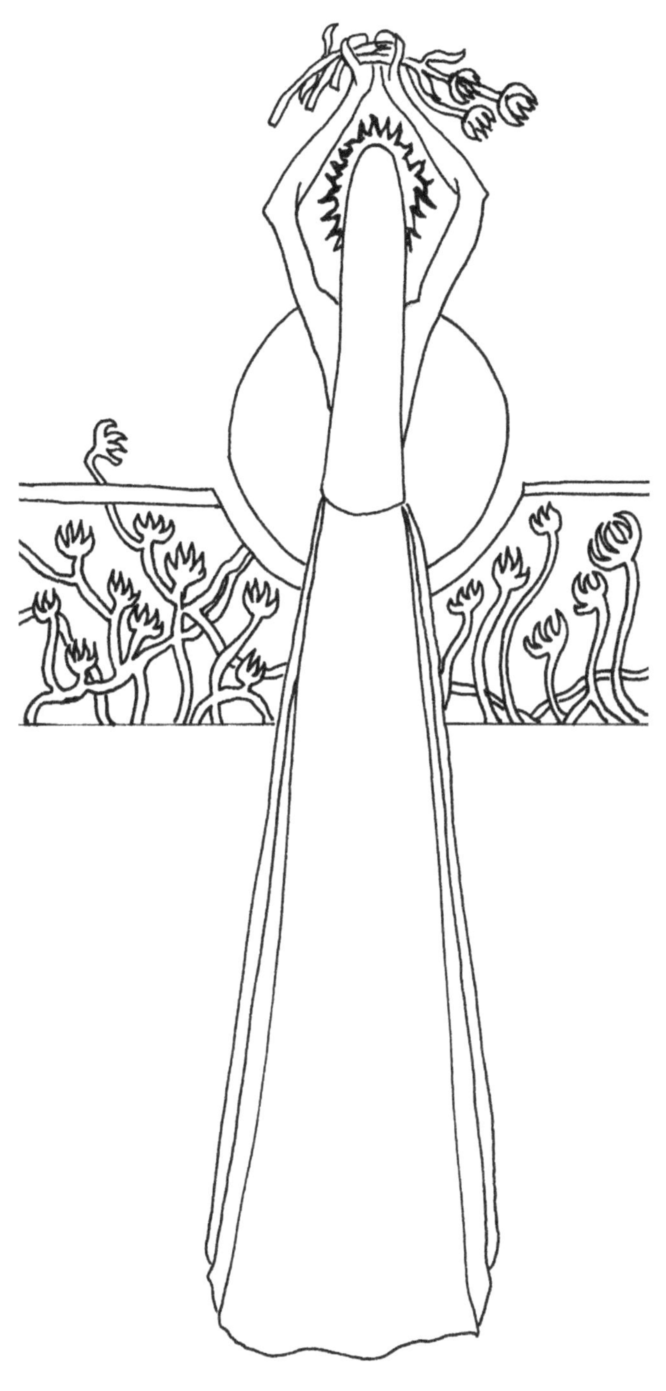

Flowers of Devotion

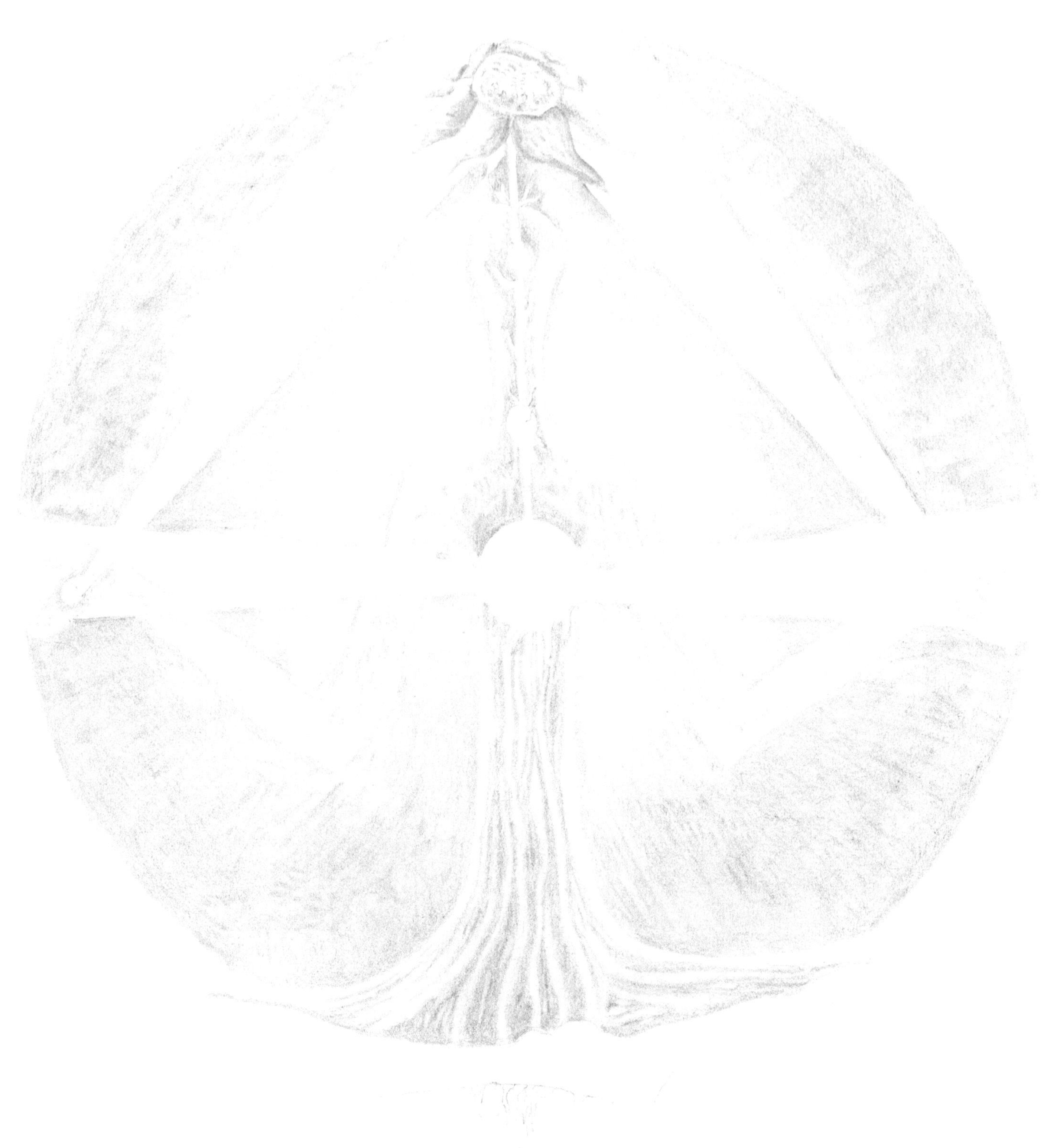

The Light of the Sun

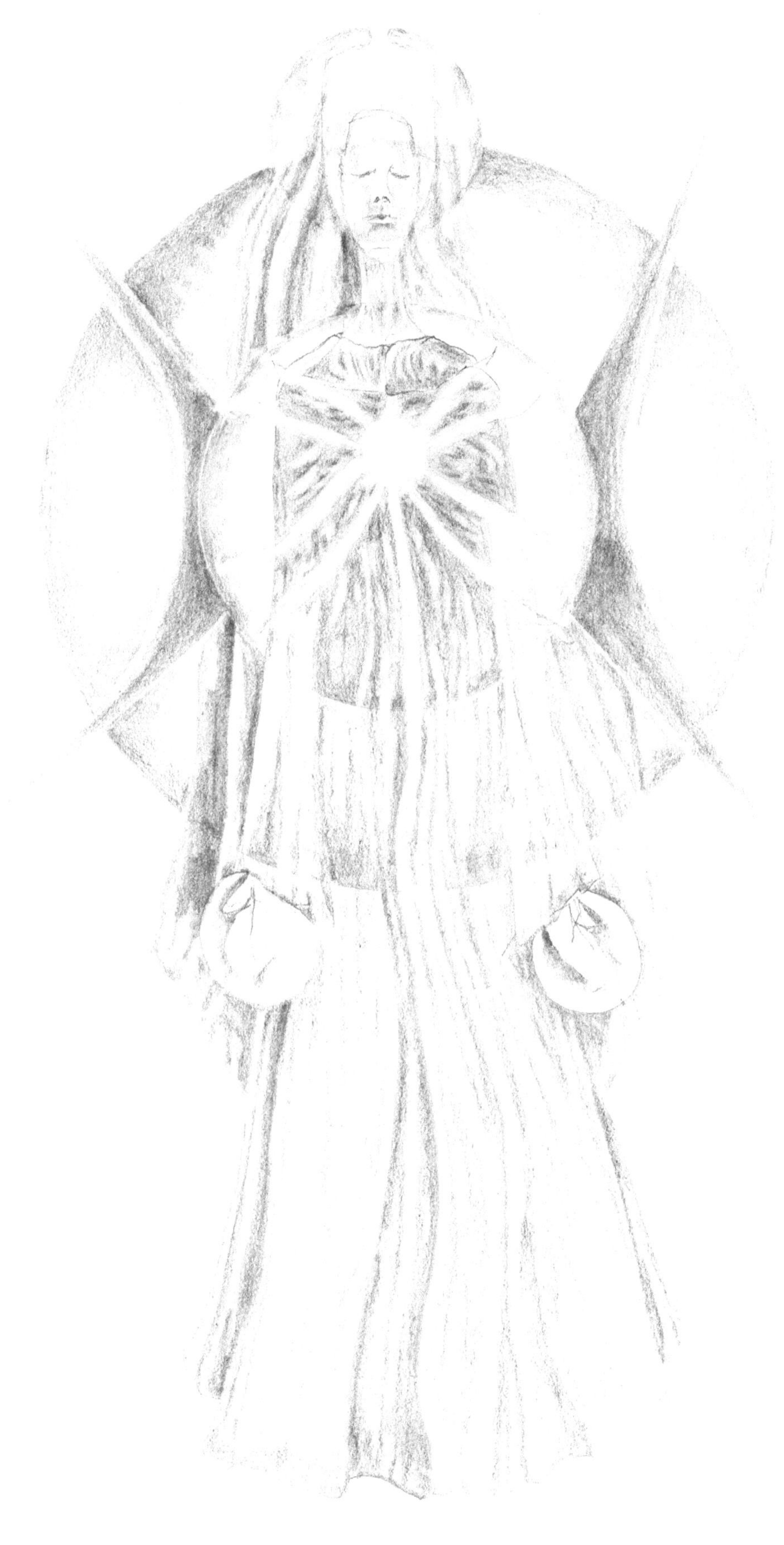

Peace

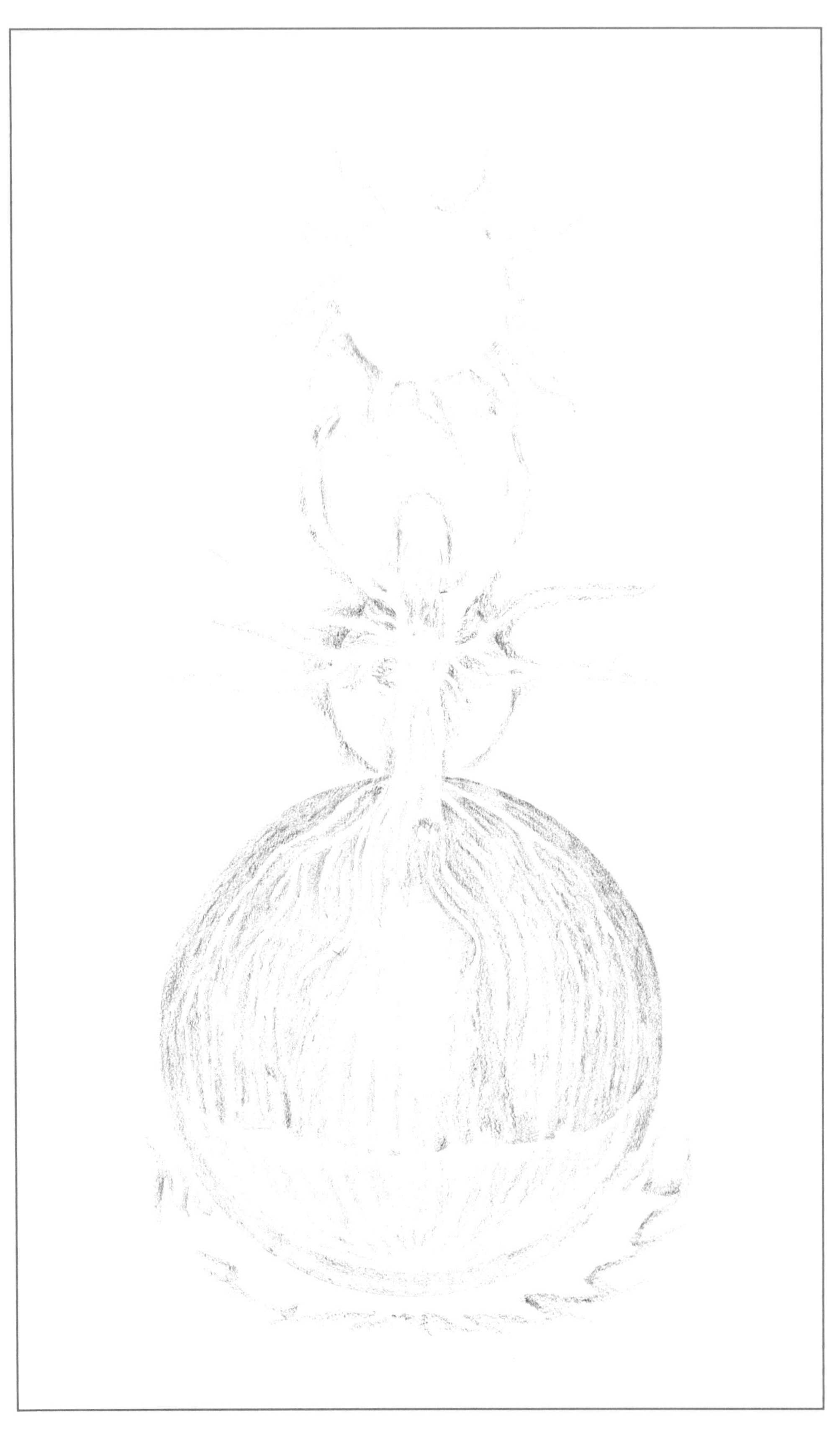

Birthing Earth's Consciousness

Thy Will Be Done

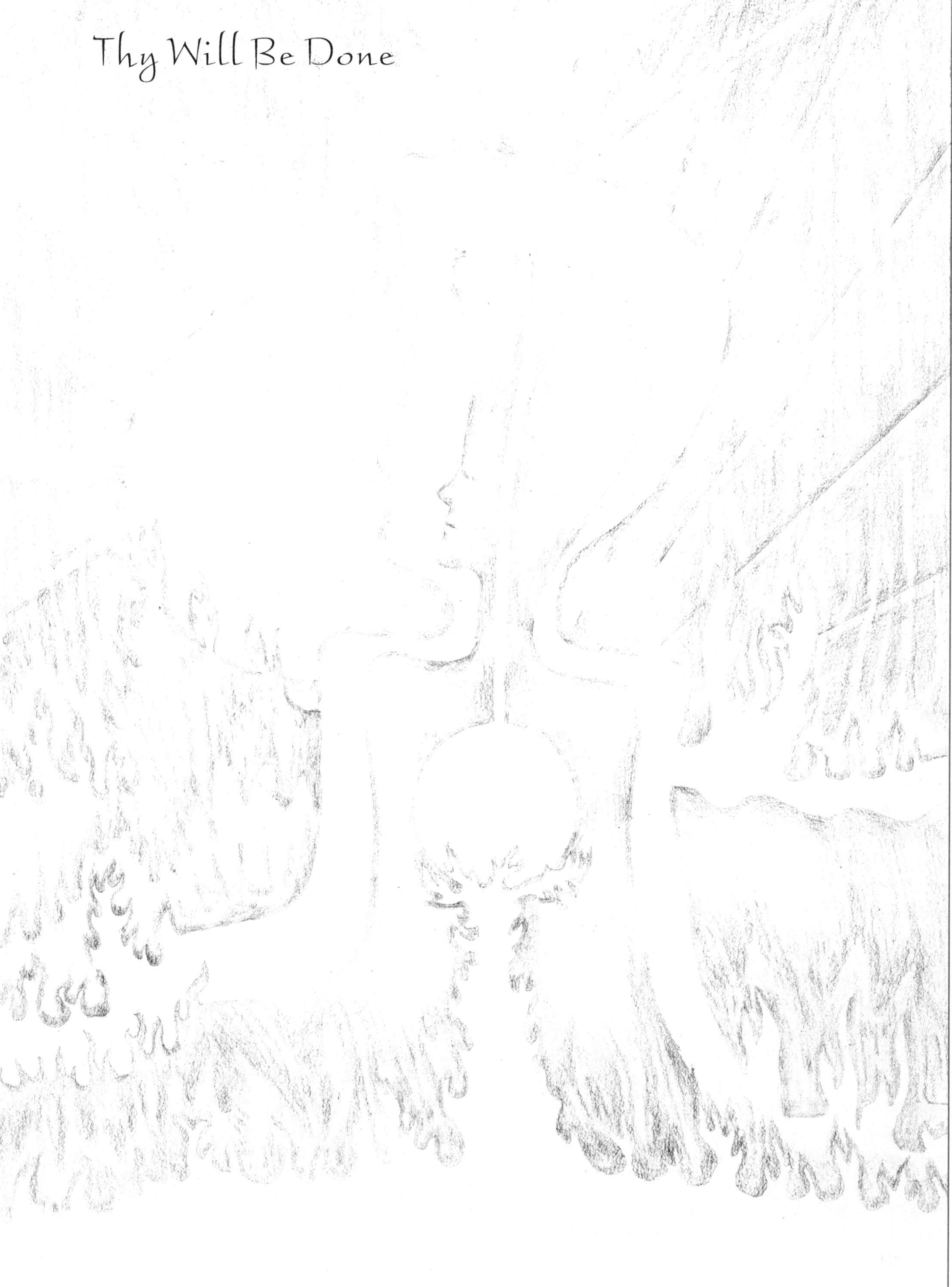

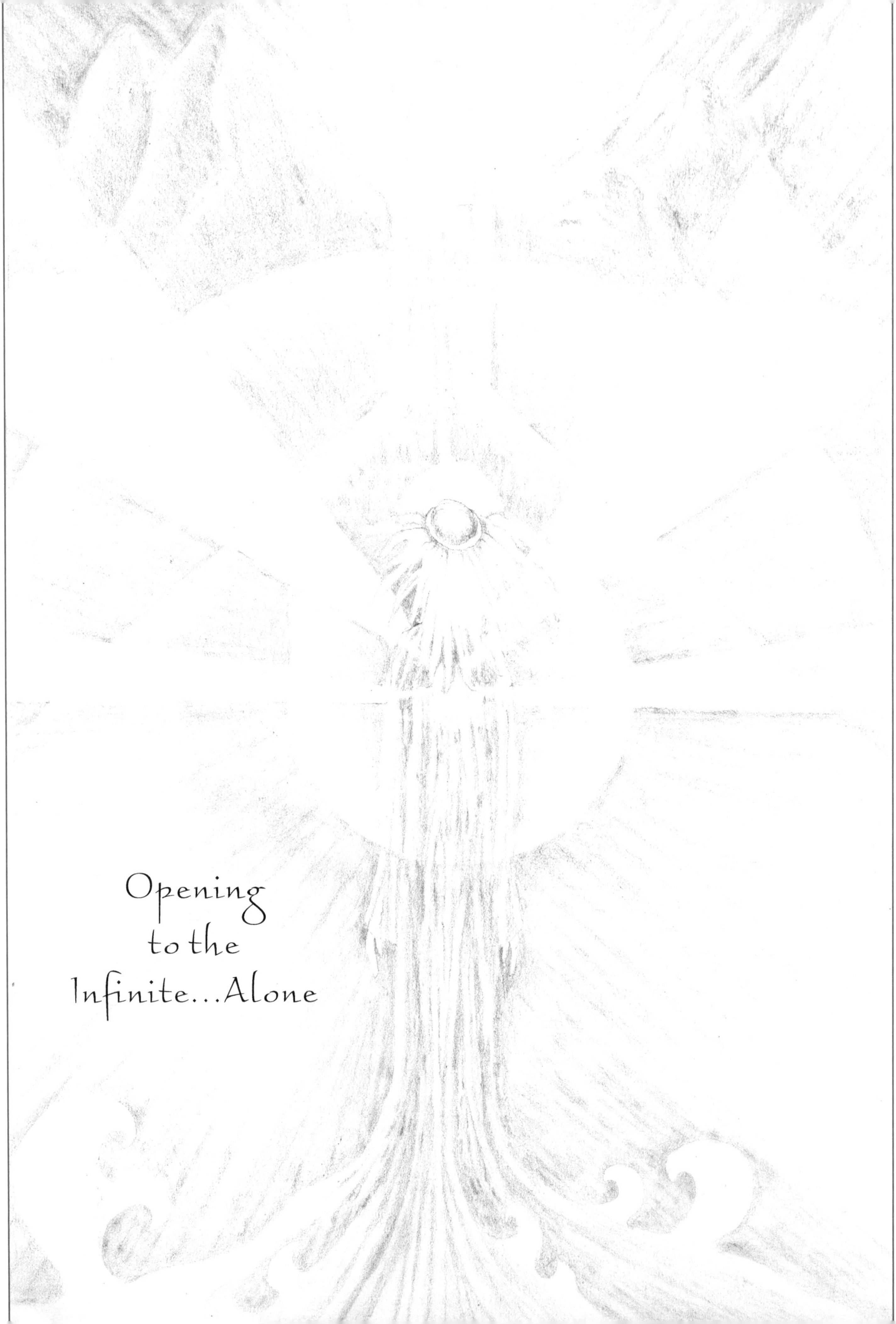

Opening
to the
Infinite...Alone

Fires of Purification

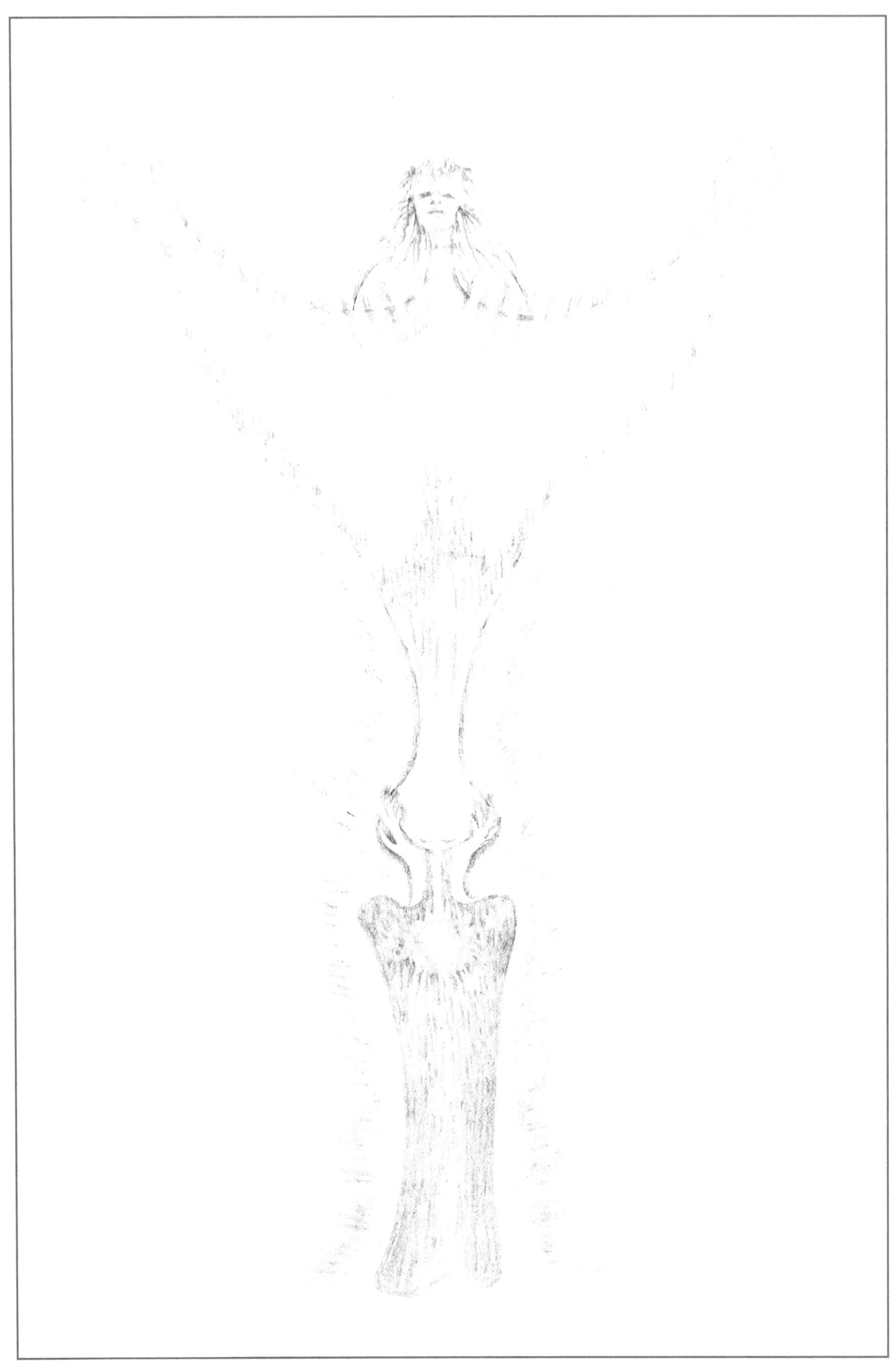

Rebirth

Balance

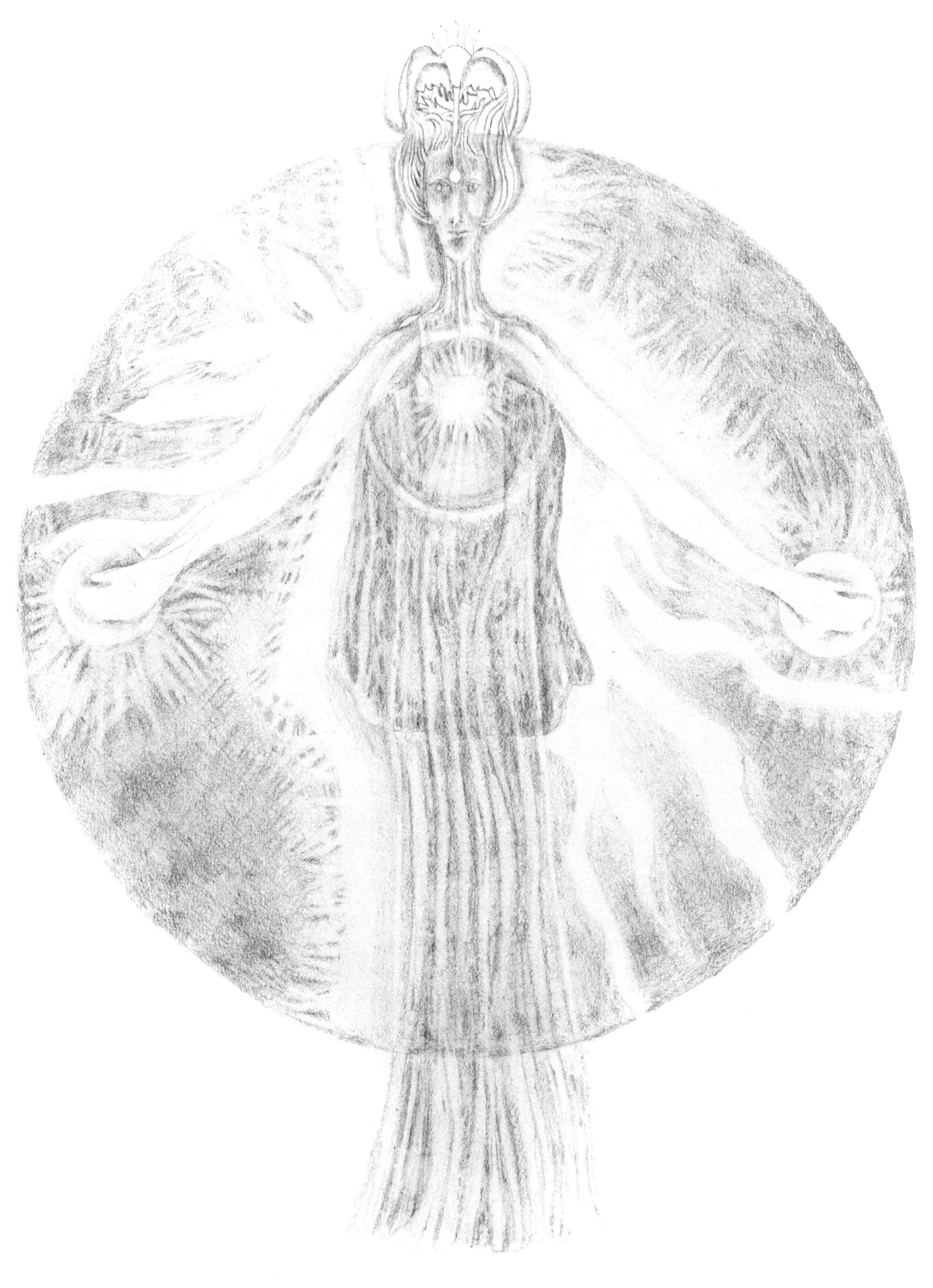

I Stand...Illumined...I Am

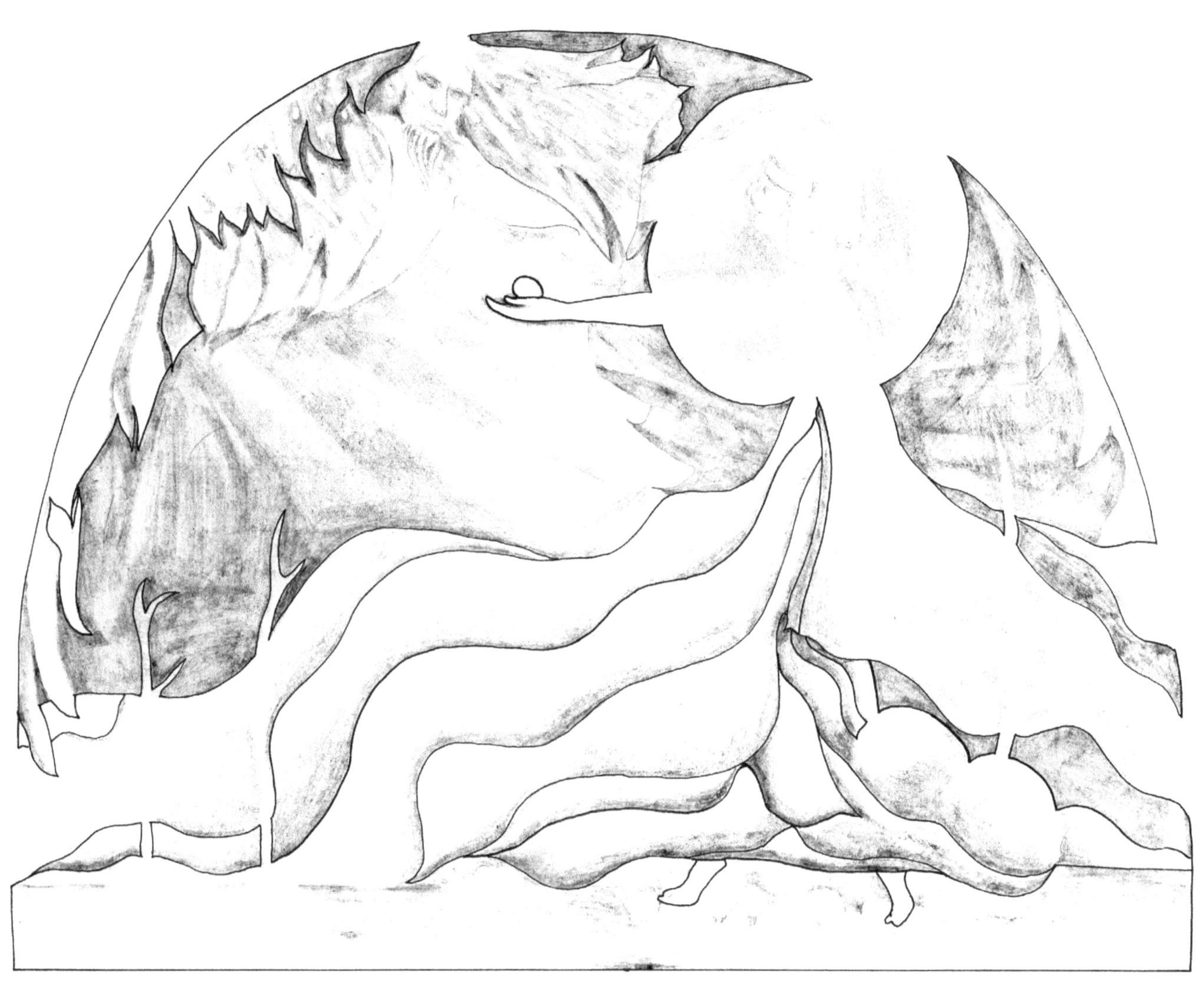

Merging

Radiance of the Heart

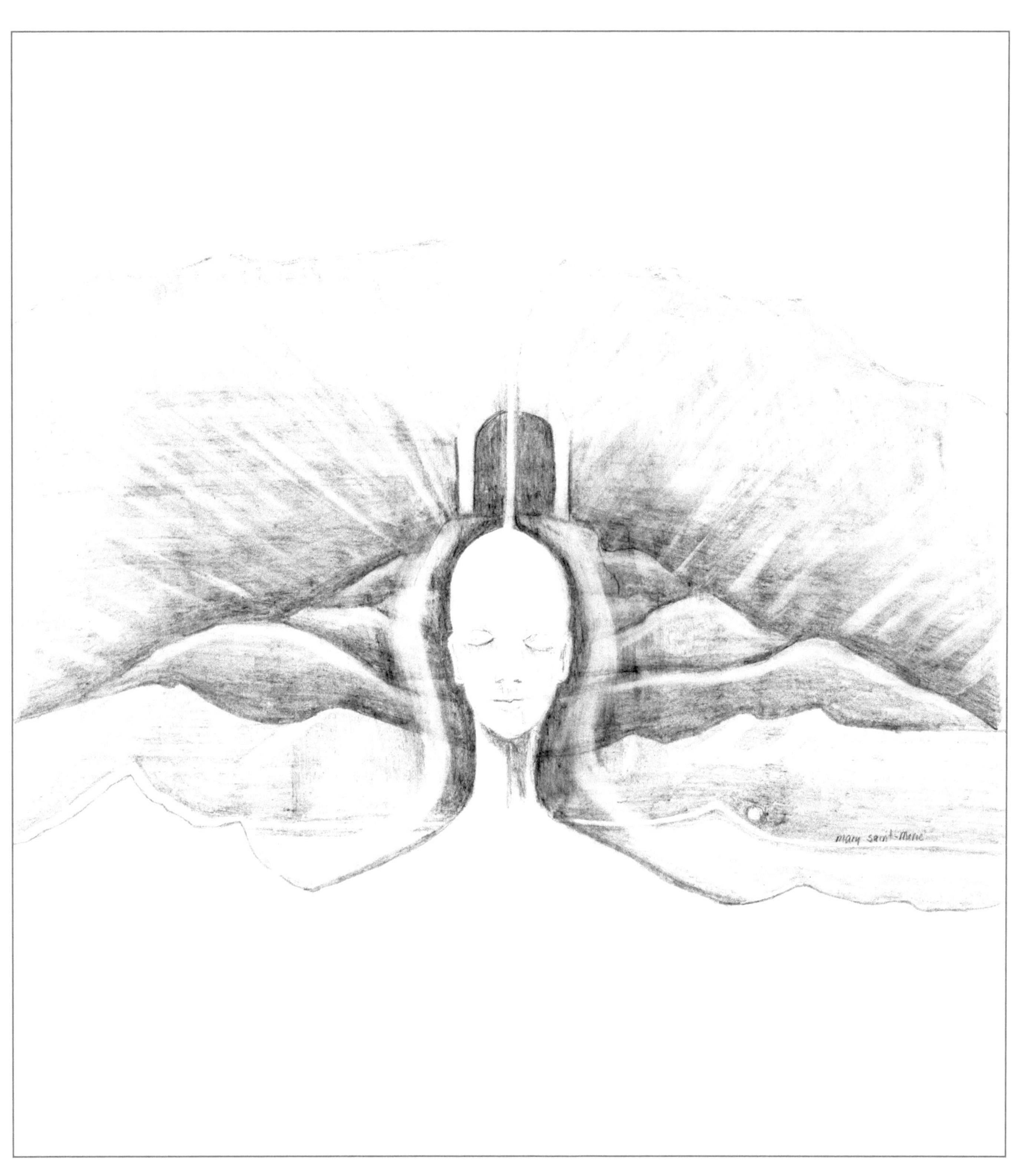

Christ, In You, I Am

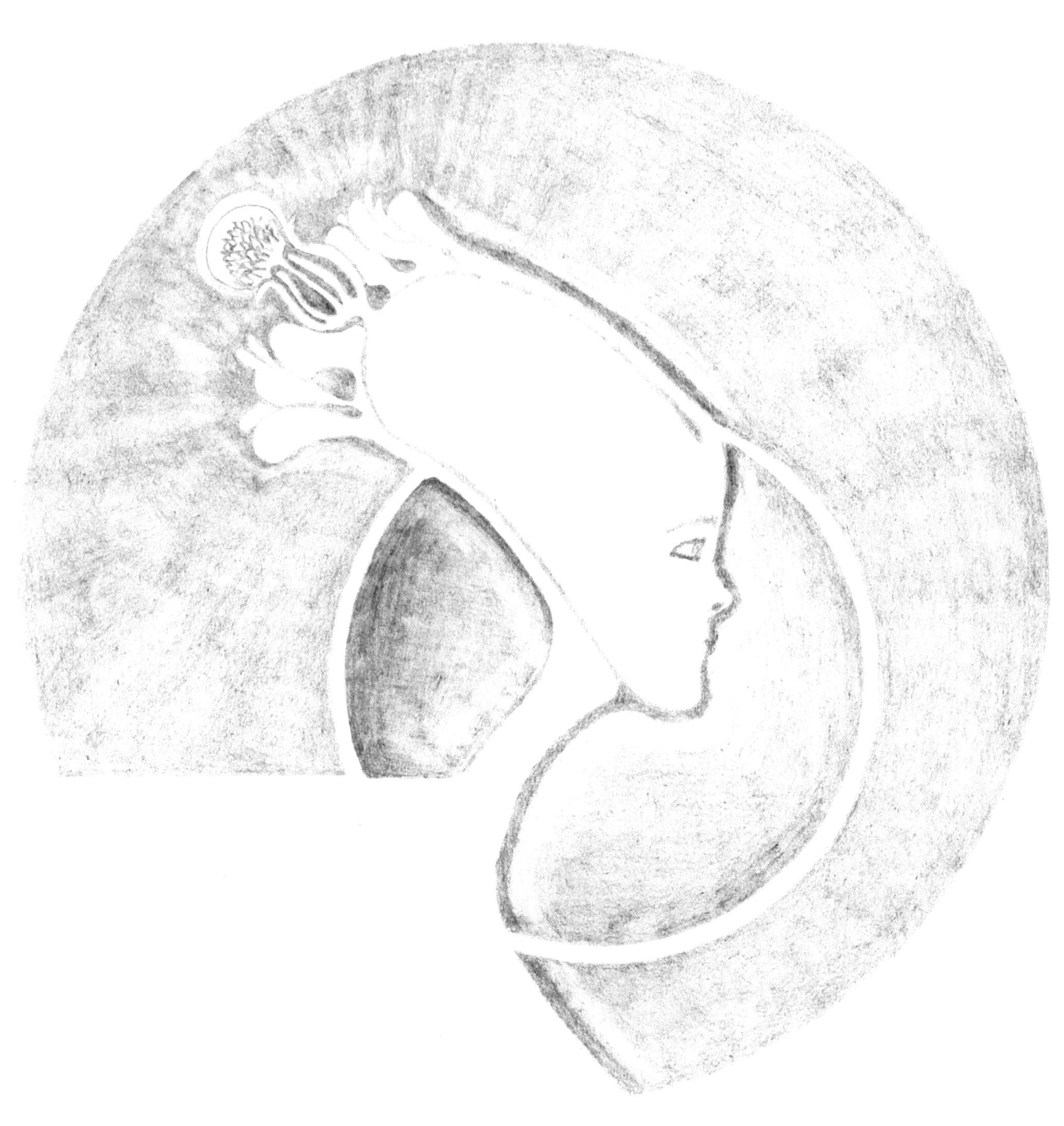

Sunflower Self

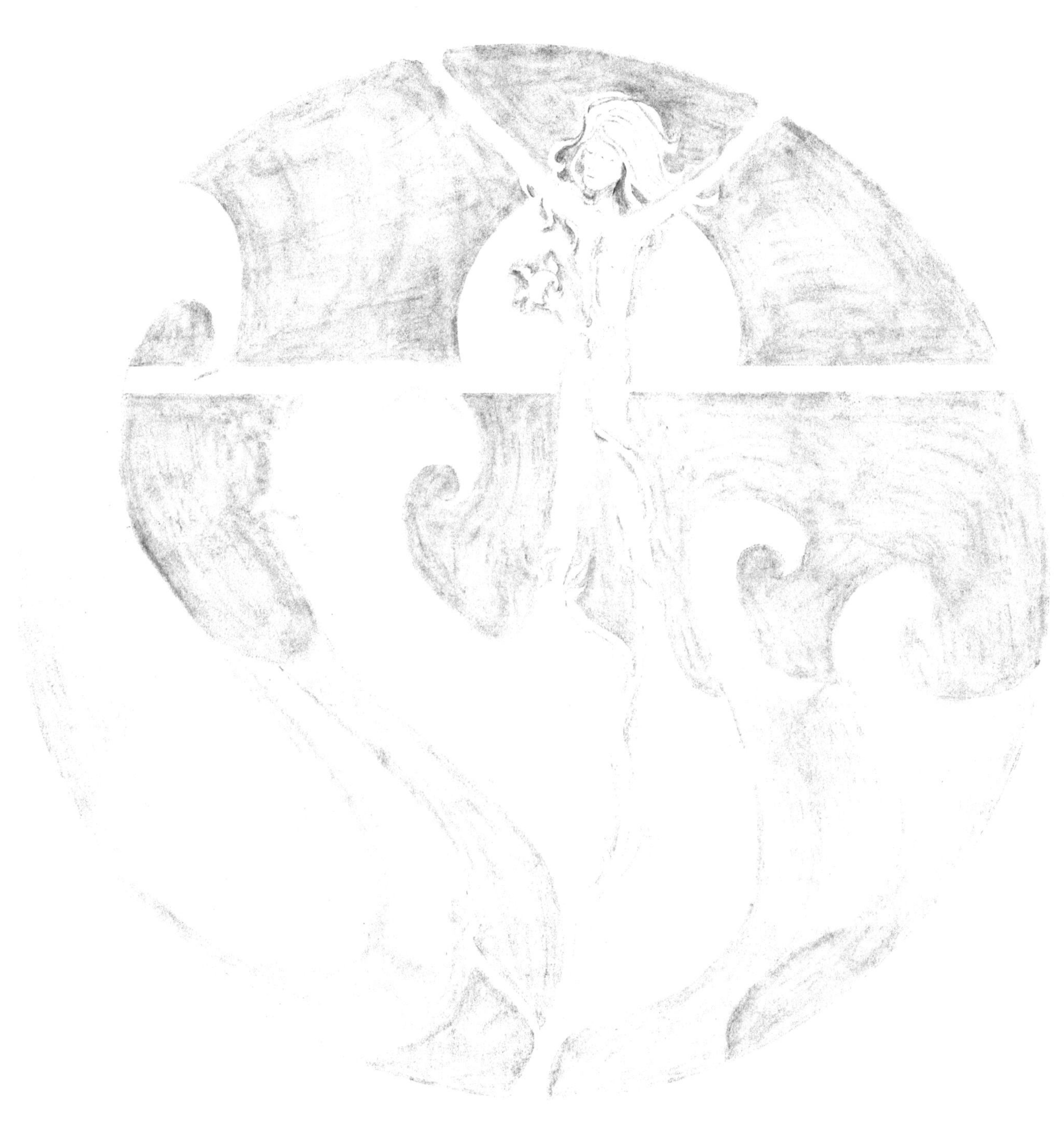

Dancing on the Ocean of Love

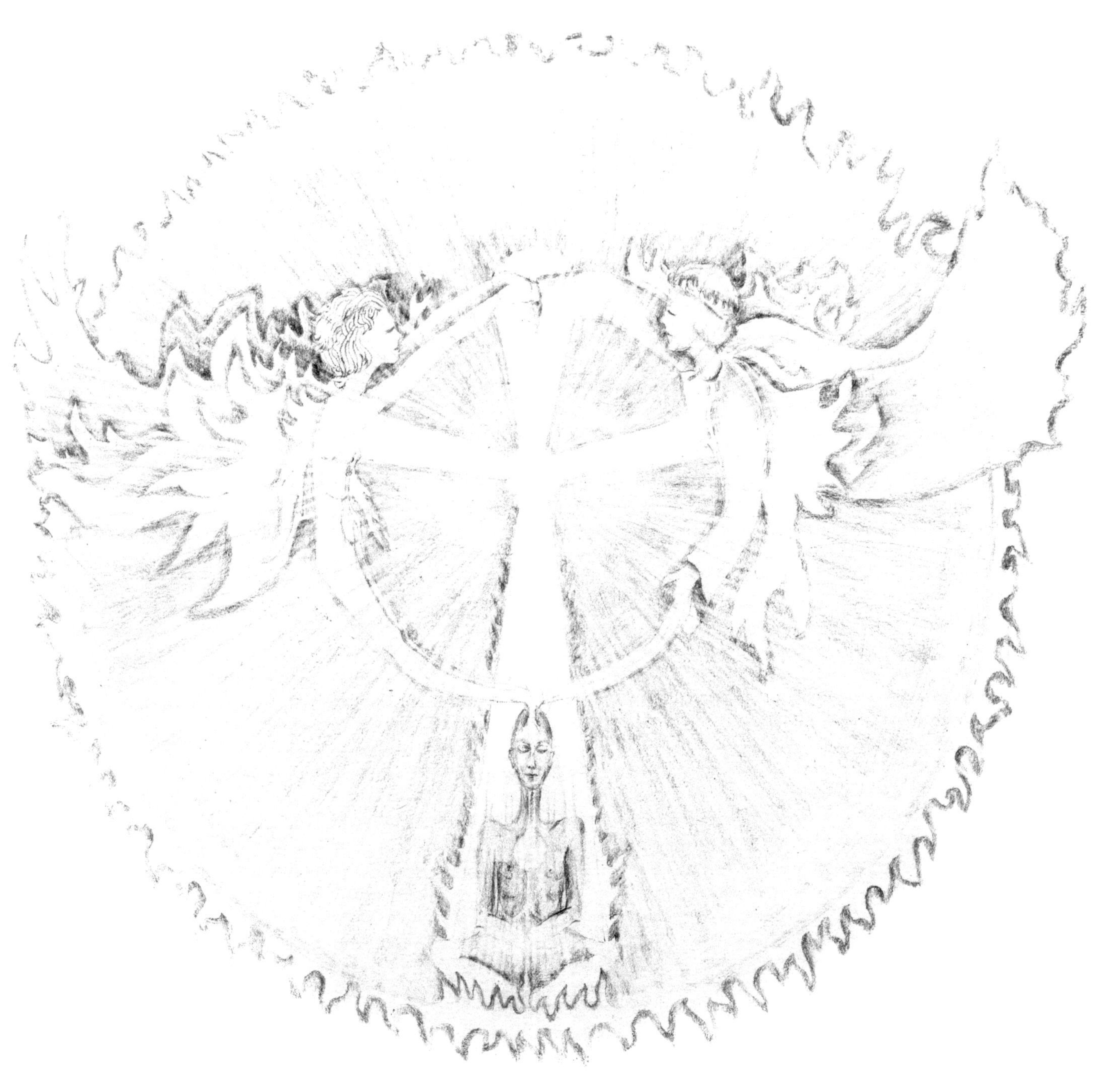

Awareness of Freedom

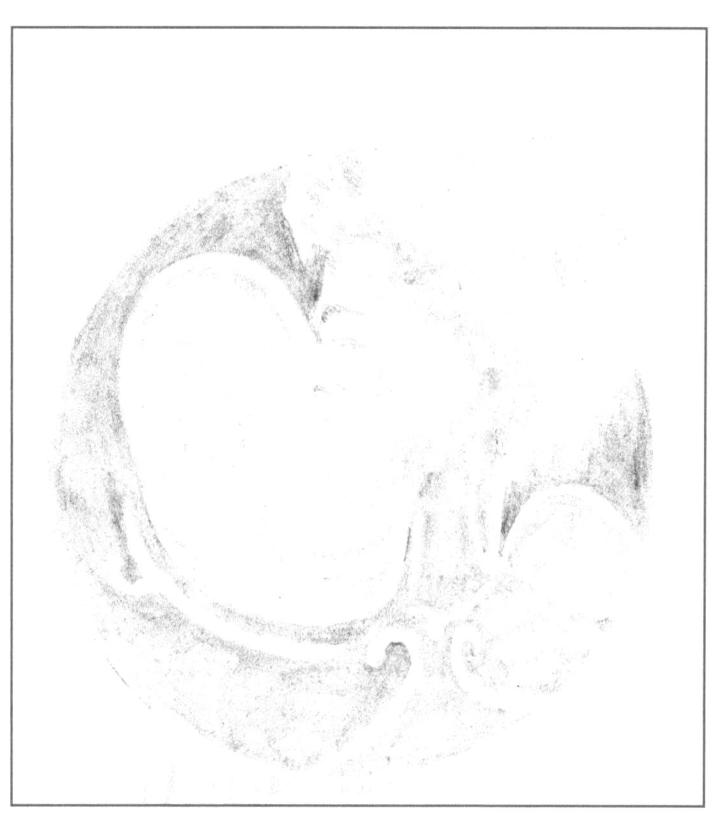

Beyond Battle

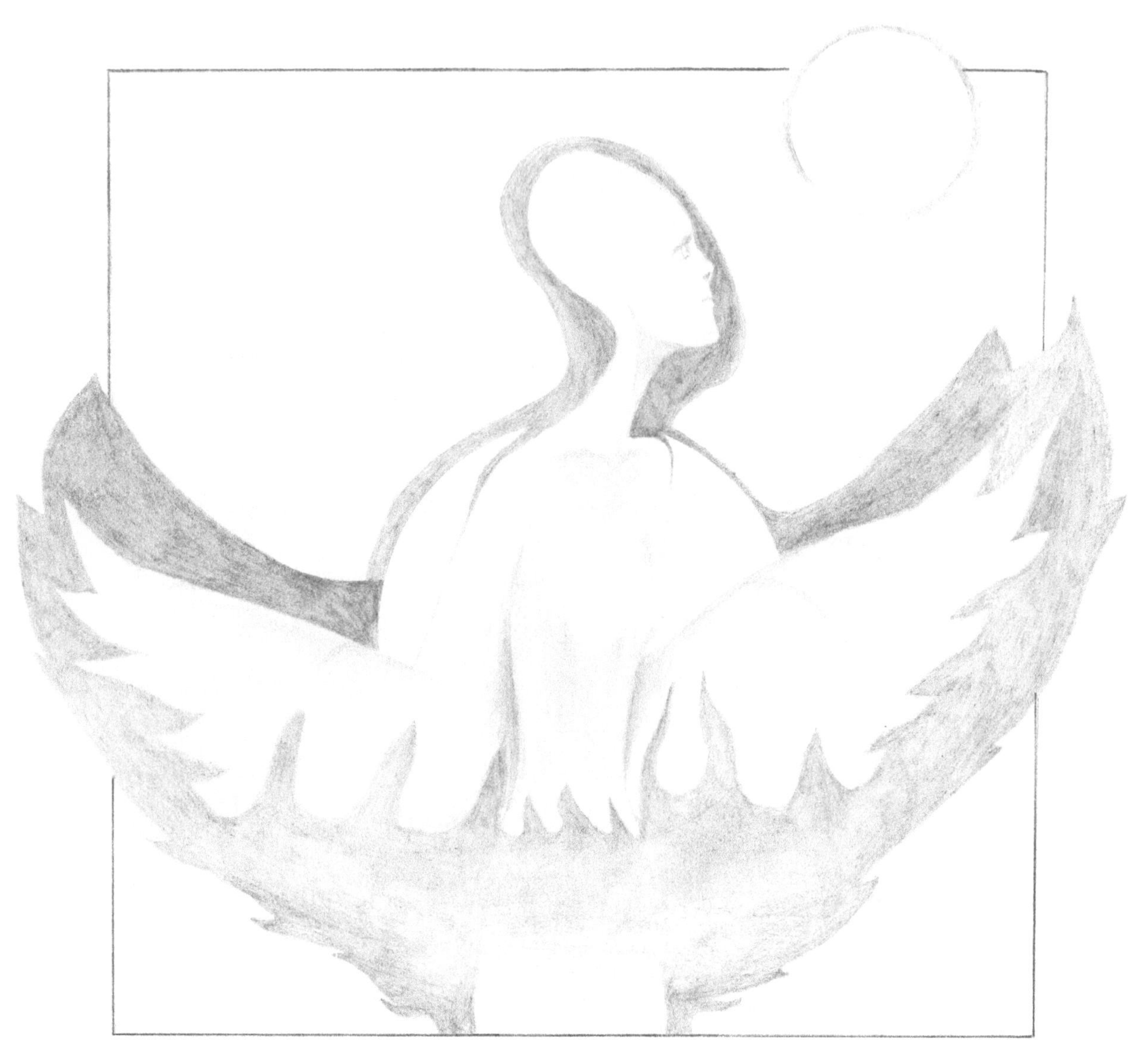

Guide Me to Thy Self

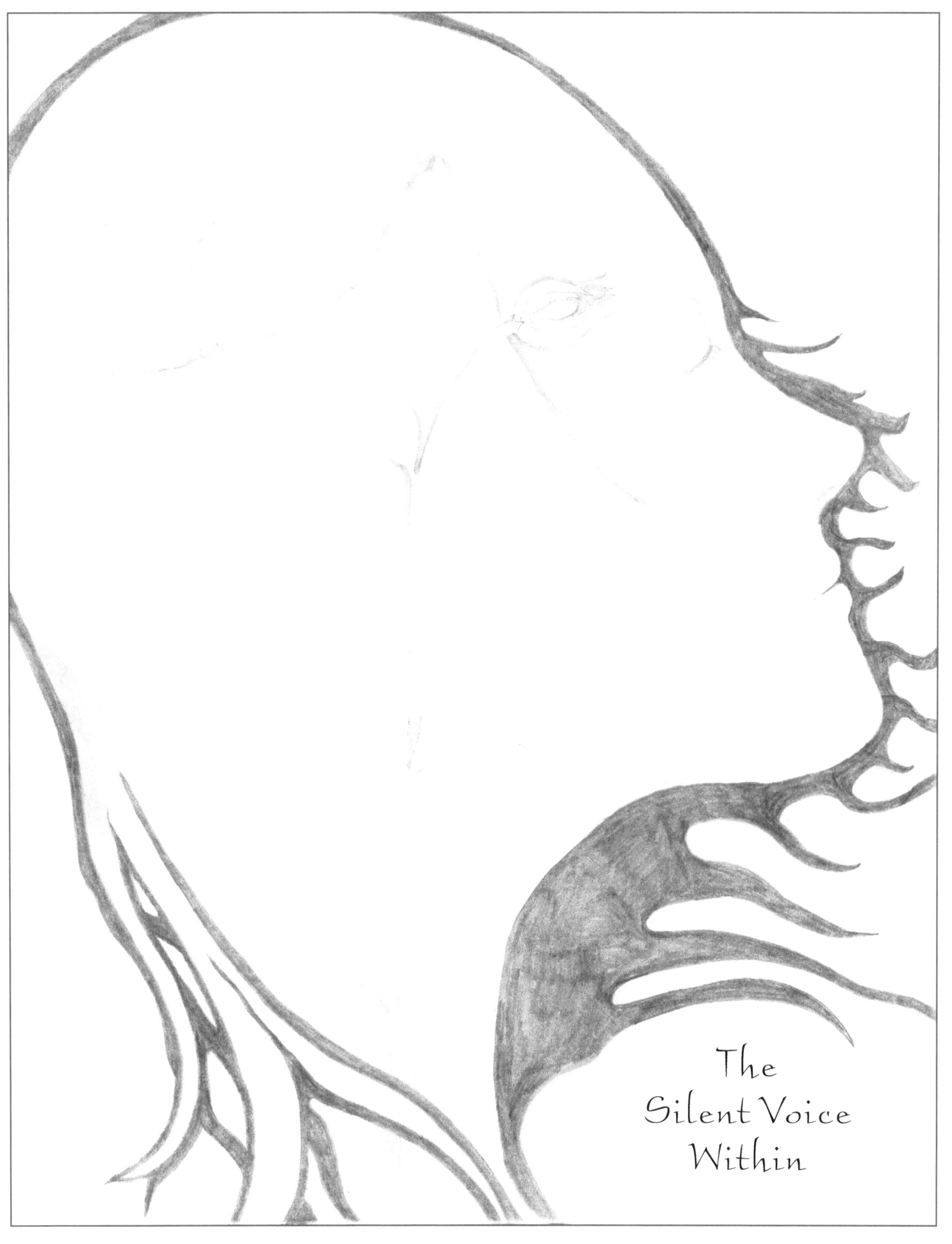
The
Silent Voice
Within

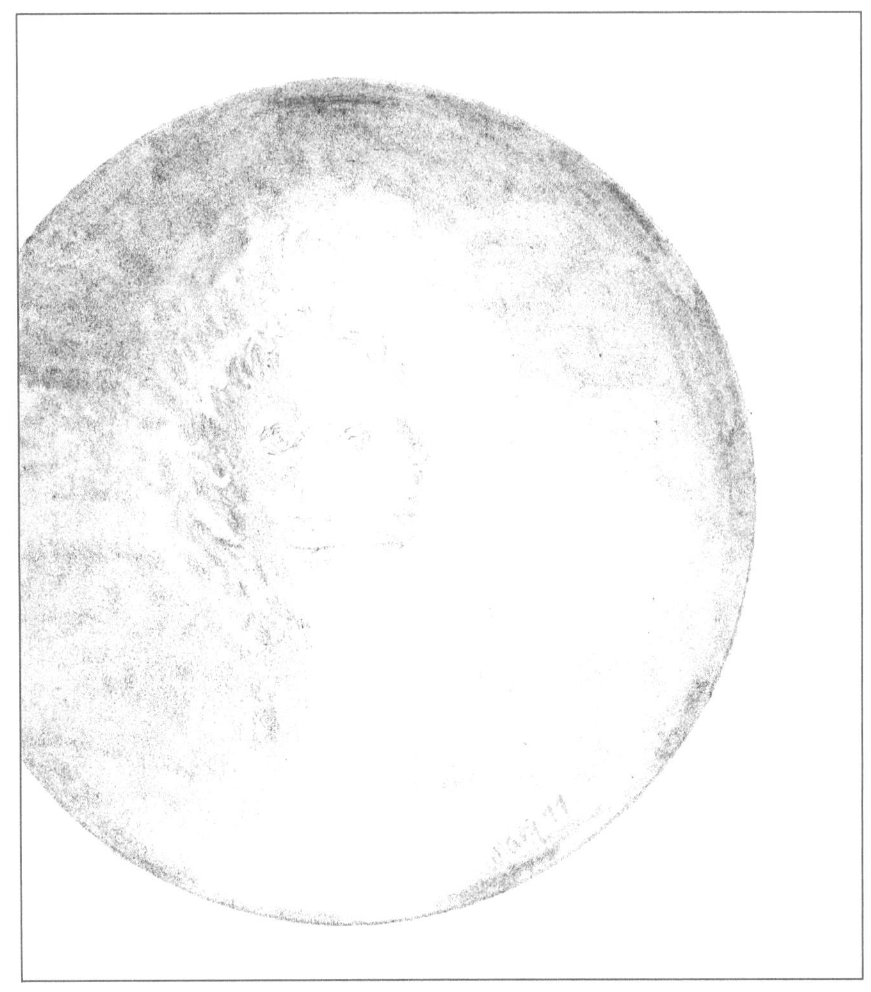

Devotion

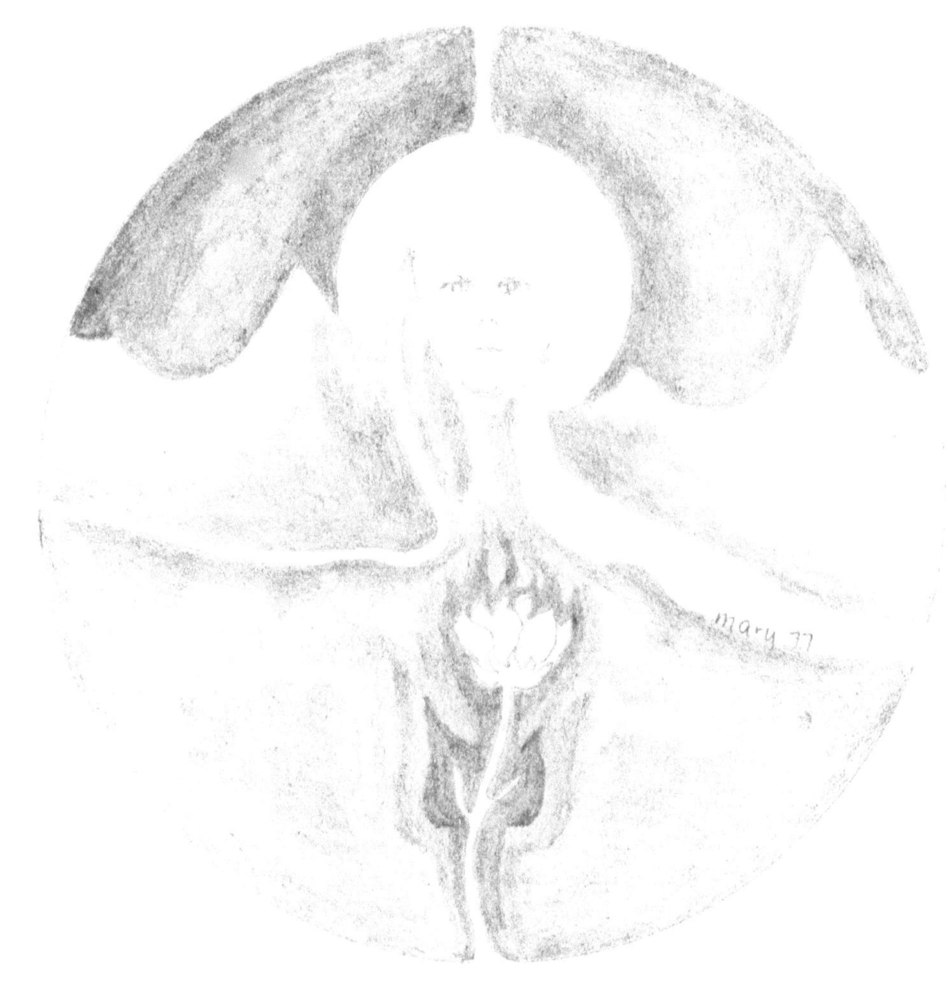

Presence Arising

Touching the Oneness

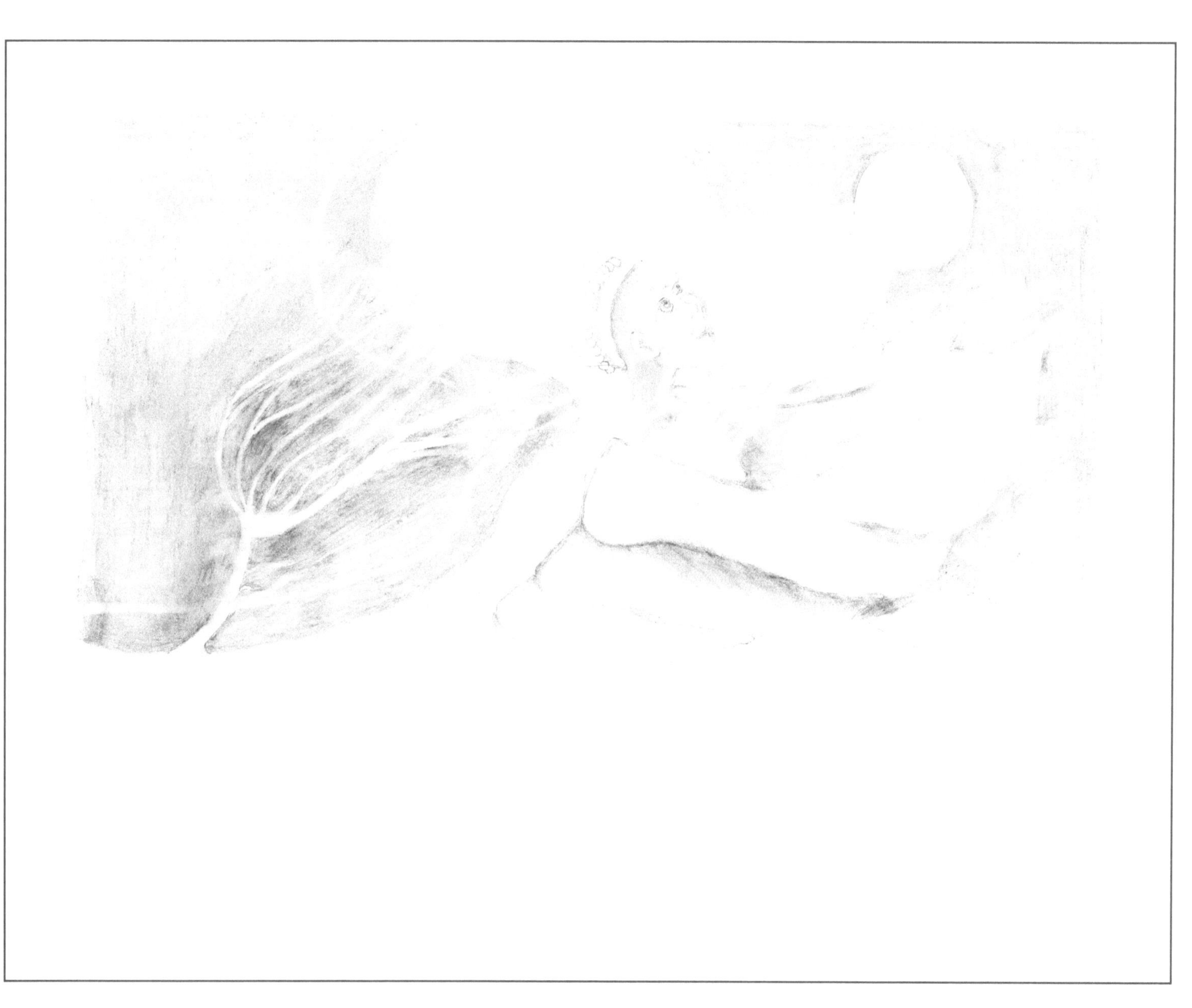

The Wind, the Beloved and Me

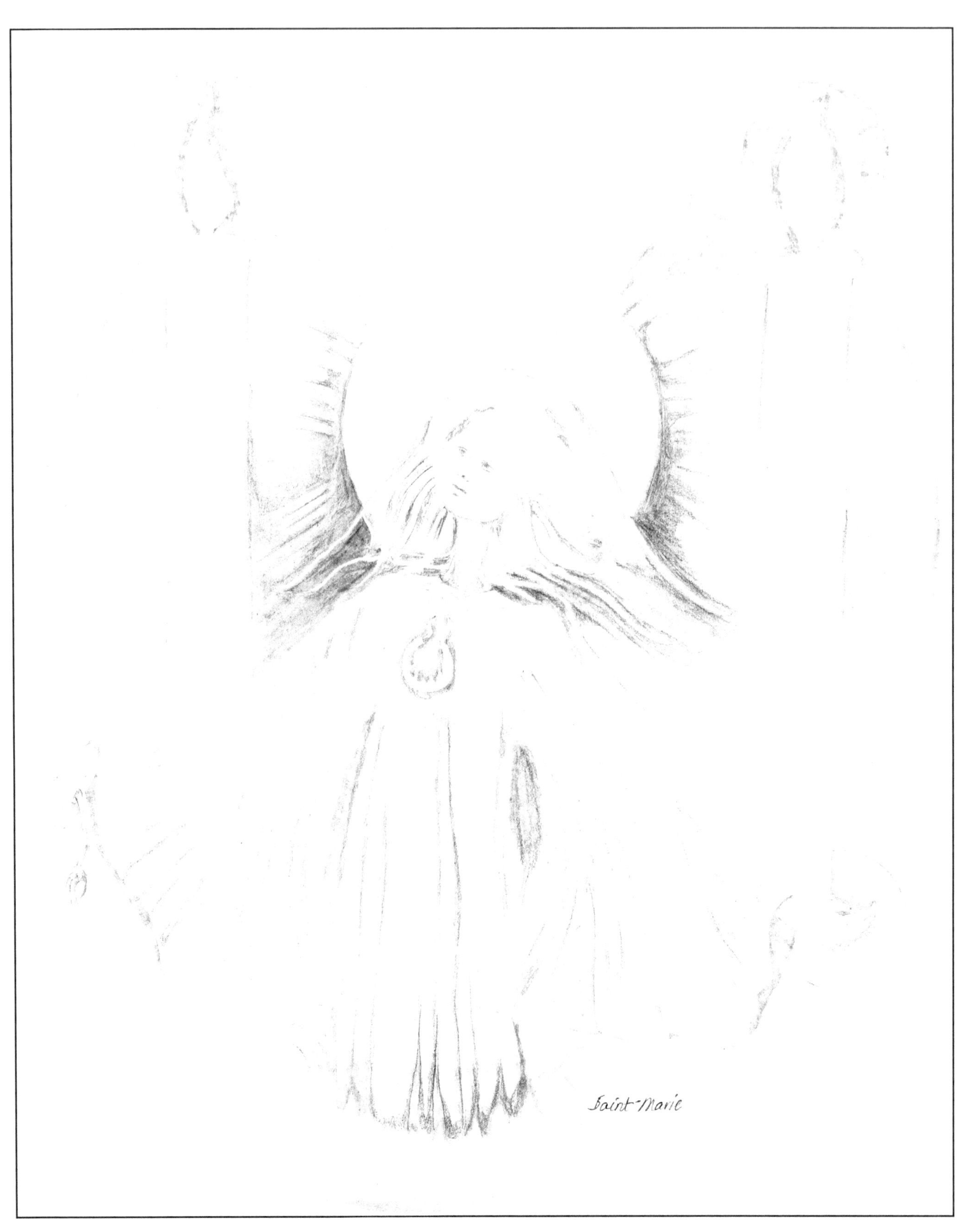

The Sanctuary of the Heart

The Light...living as my very being

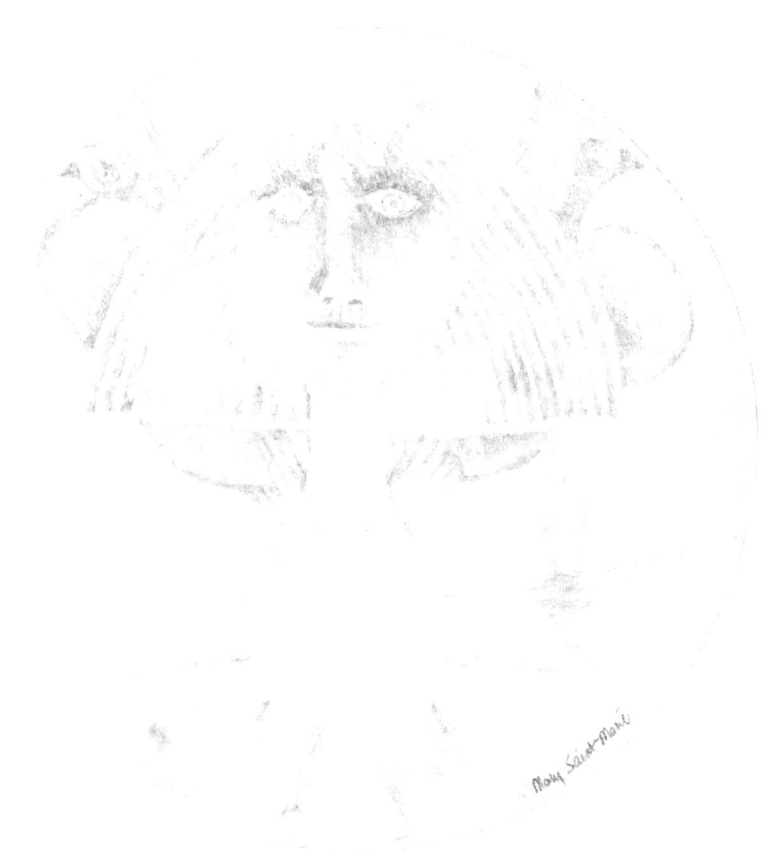

Face the Sun of Your Being

Animated by Presence

The Sacred Vision

The Light of Being

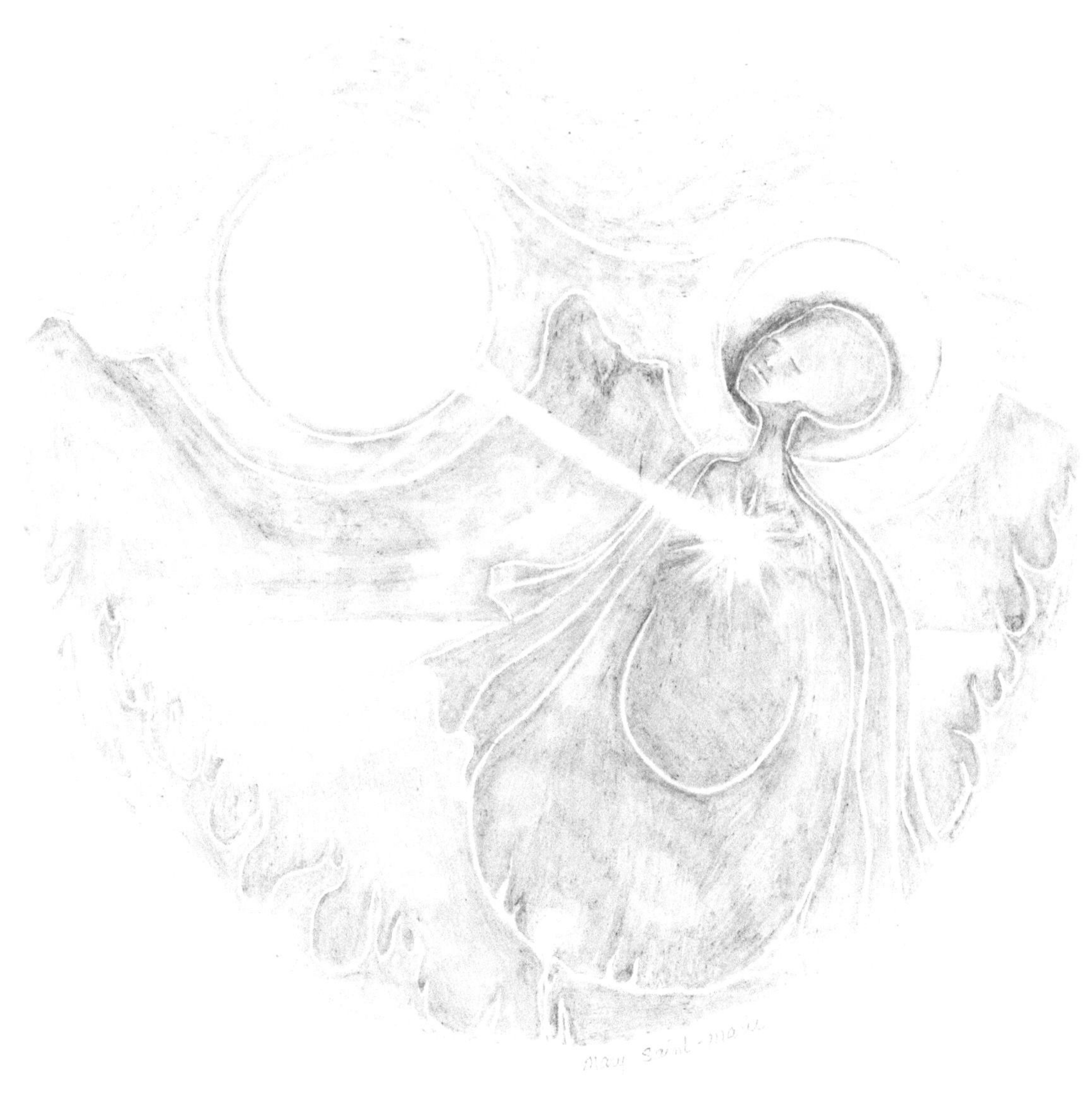

Revelations of the Heart

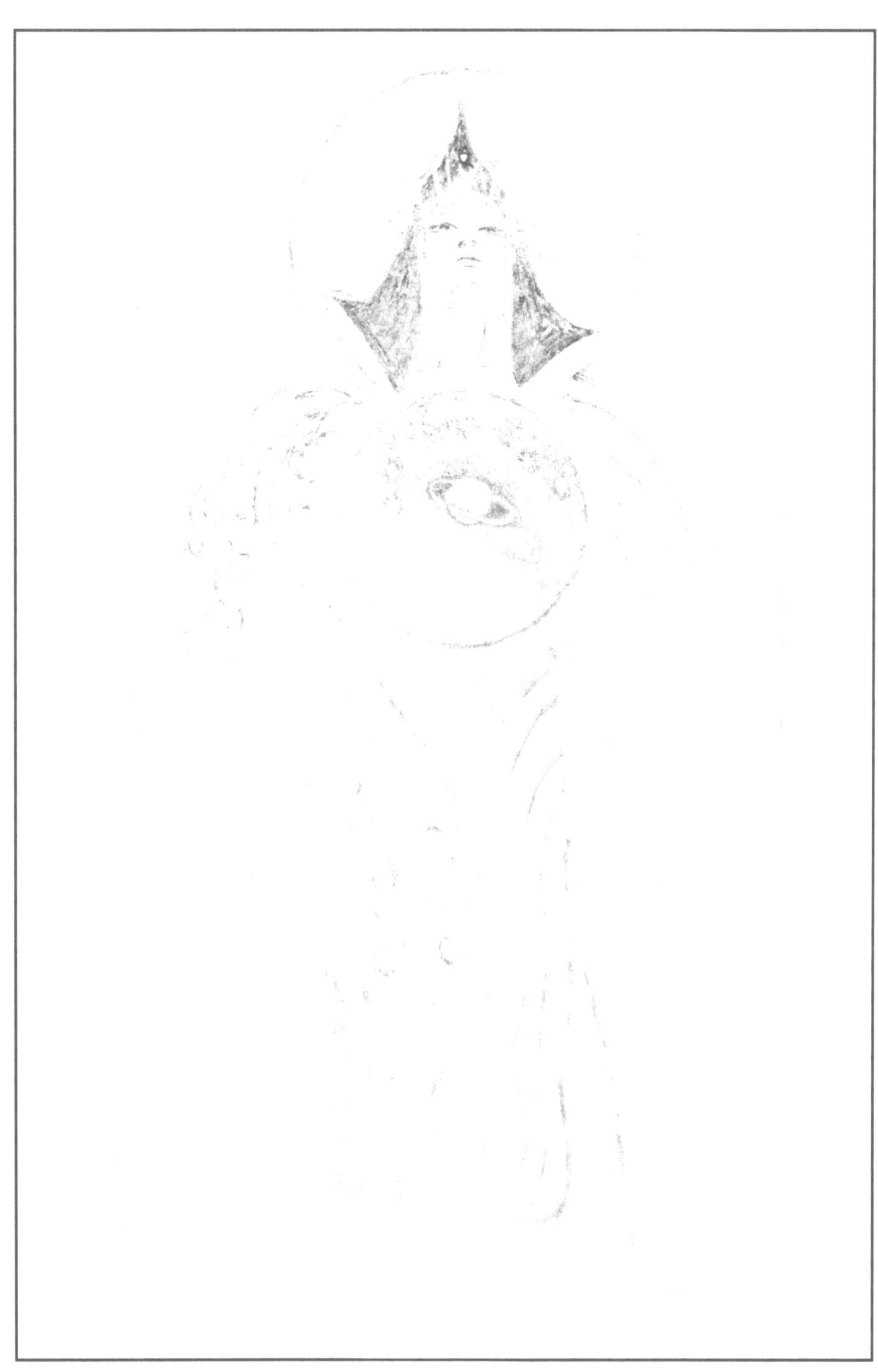

Cosmic Mother

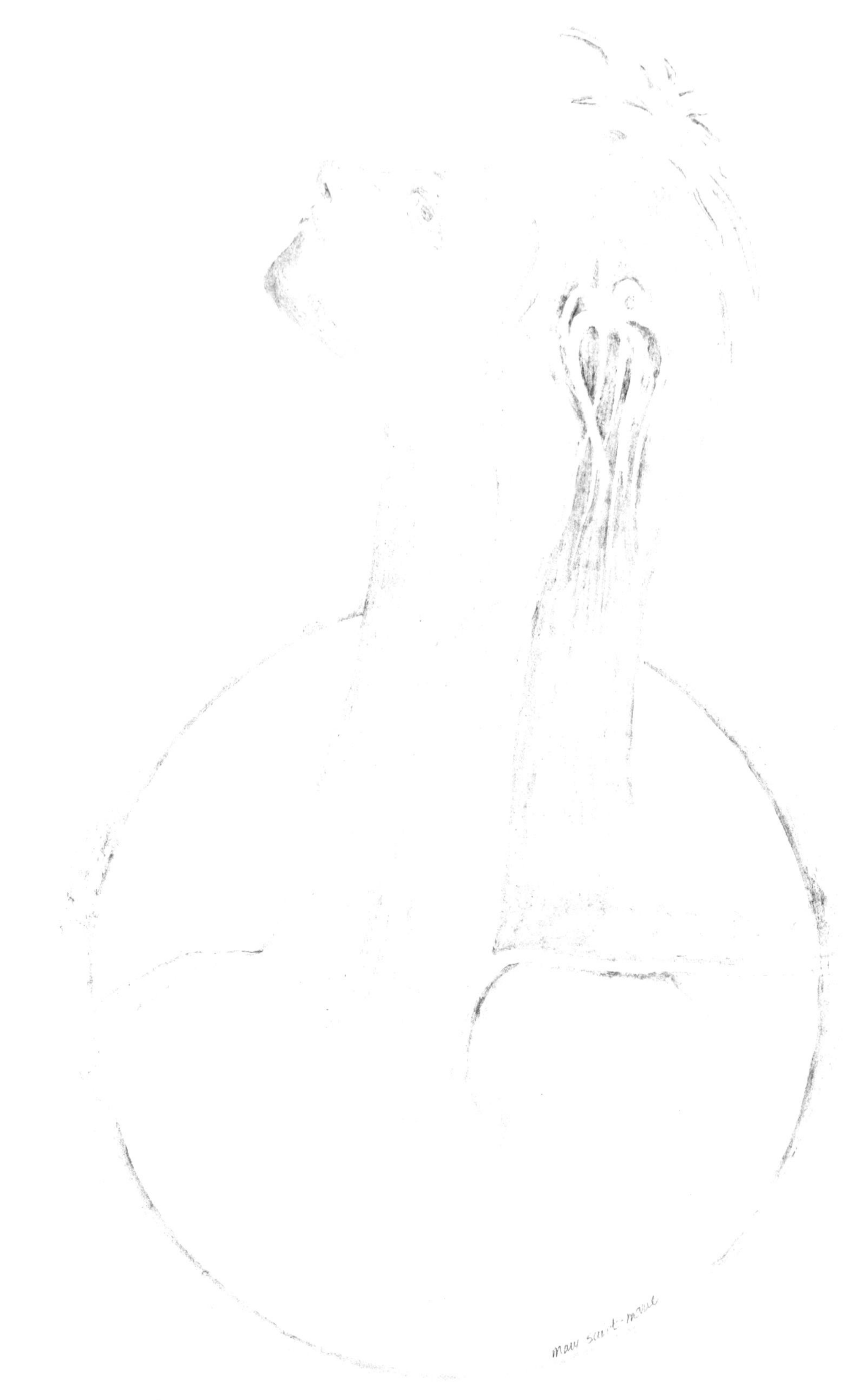

The Light of Being

Holy Sight…a Bringer of Illumination

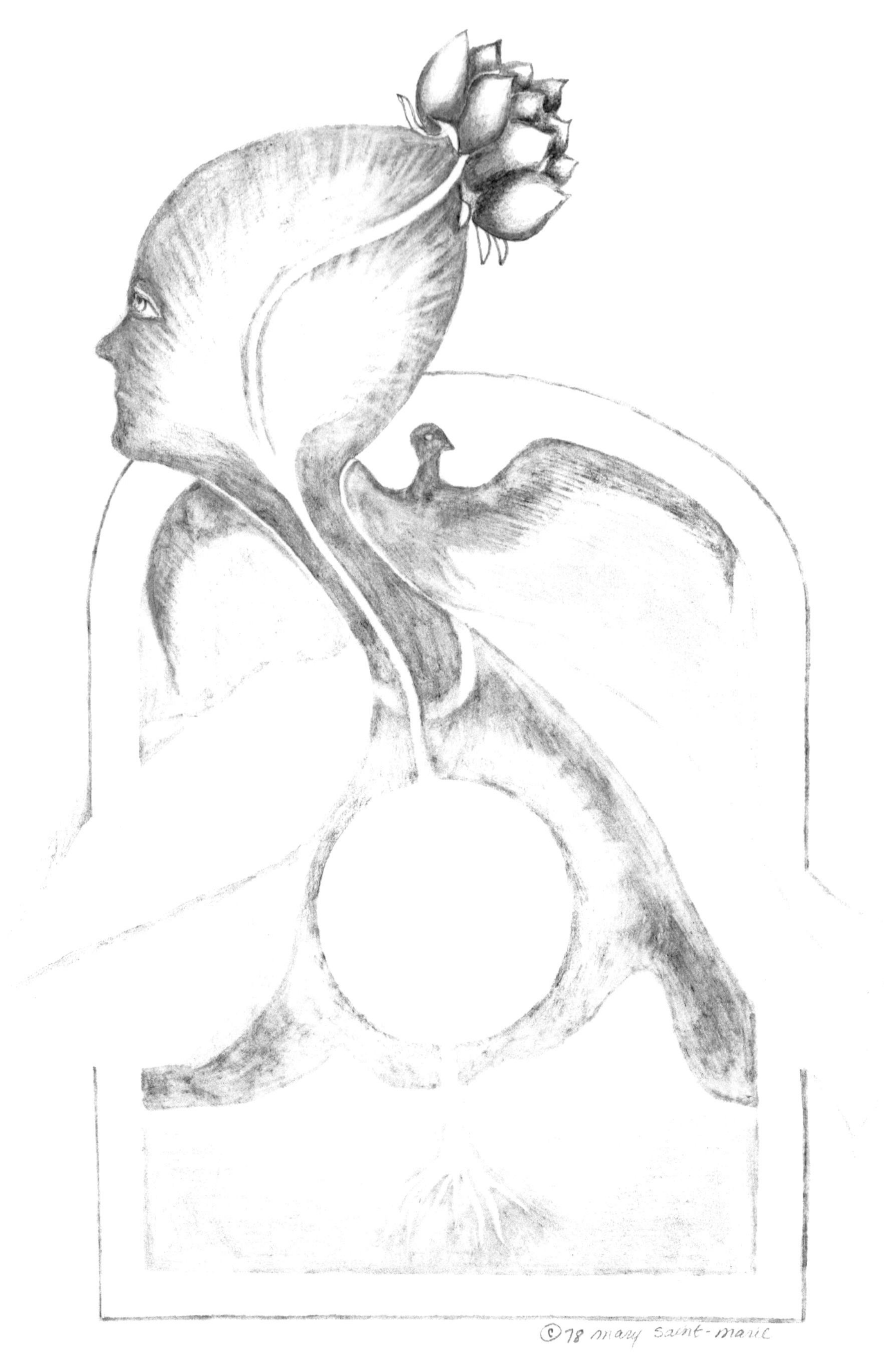

Devotion to the Heart's flame

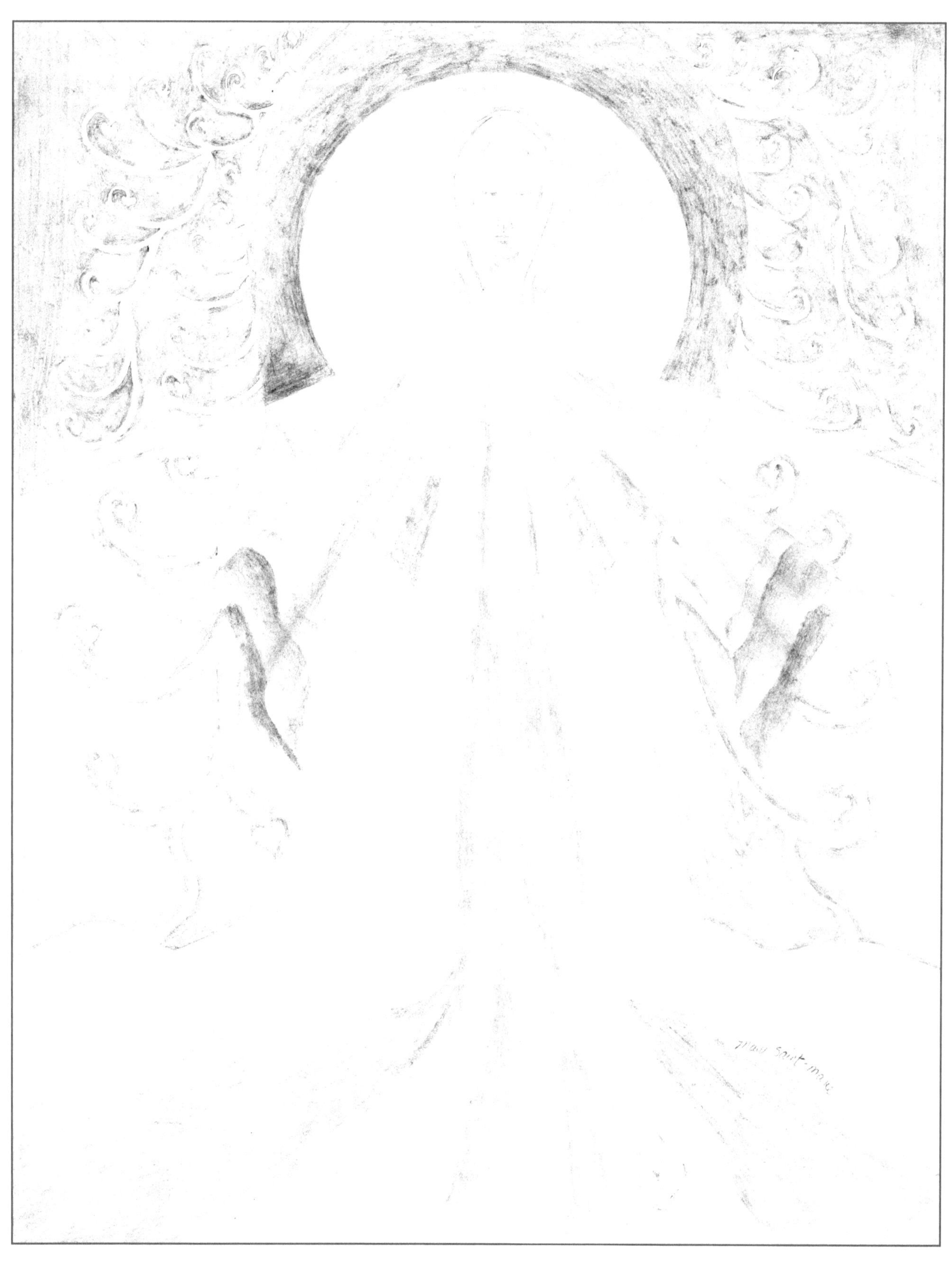

Love Lights Your Way

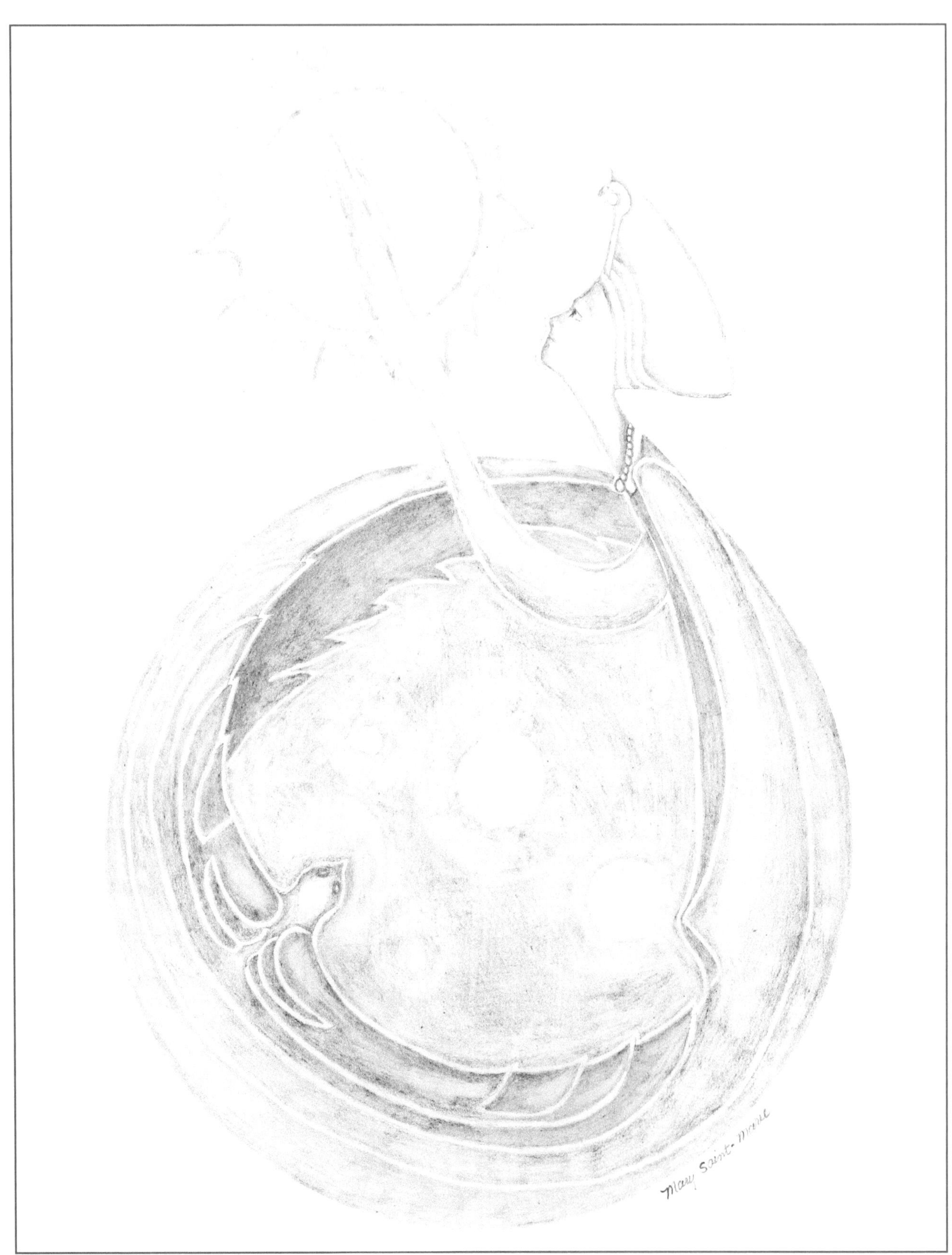

Sword of Truth

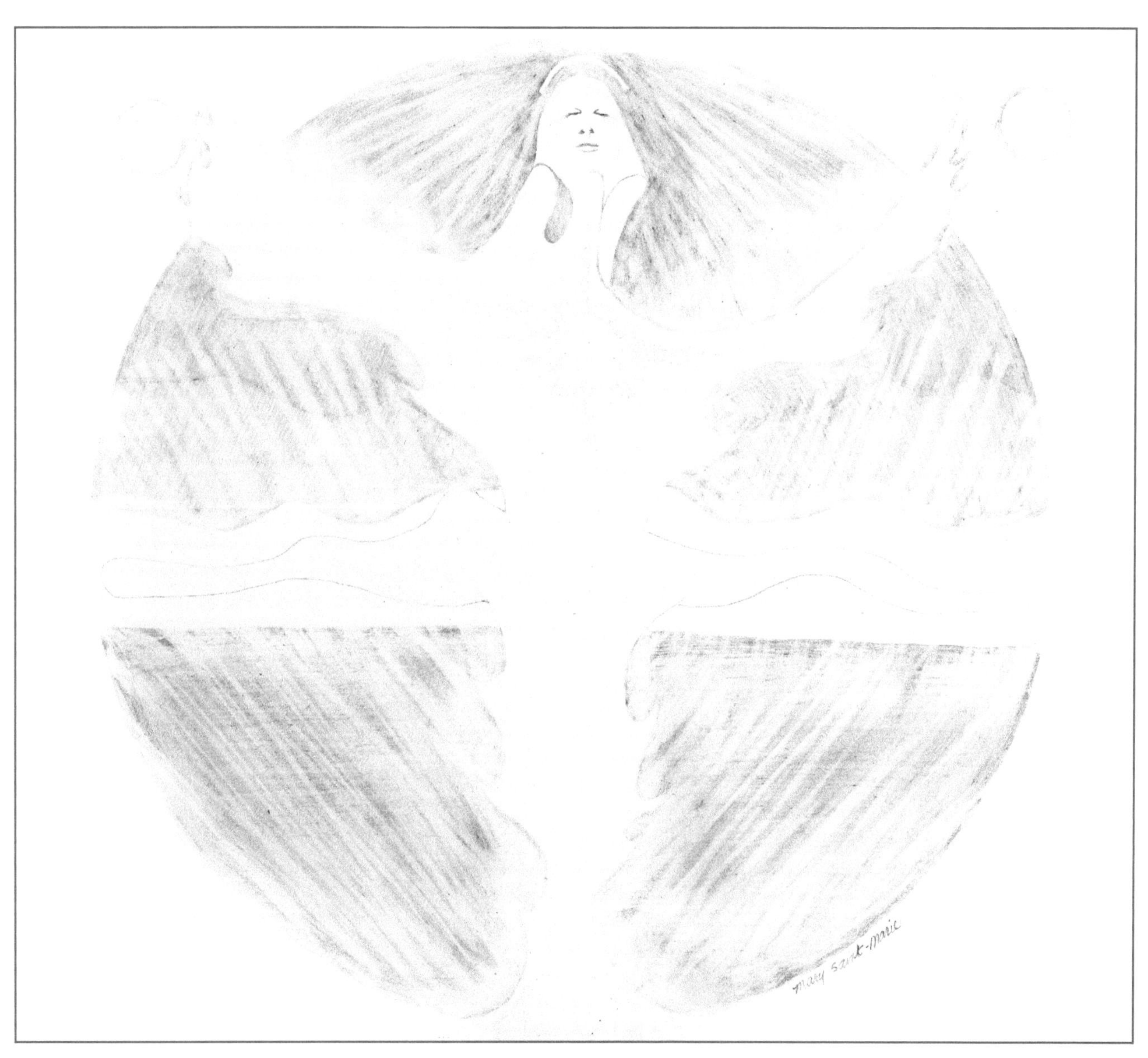

Feeling Love's Flame...Everywhere Present

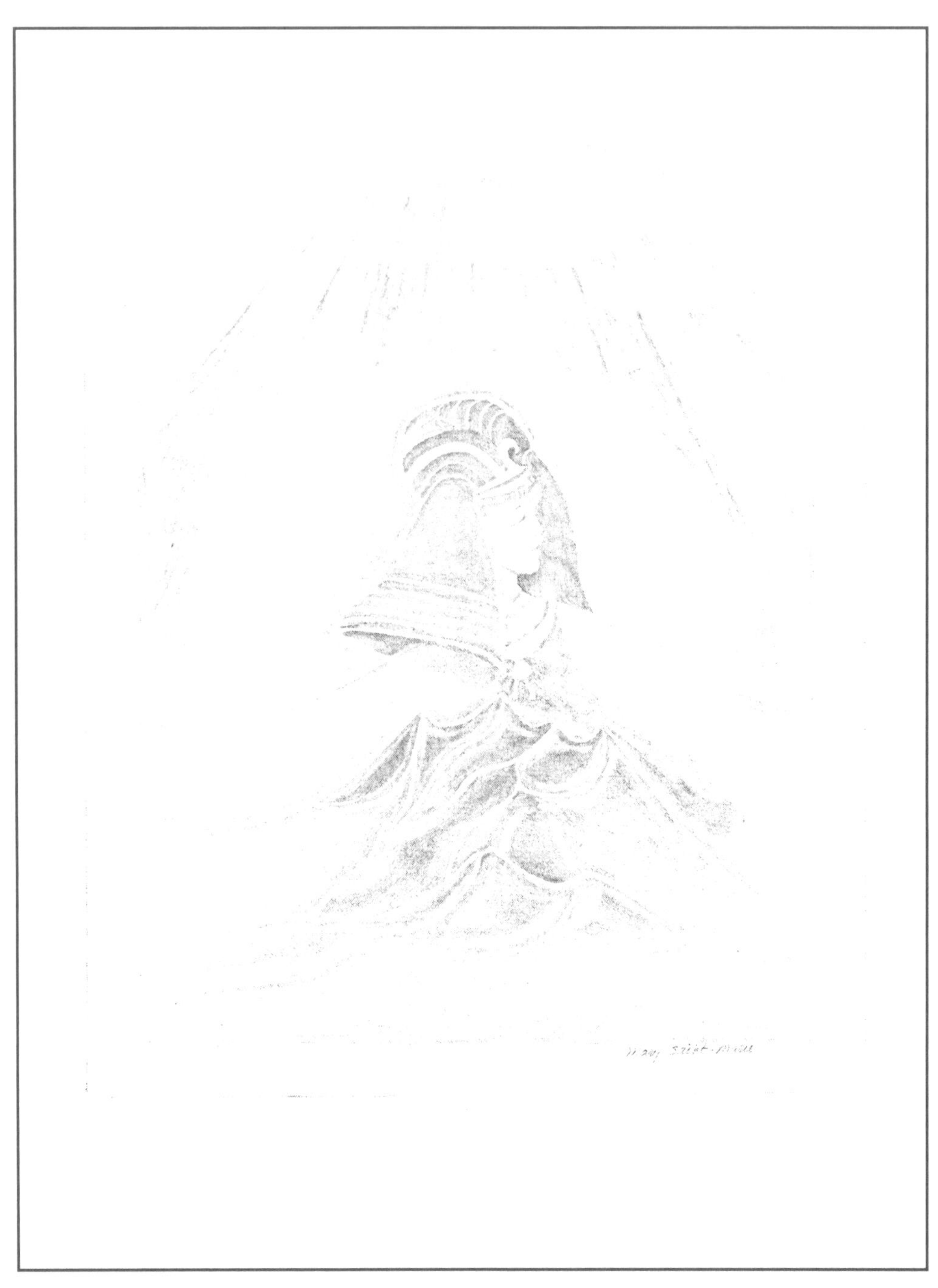

Cosmic Mother of the Mountain

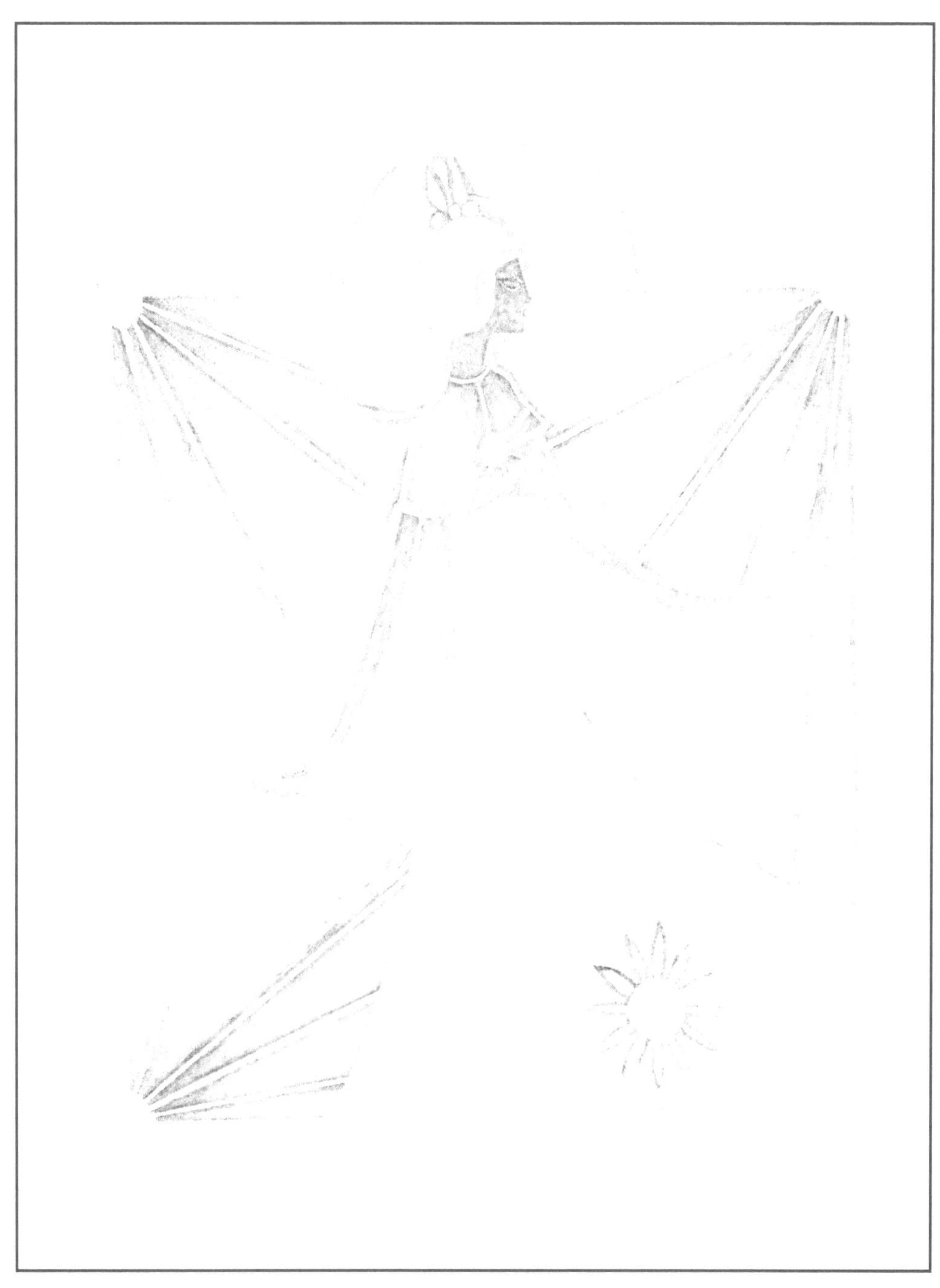

Priestess from the Higher Realms

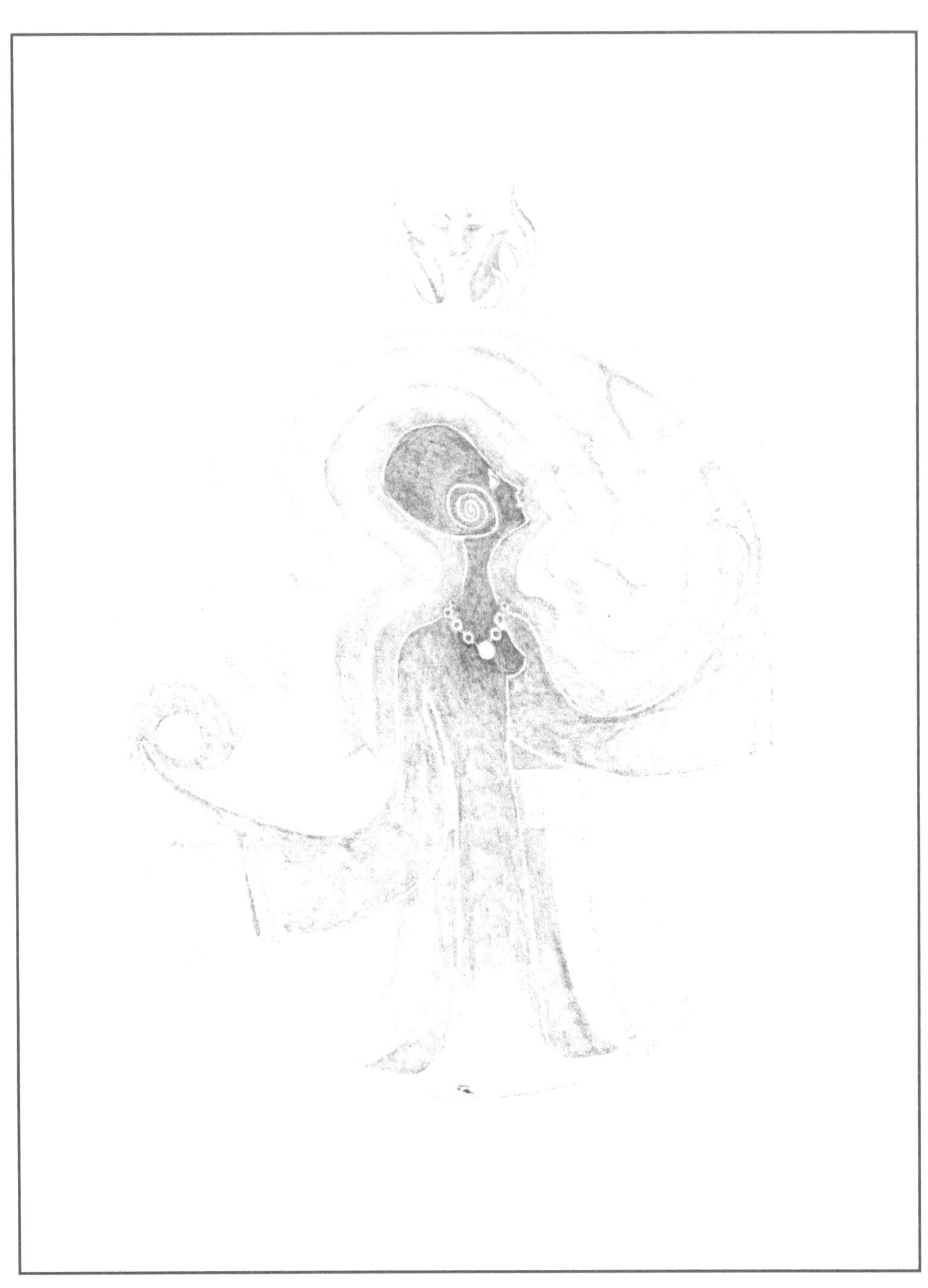

Emanating Light

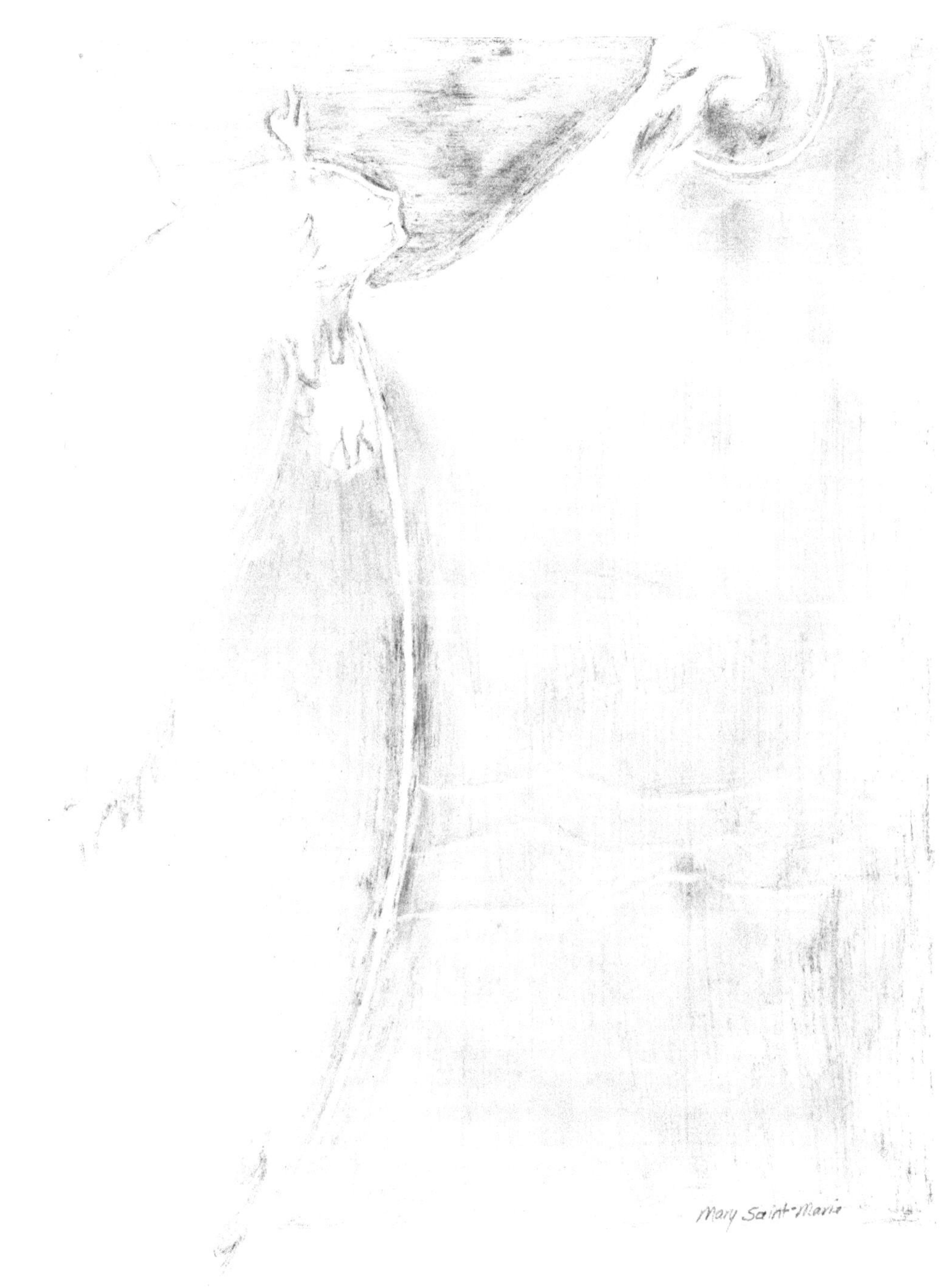

Ecstatic flame

The Call of the Invisible One

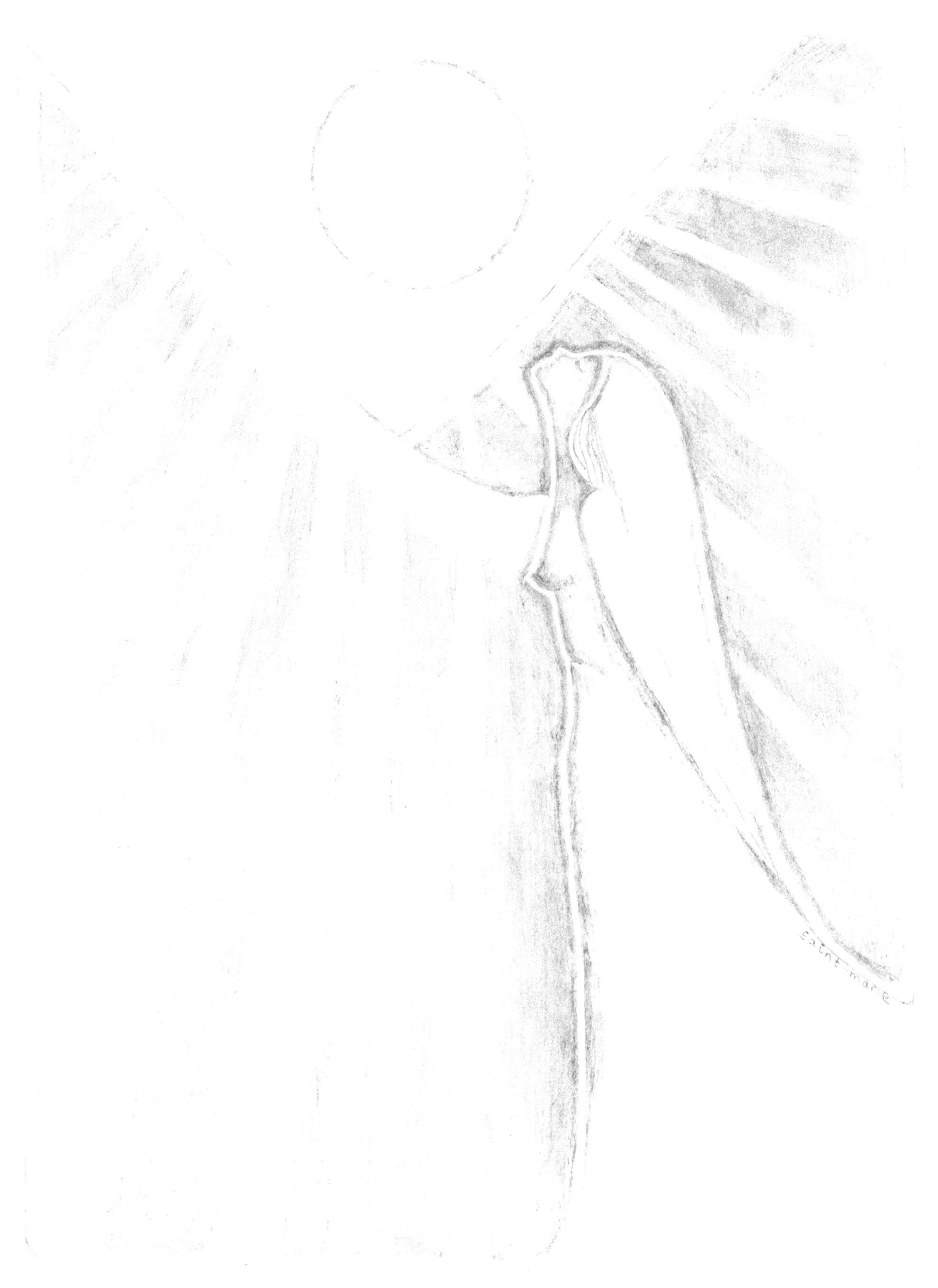

A Flight of Consciousness

Behold...the Christ

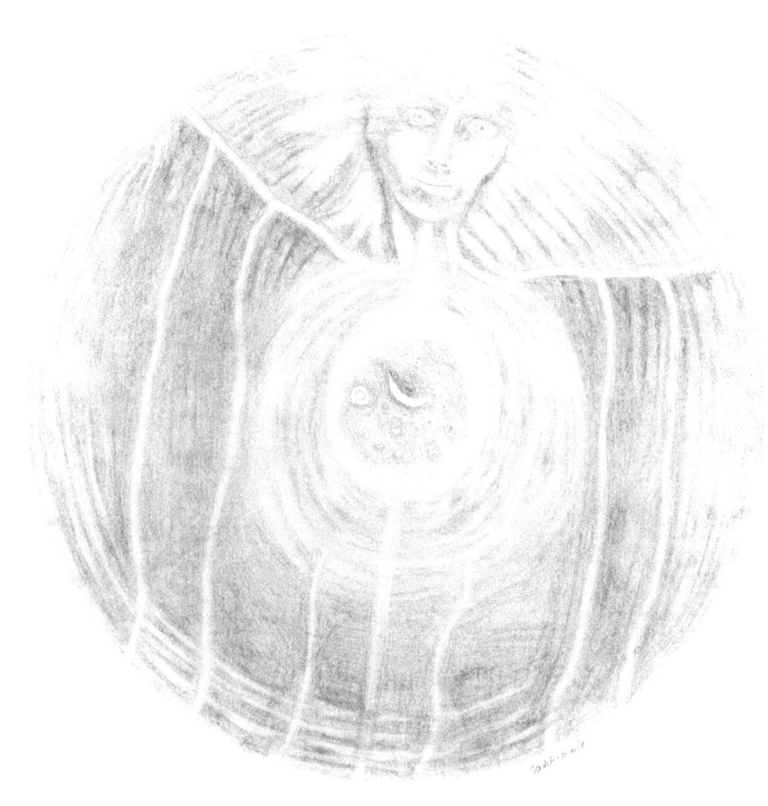

Behold...the Mother of the World

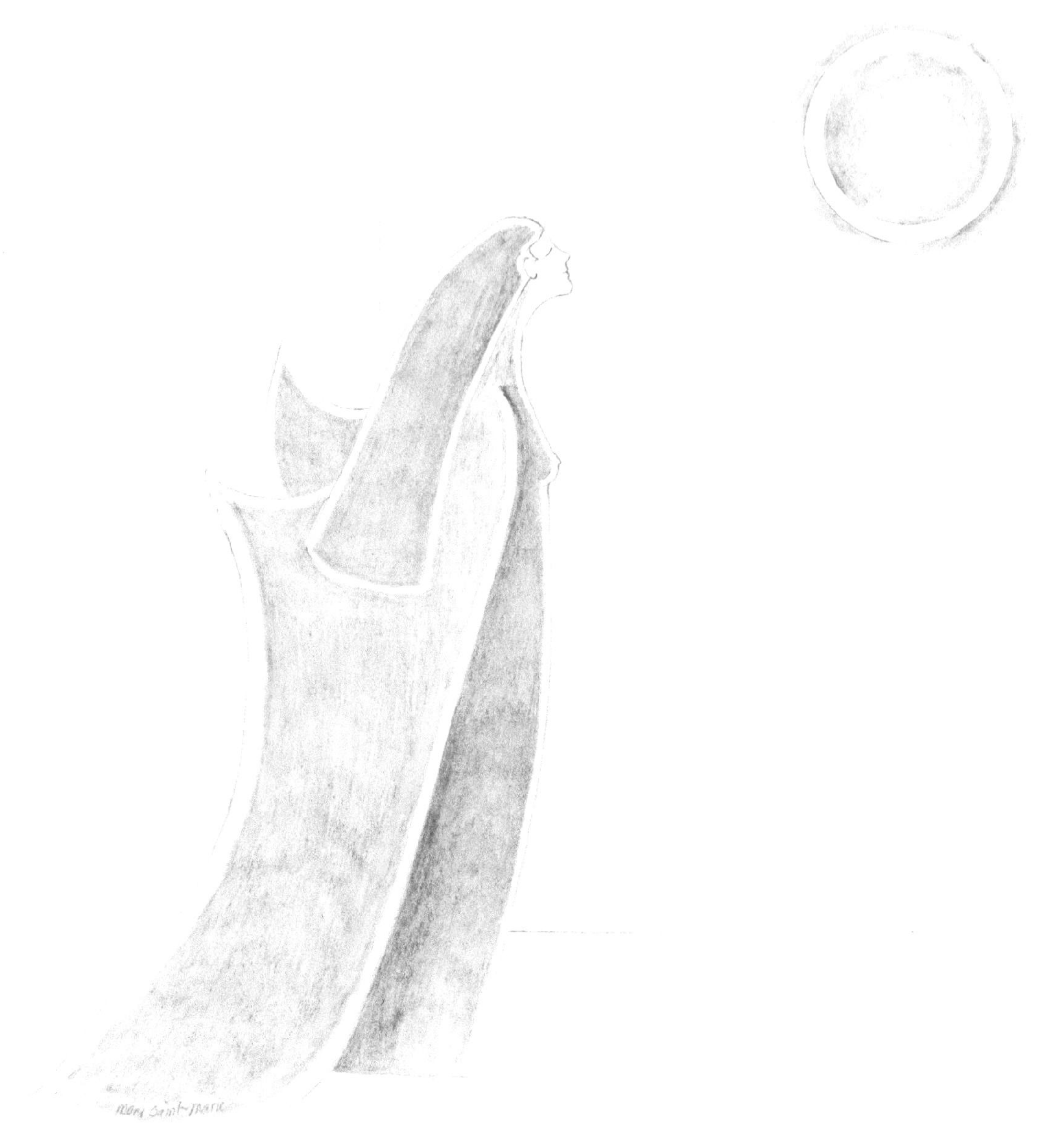

The Light that IS

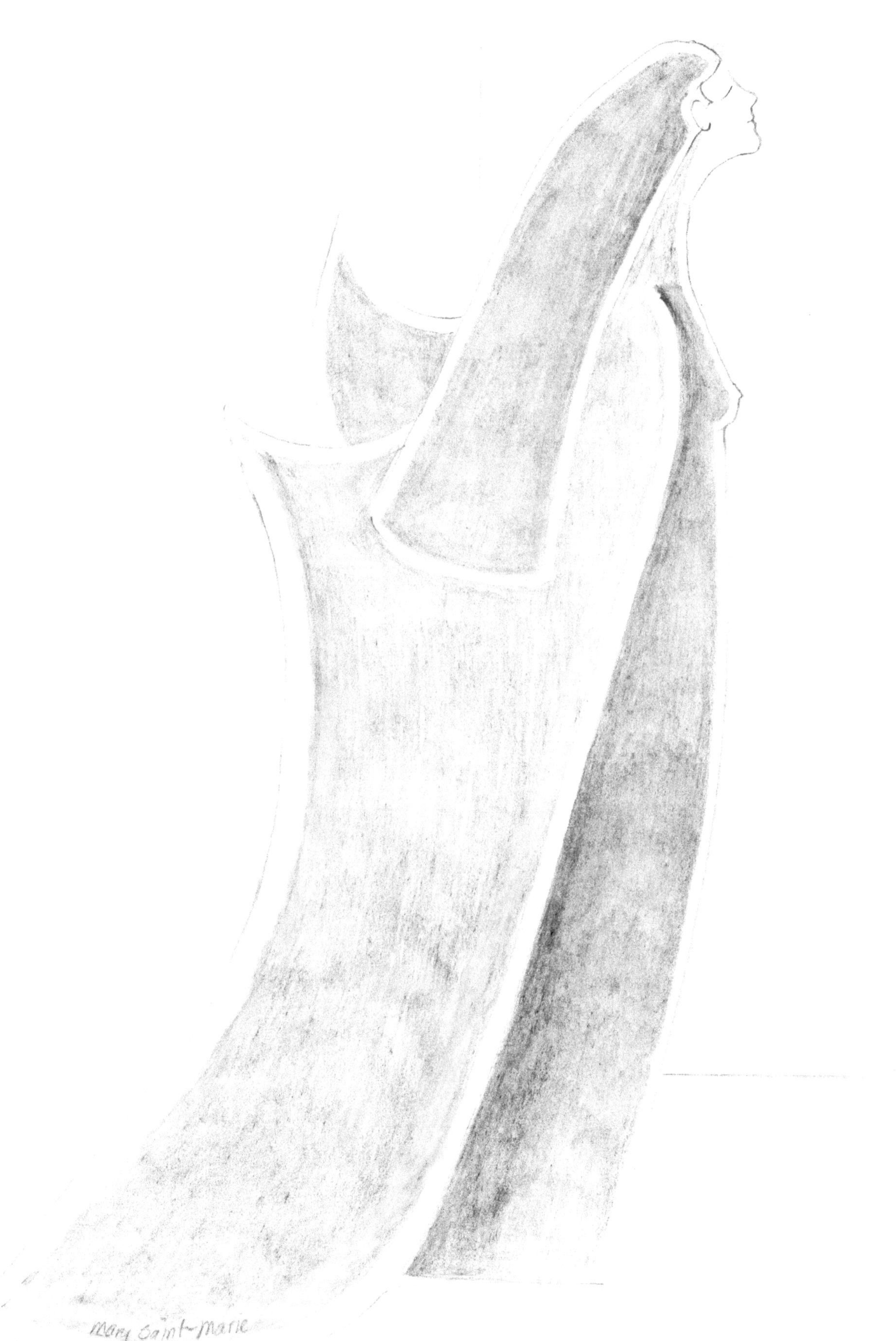
Mary Saint-Marie

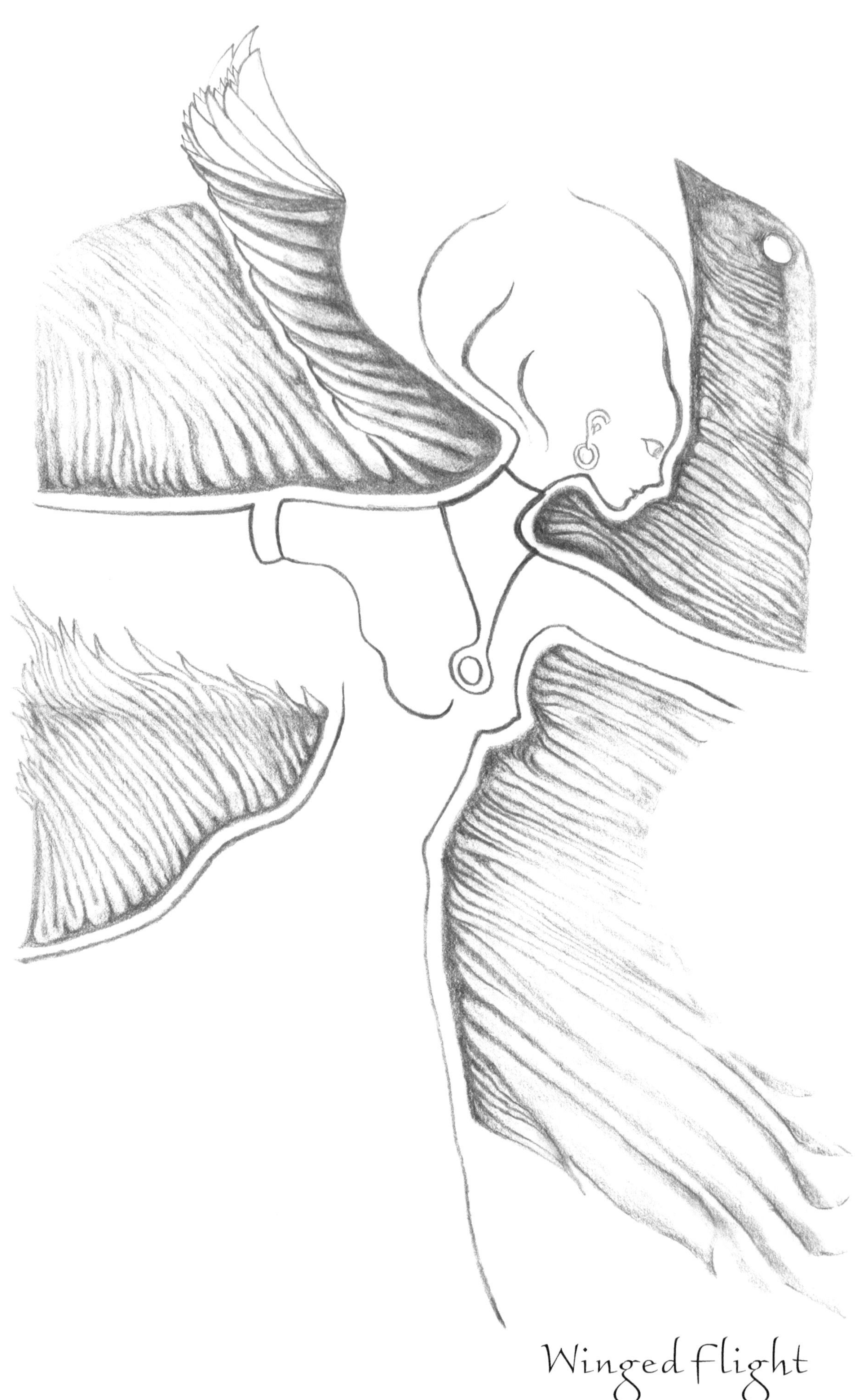

Winged flight

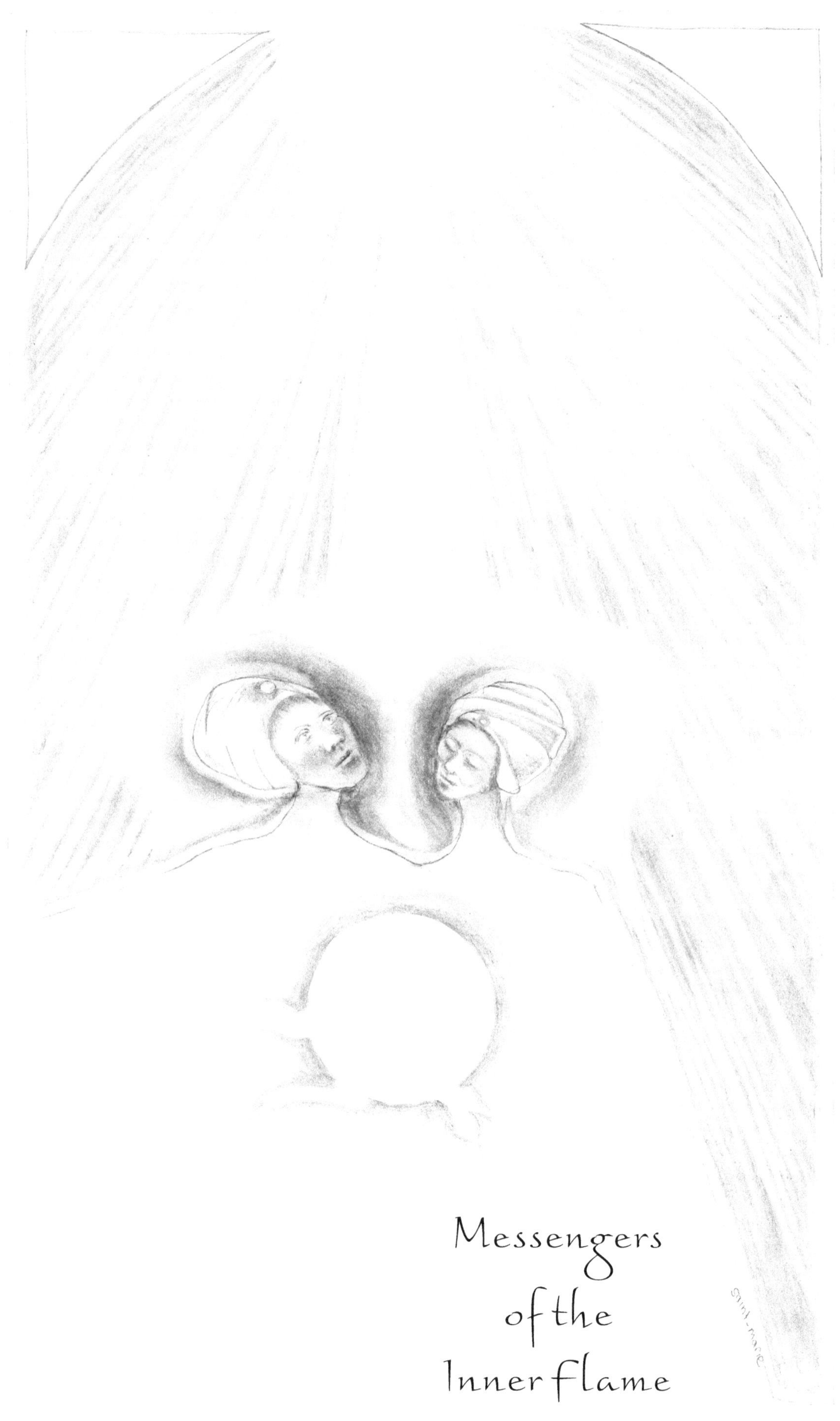
Messengers
of the
Inner flame

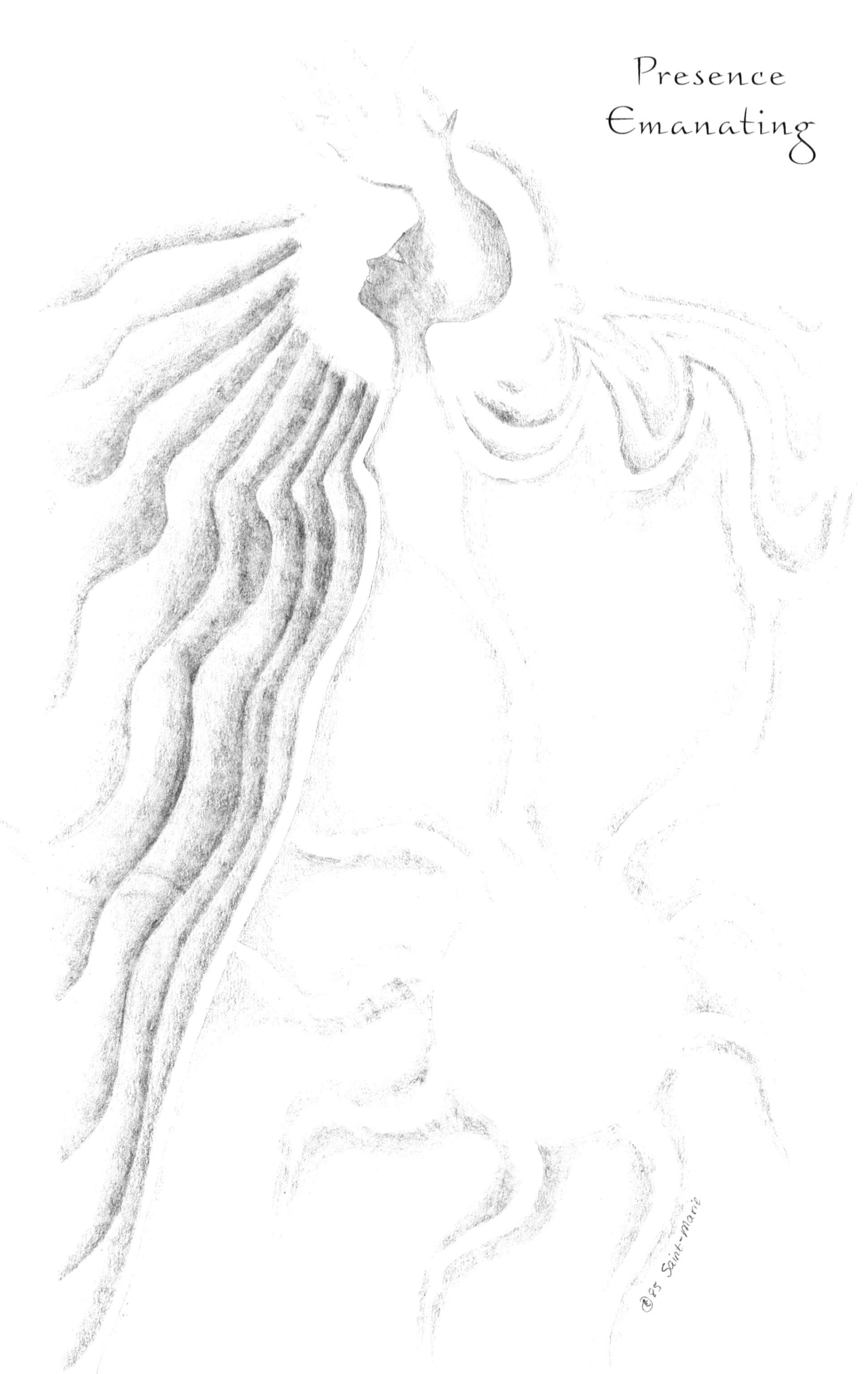
Presence
Emanating
©85 Saint-Marie

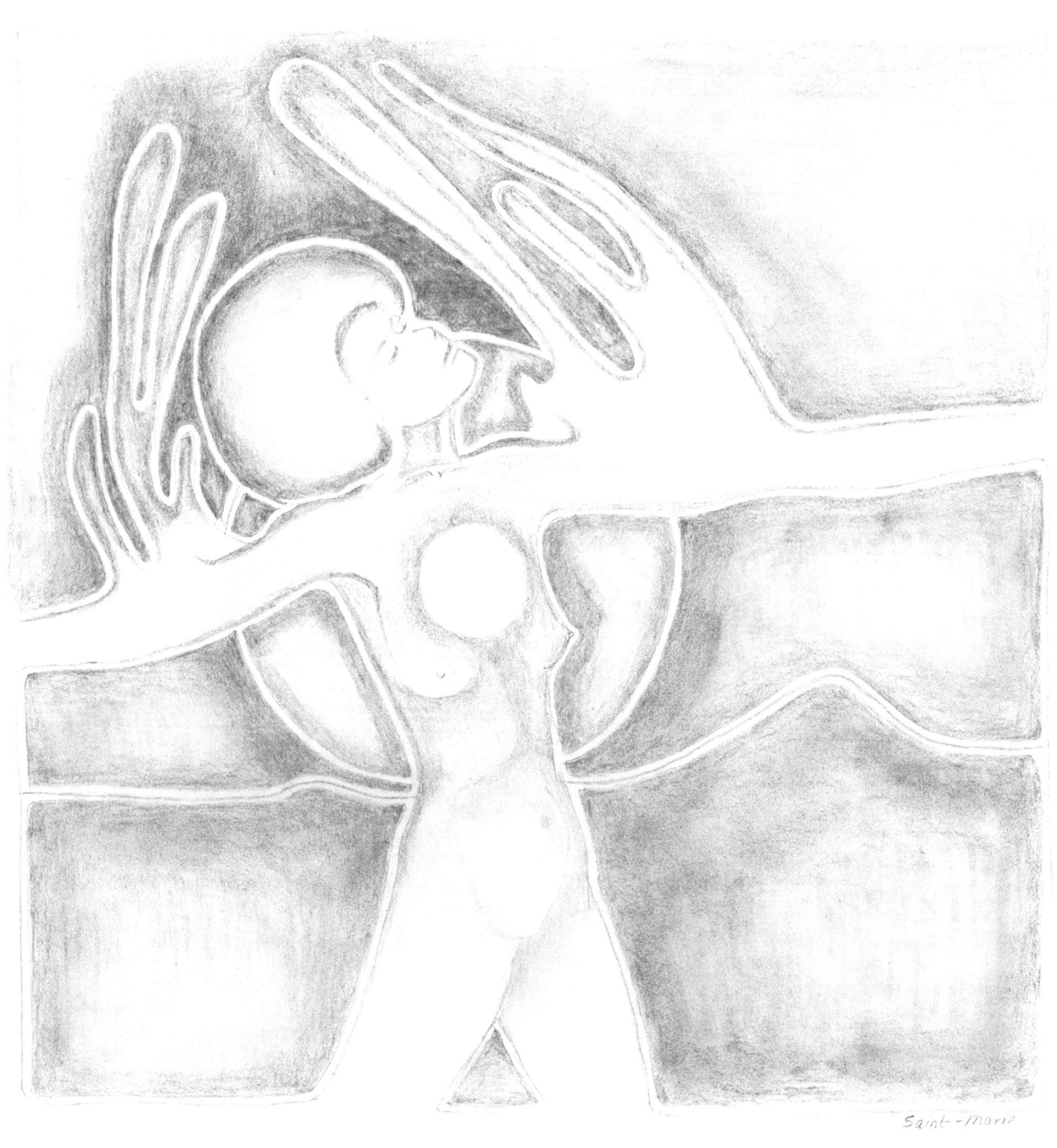

The Heart's Flow of Imagination

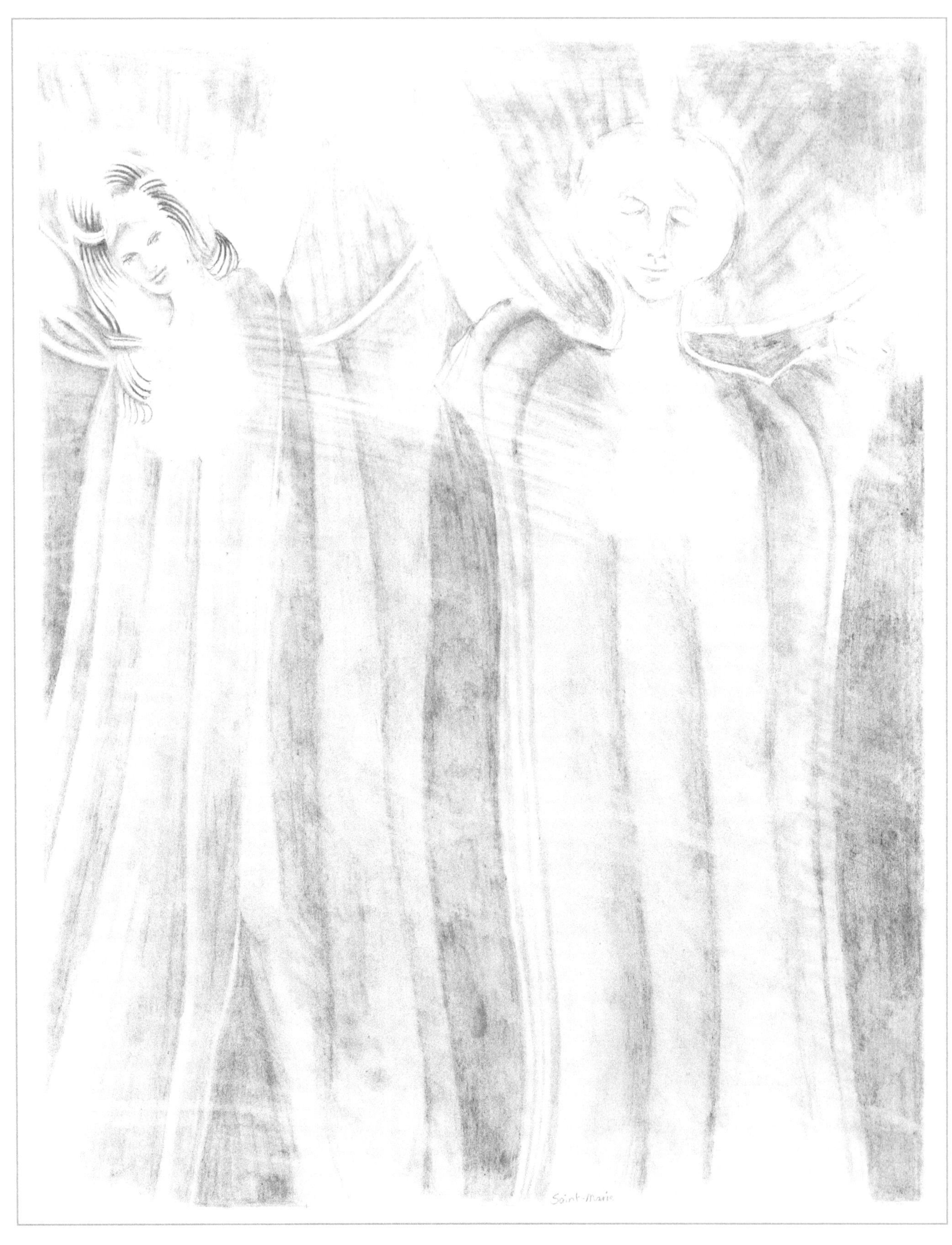

Union in Service to the Infinite

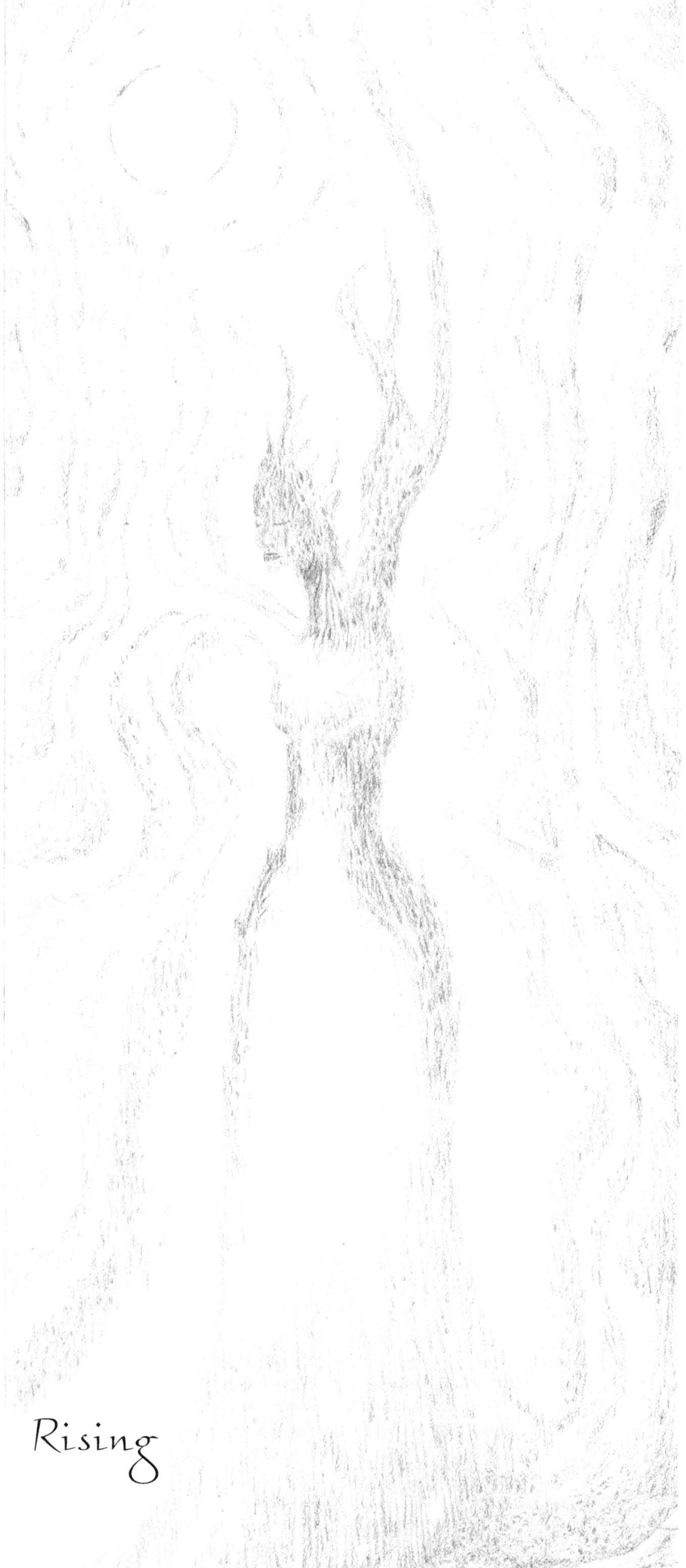
Rising

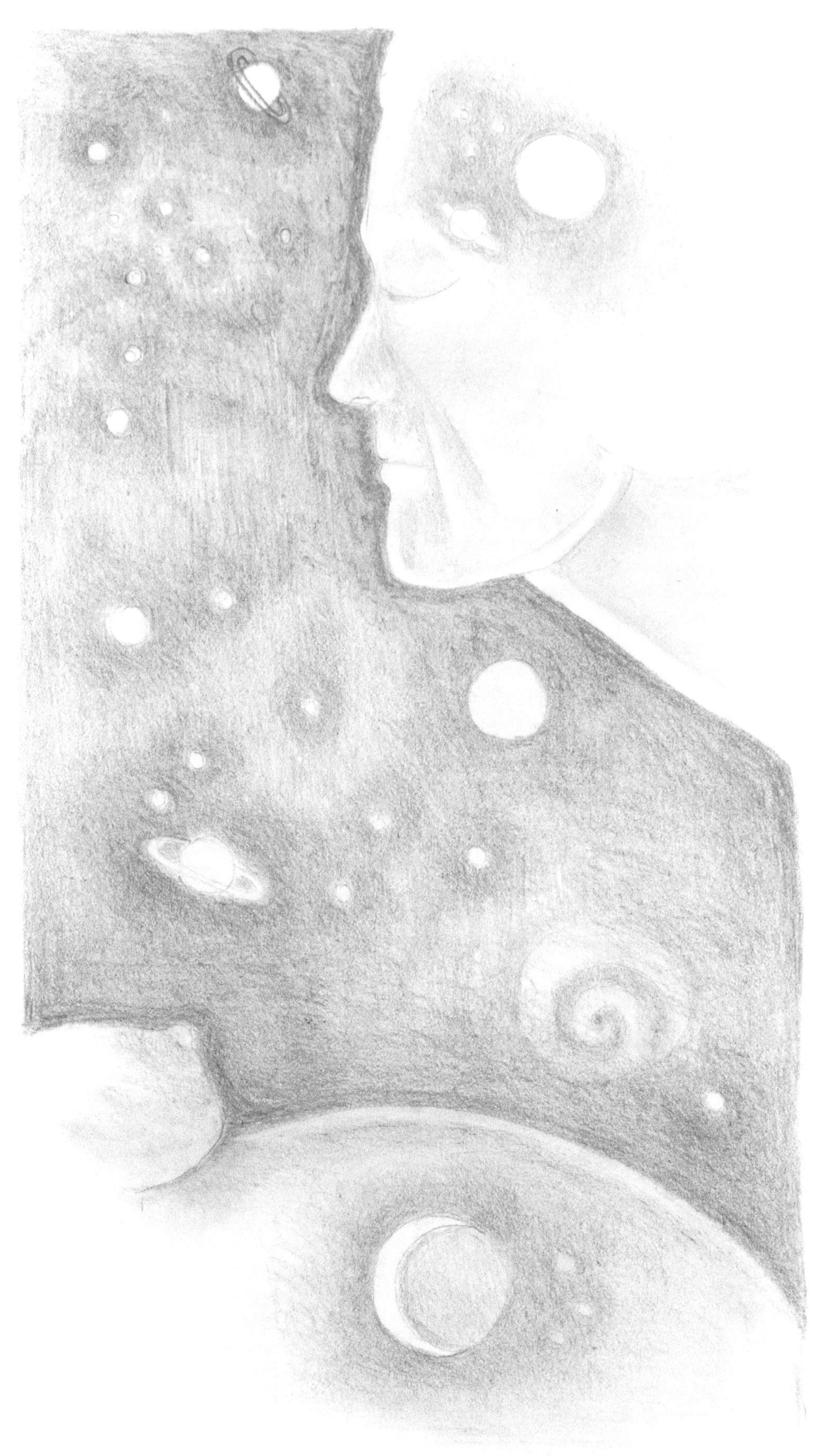

Harmony with the Cosmos

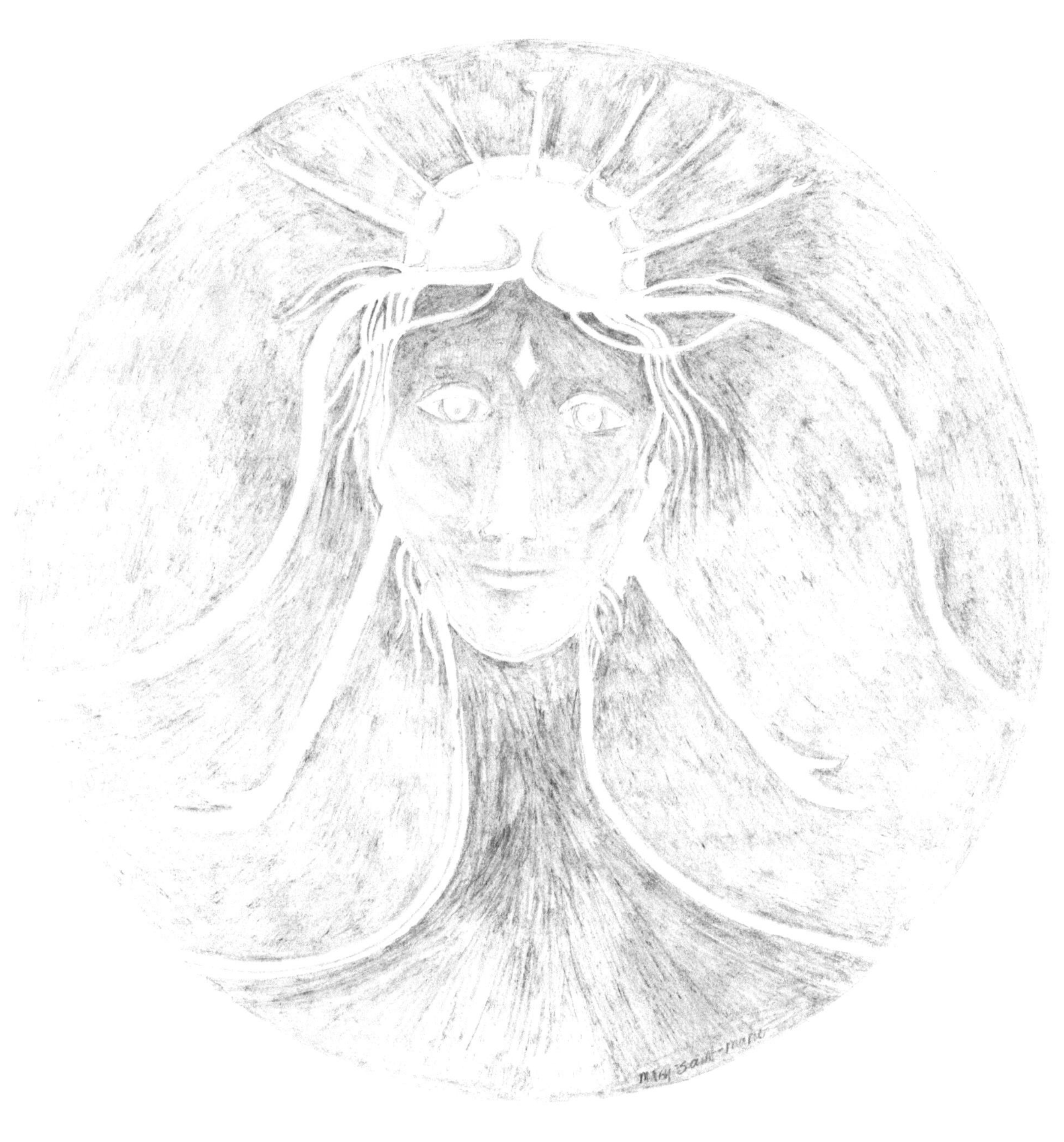

I Am the Light that Is

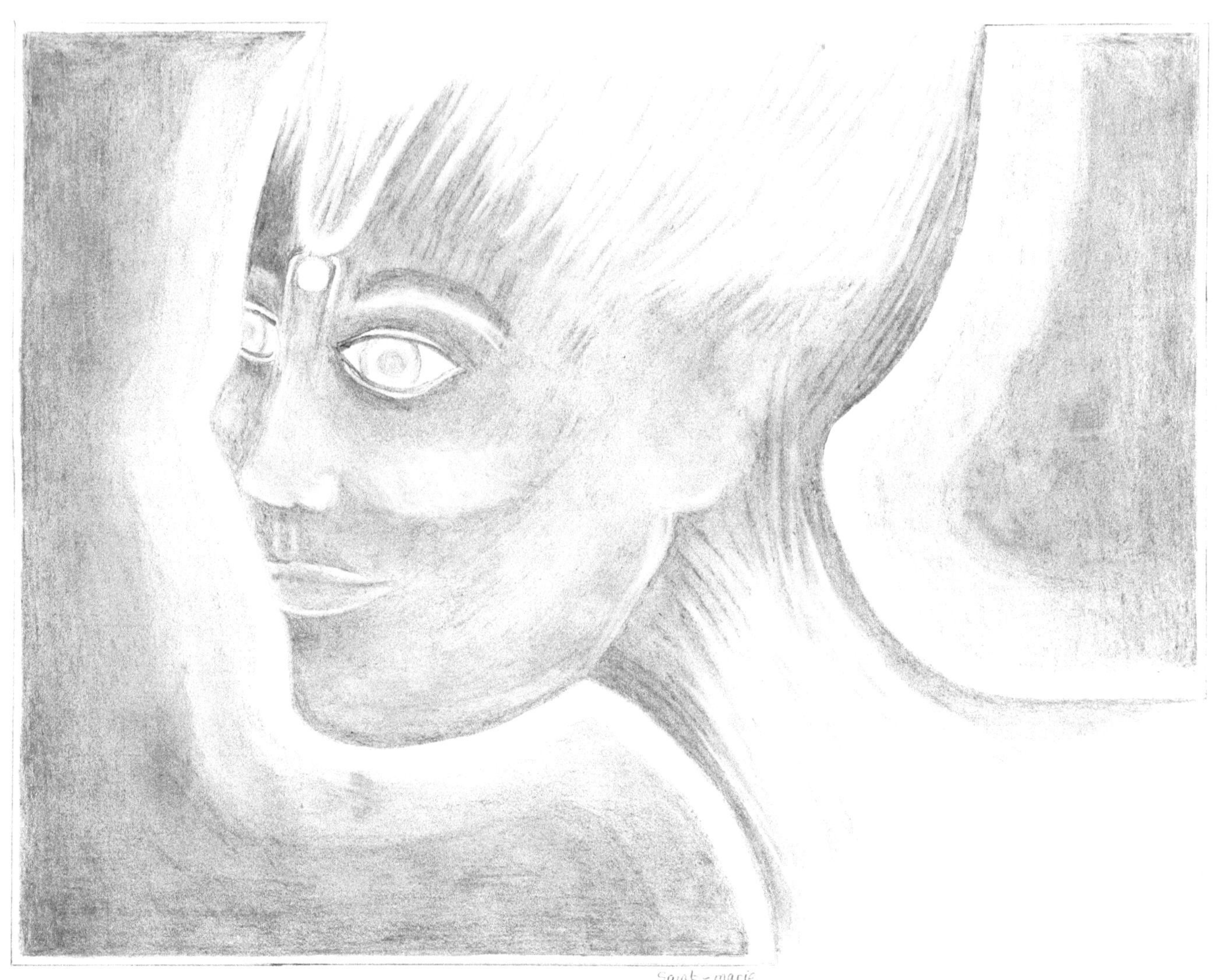

the formed and formless…in balance

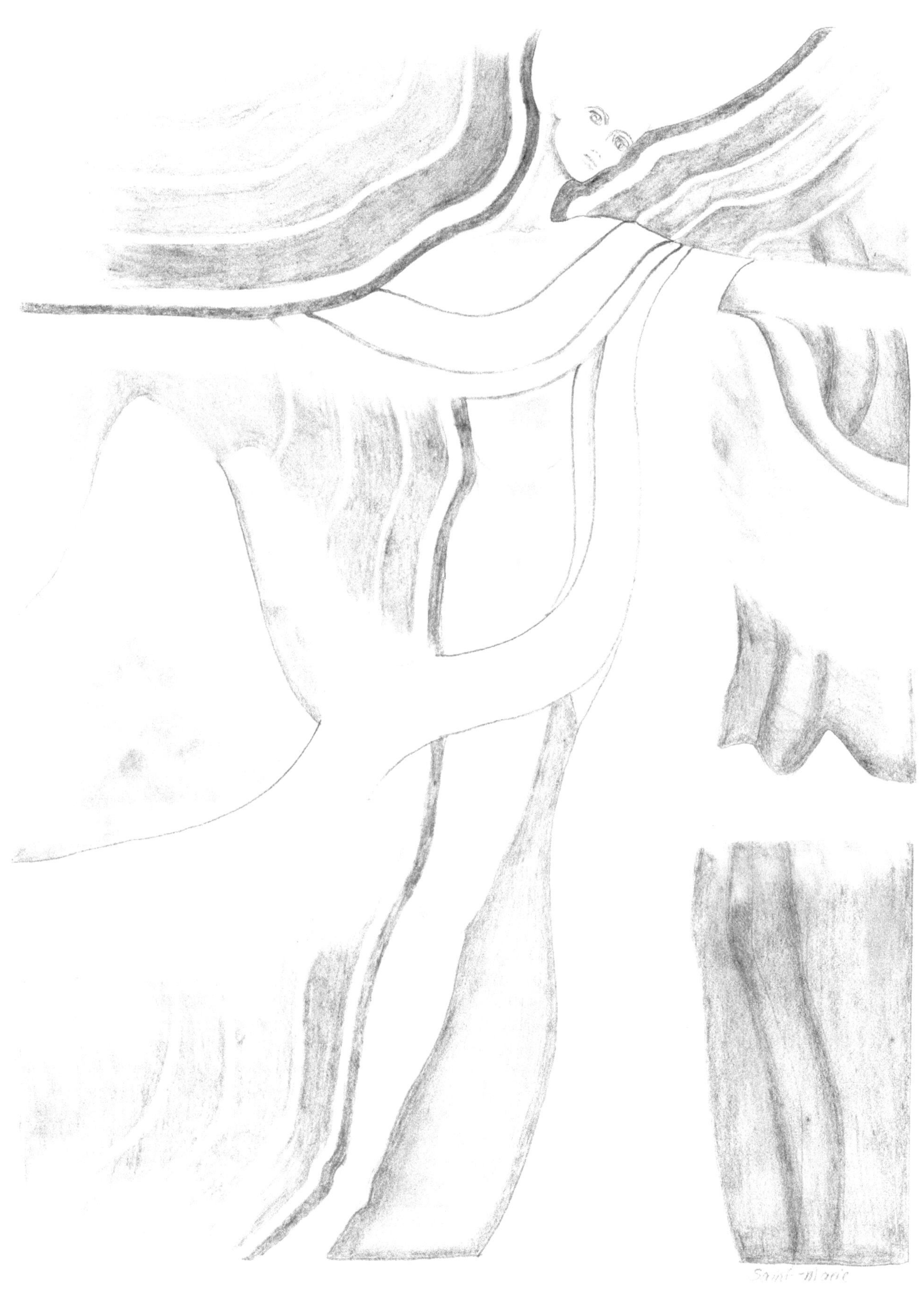

Open to the World Within

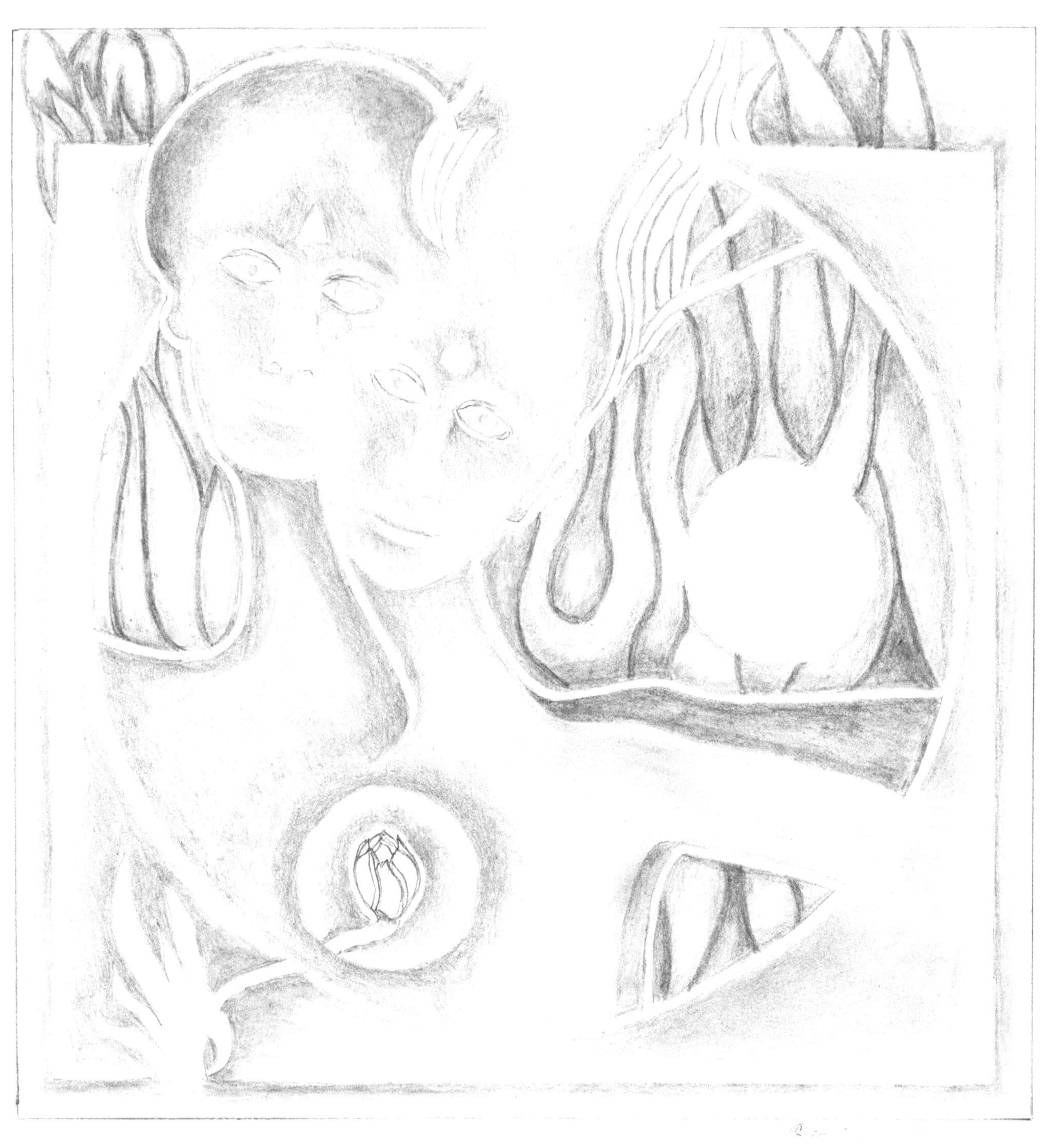

The Heart's Flowering

Heart Essence

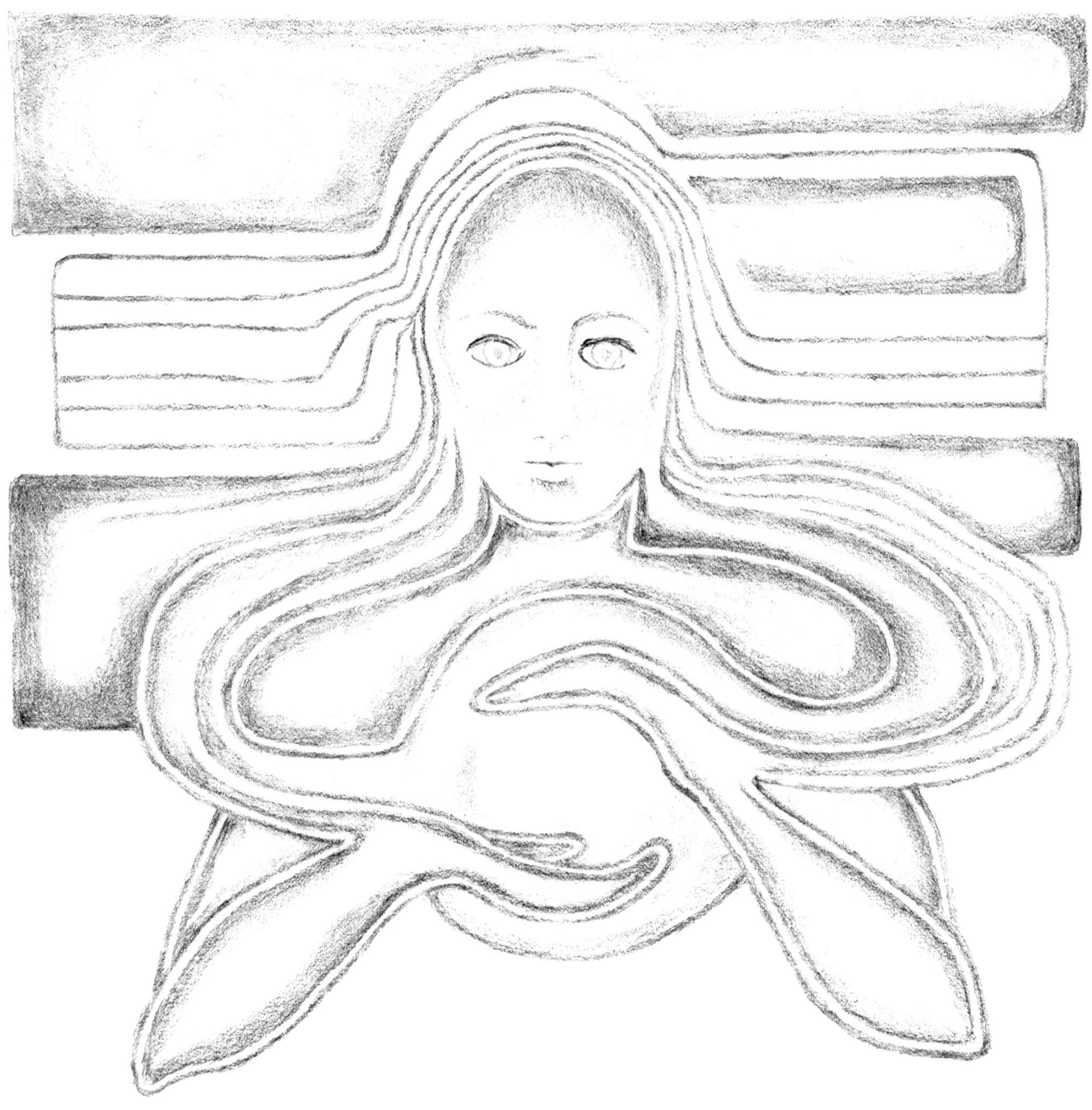

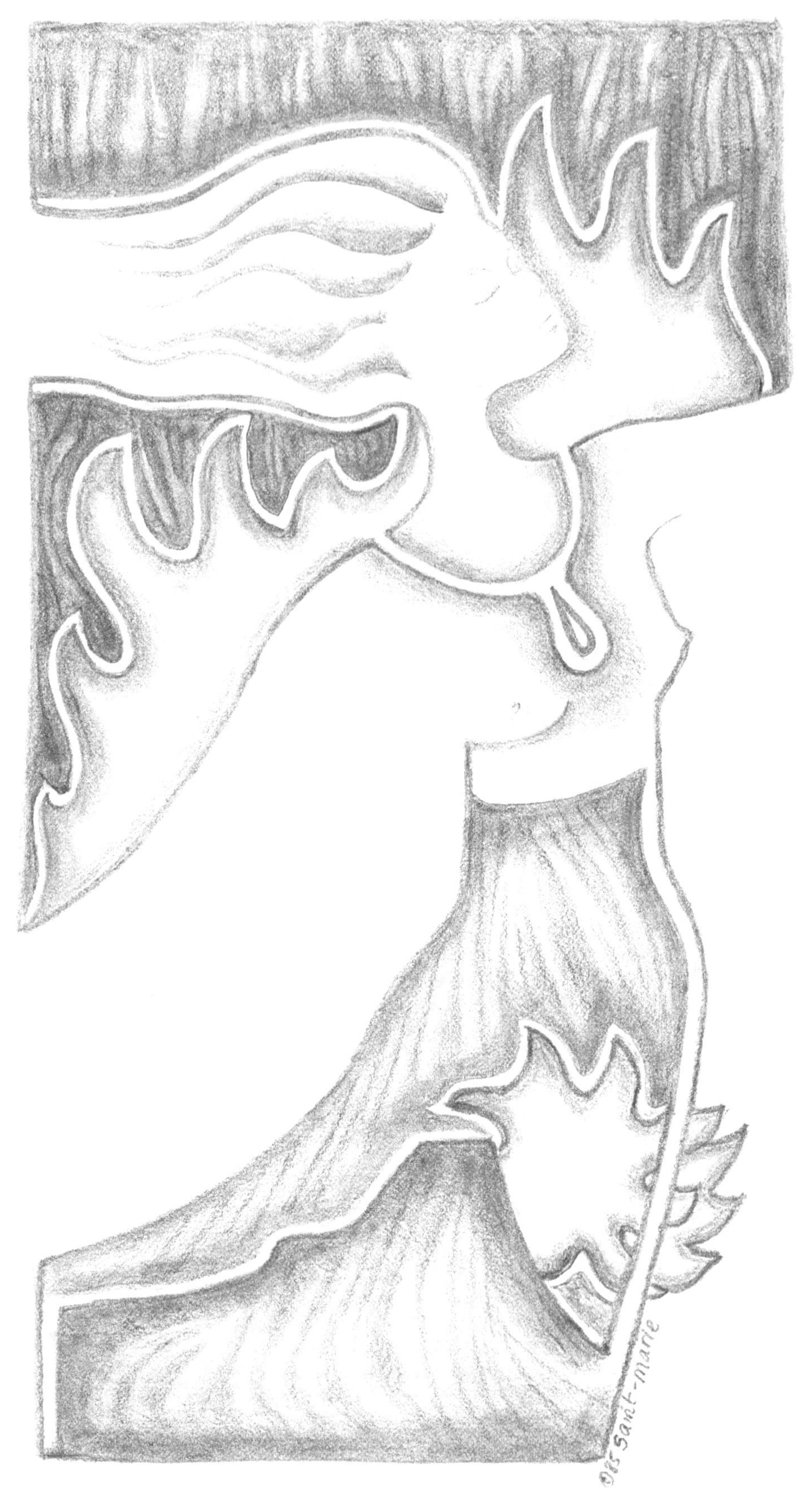

The Fiery Dance of Oneness

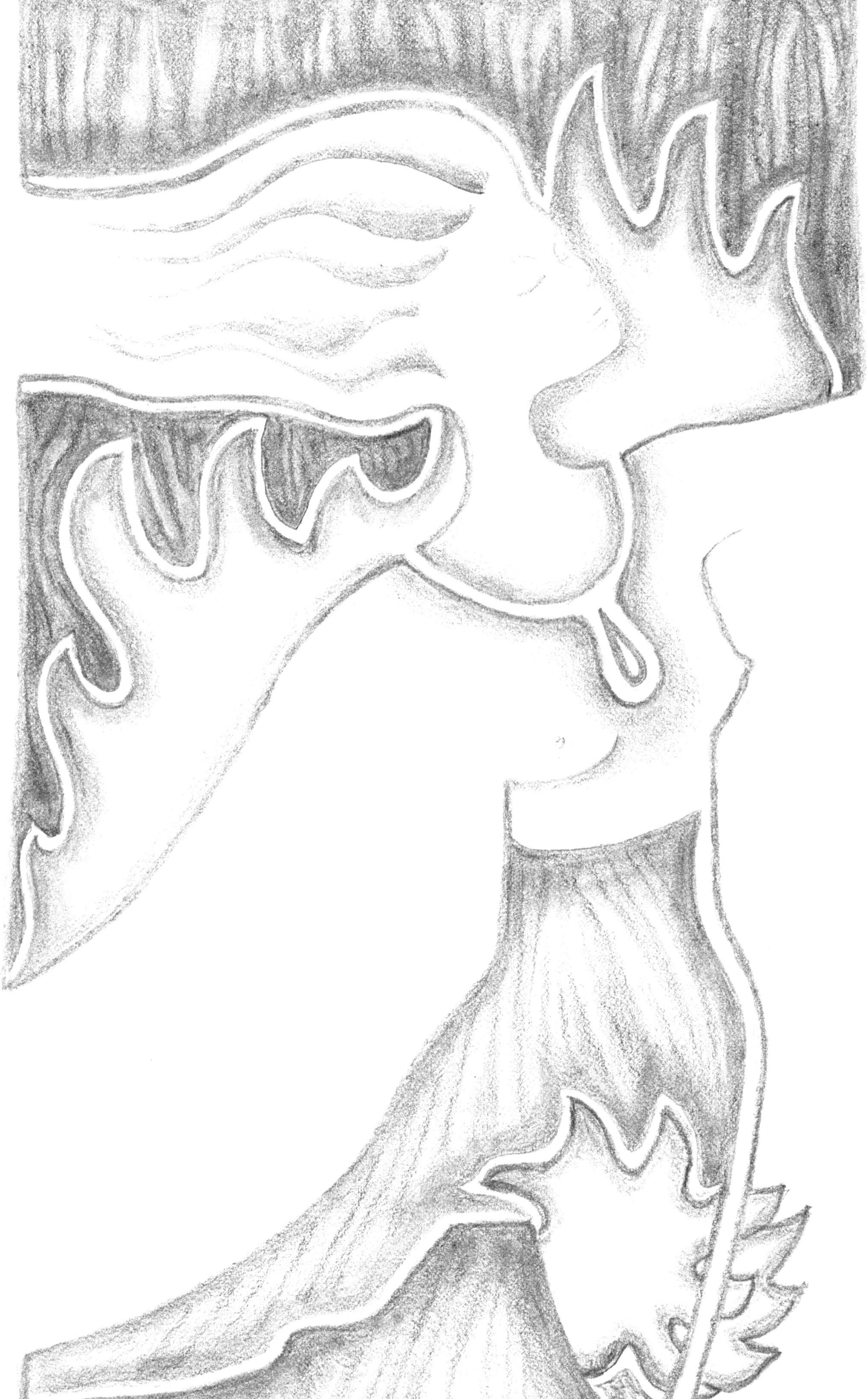

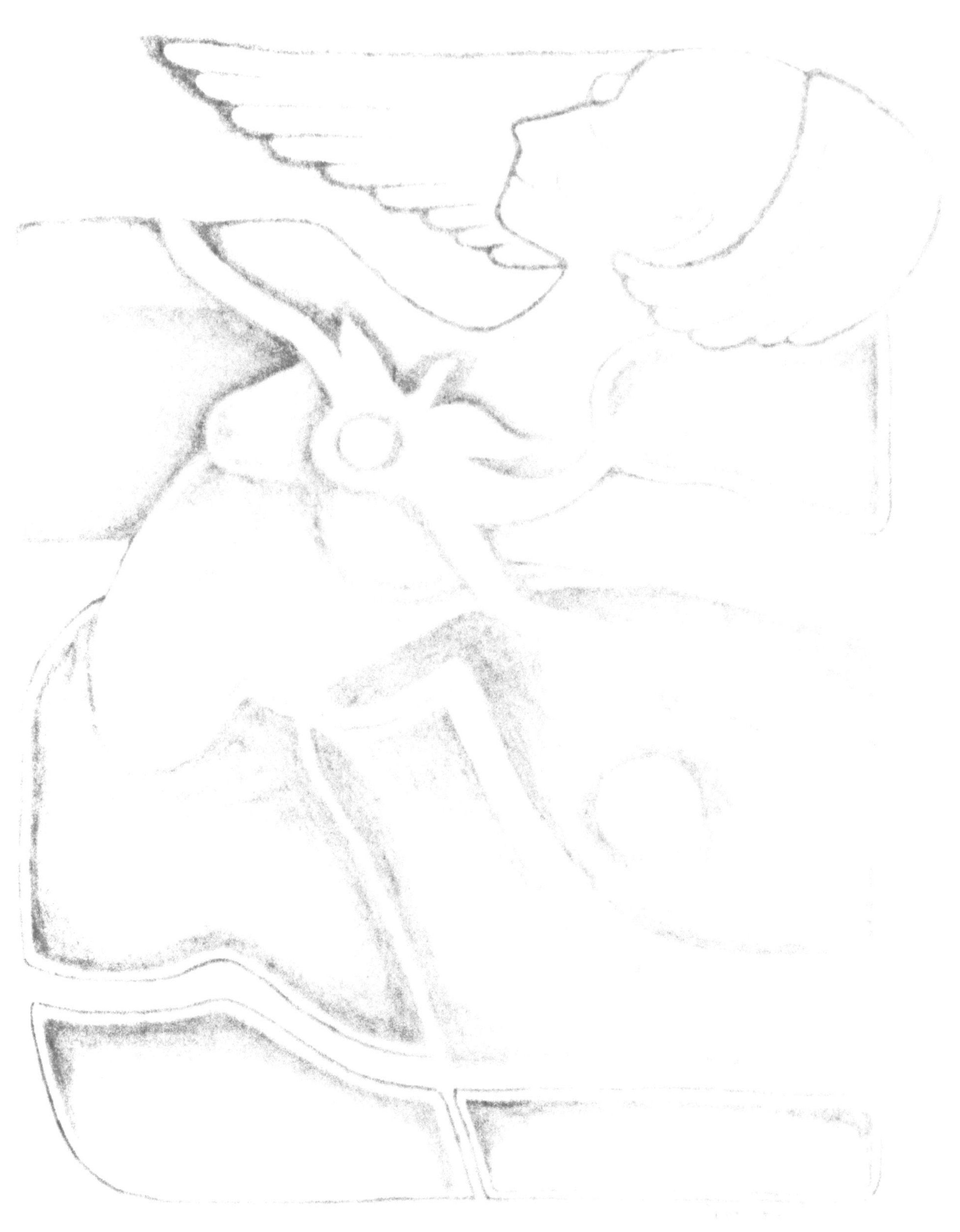

A Heart Conversing with Other Realms

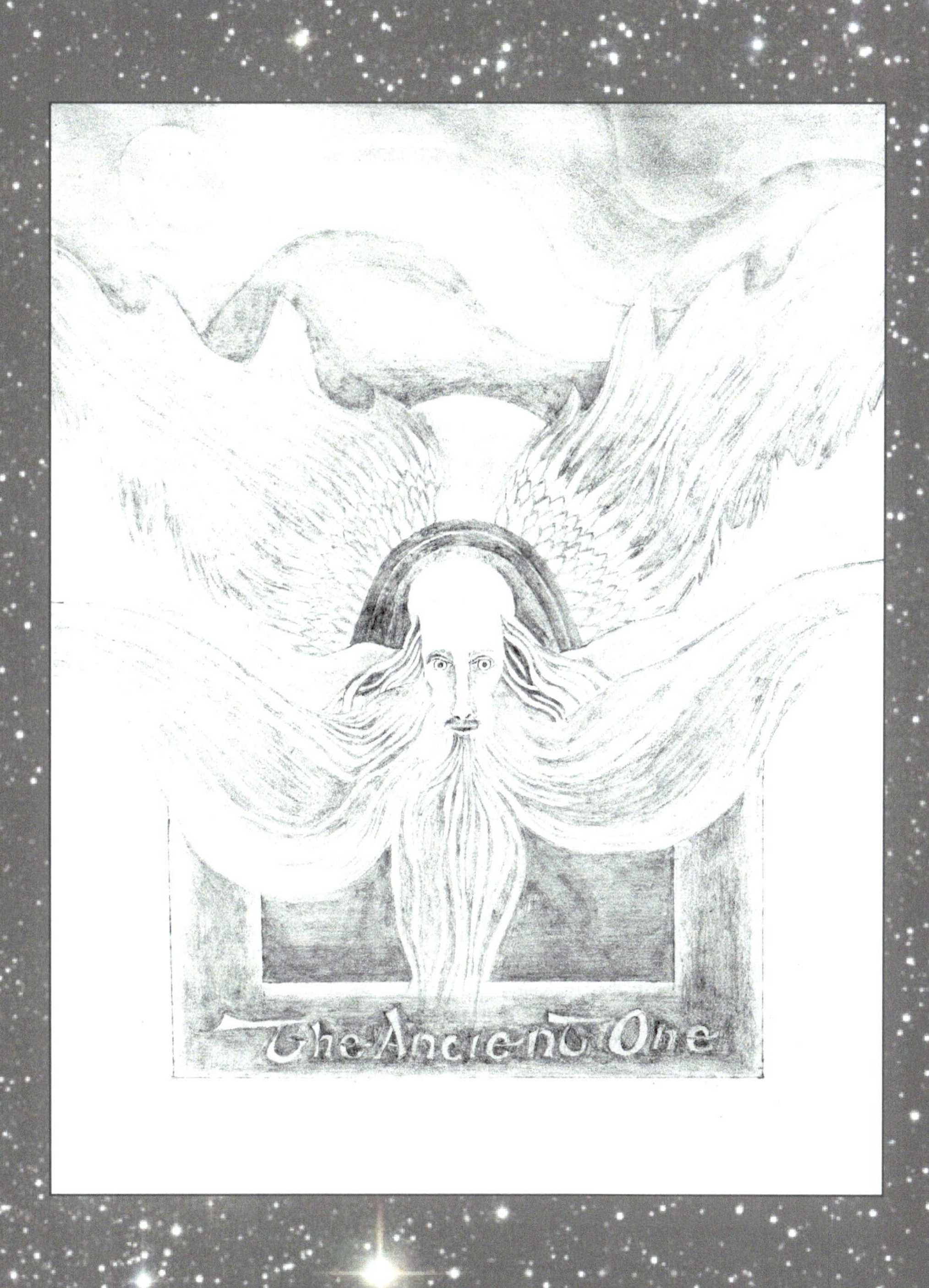

The Ancient One

a soul connection

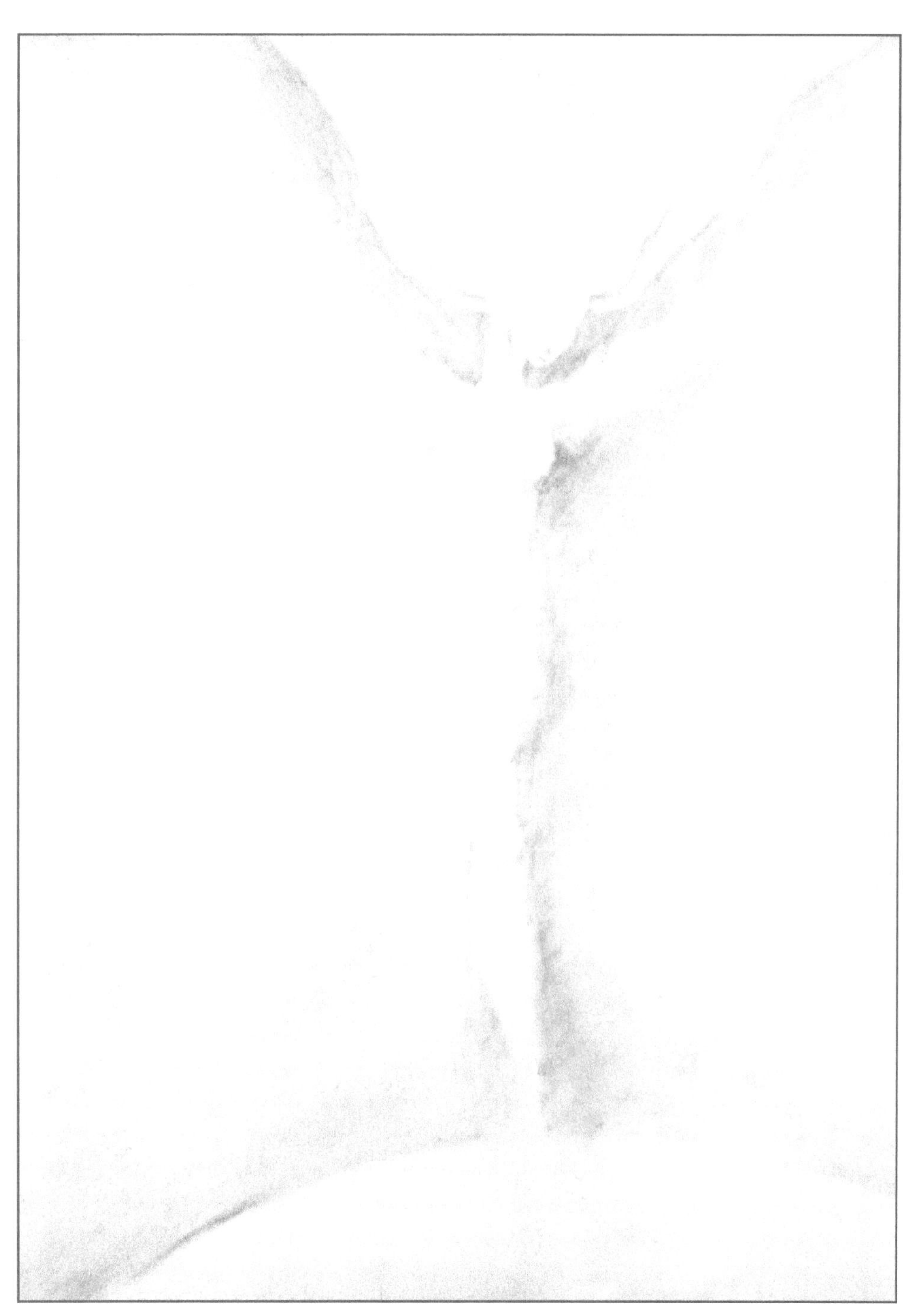

Being Here

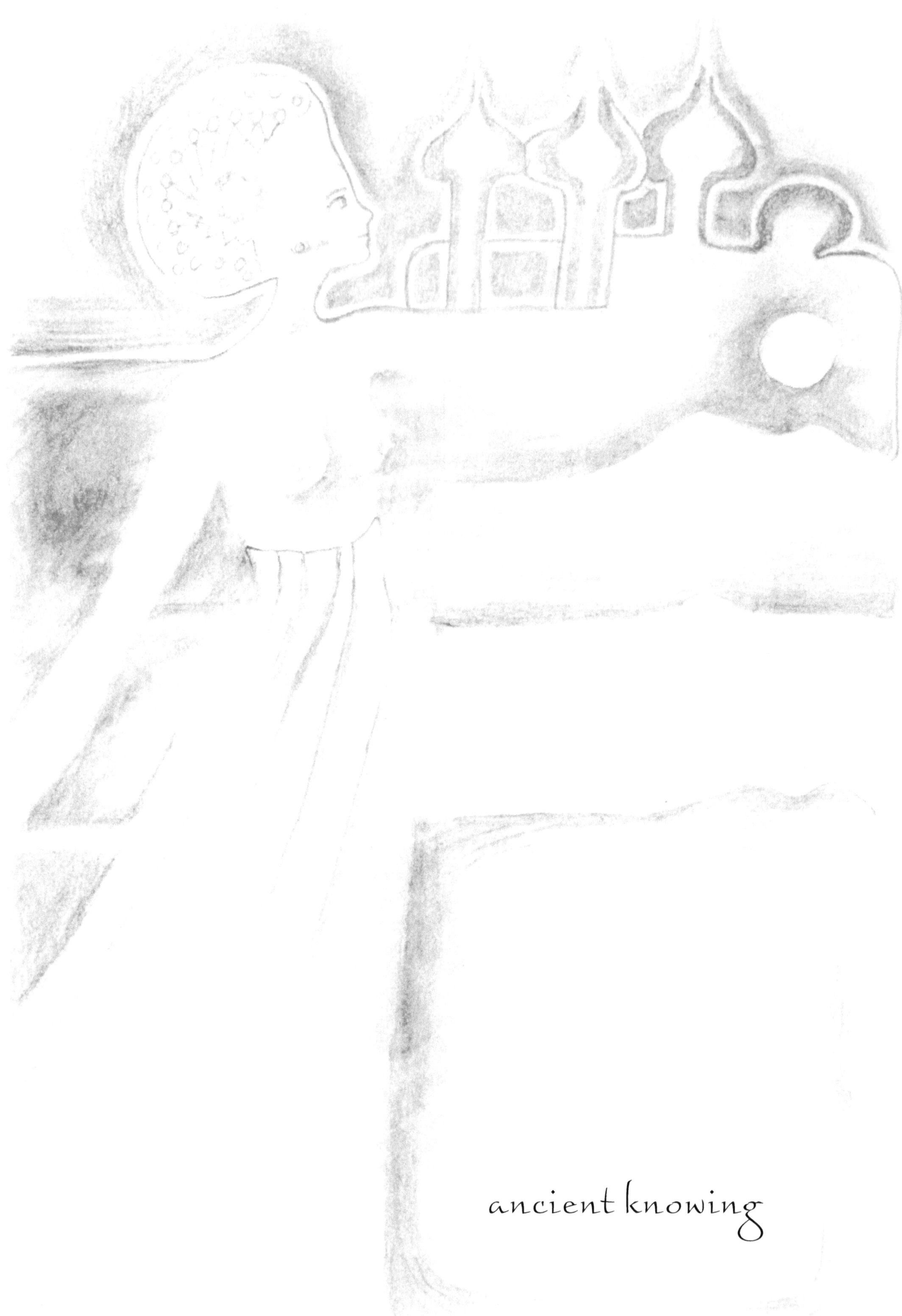
ancient knowing

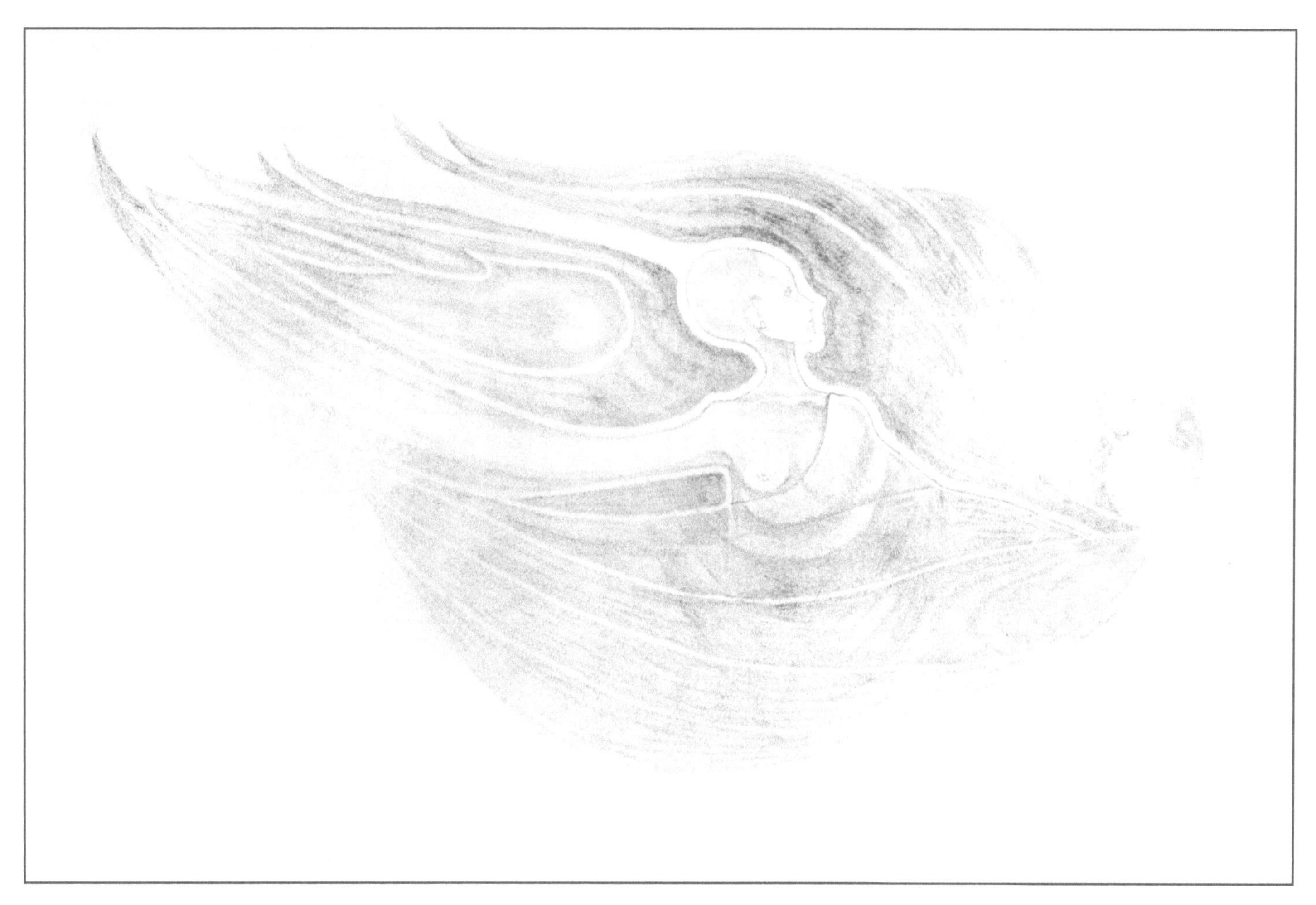

the messenger

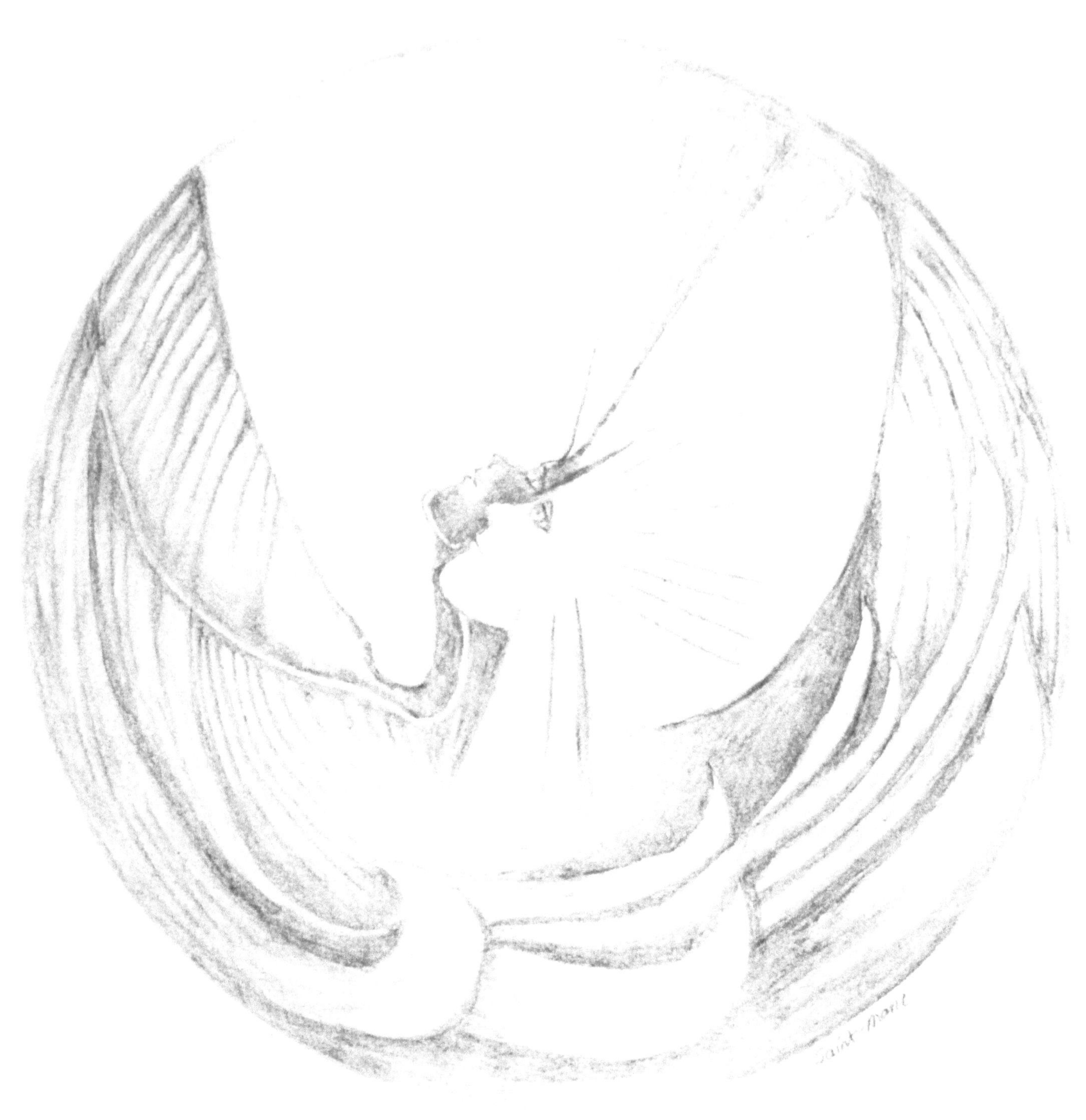

Attuned to Oneness

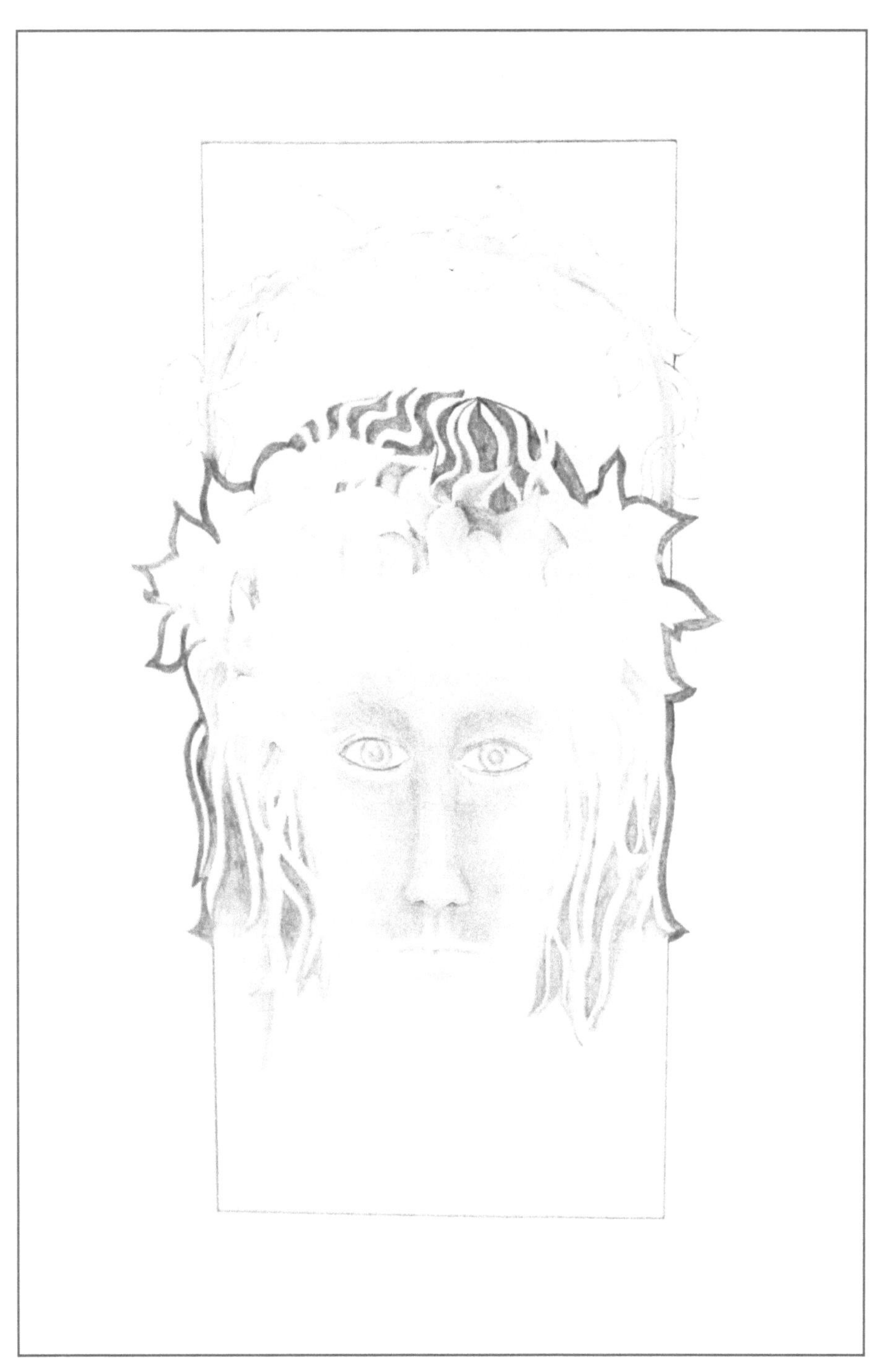

I Am…Here

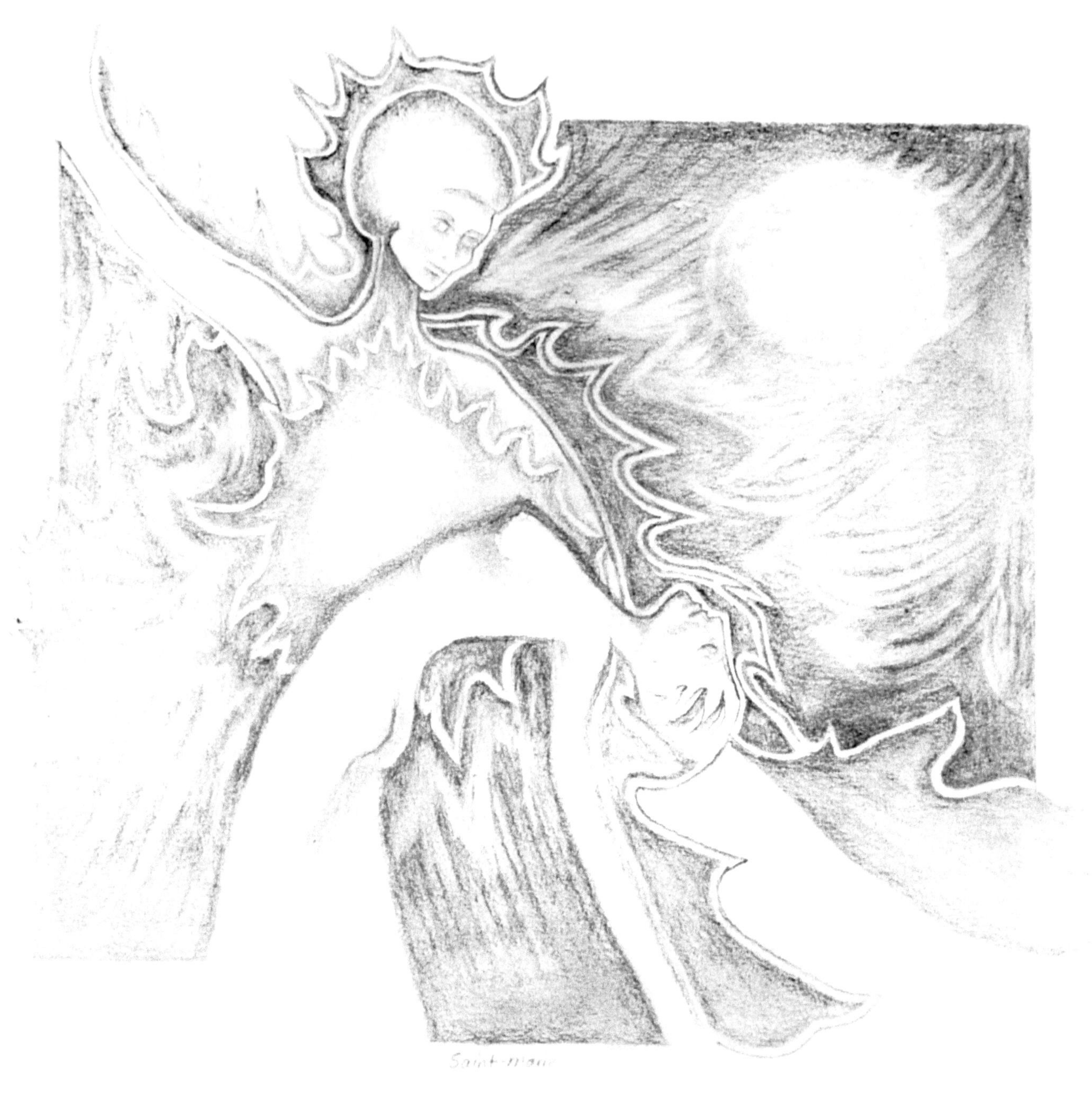

Light...Alone...

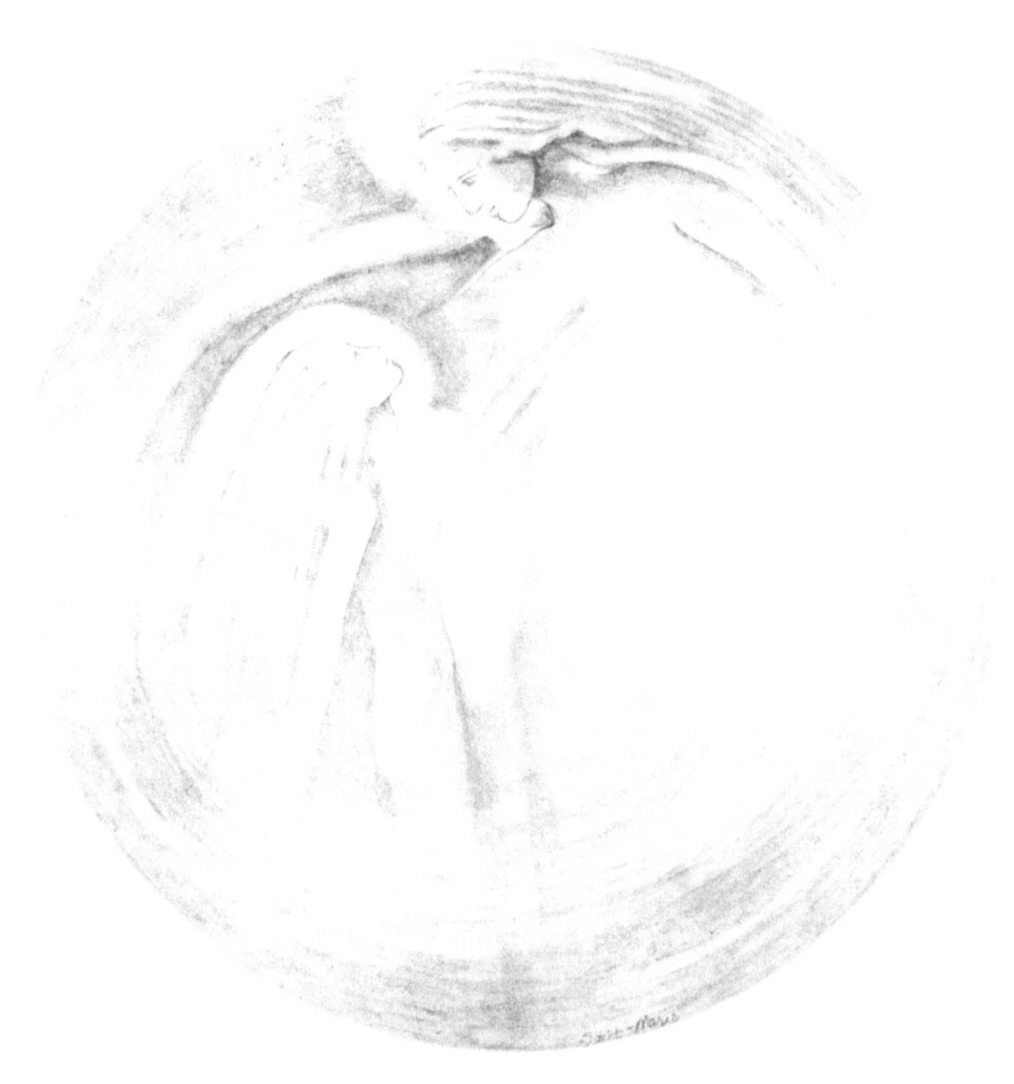

the heart's knowing

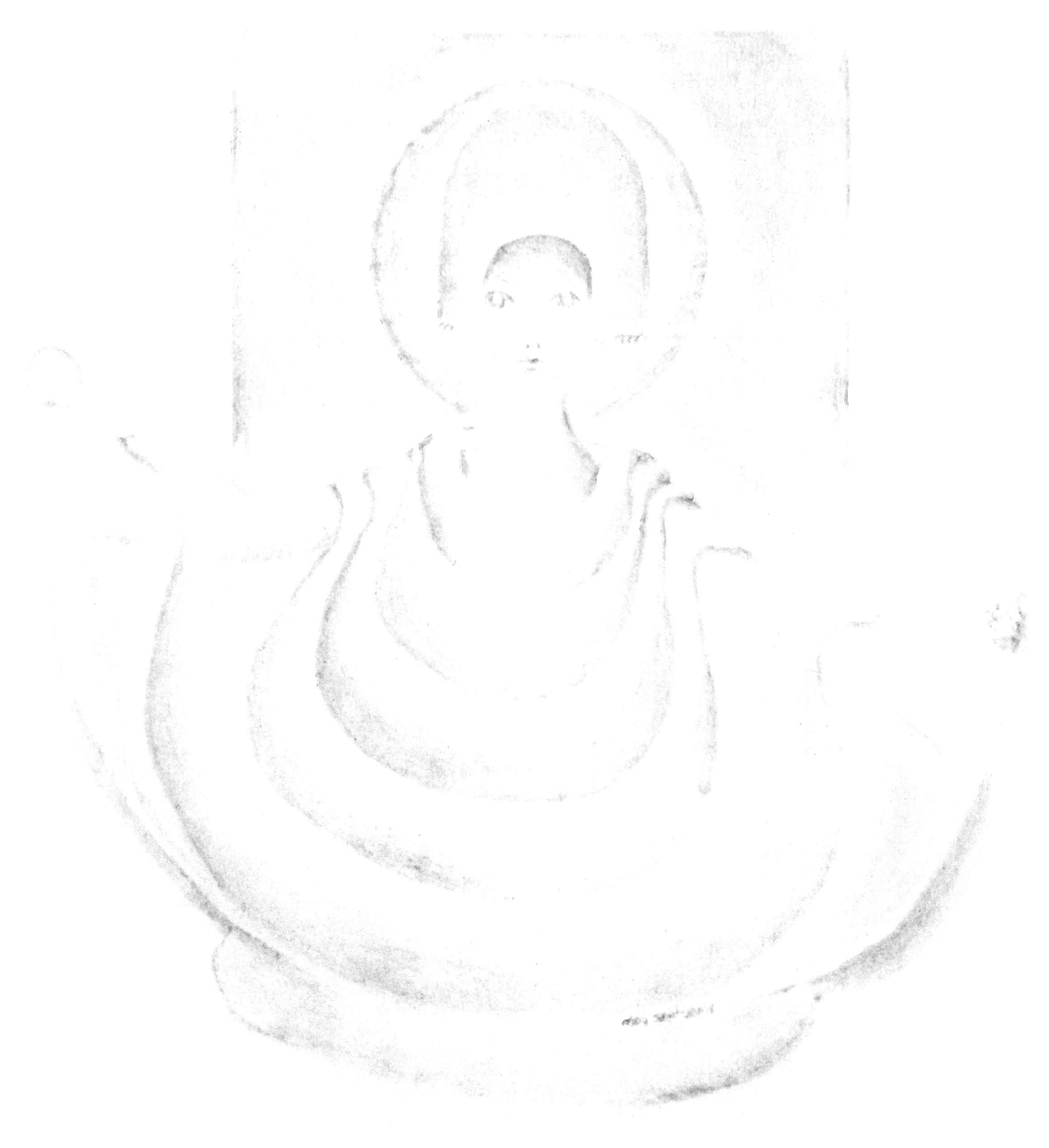

purity manifest

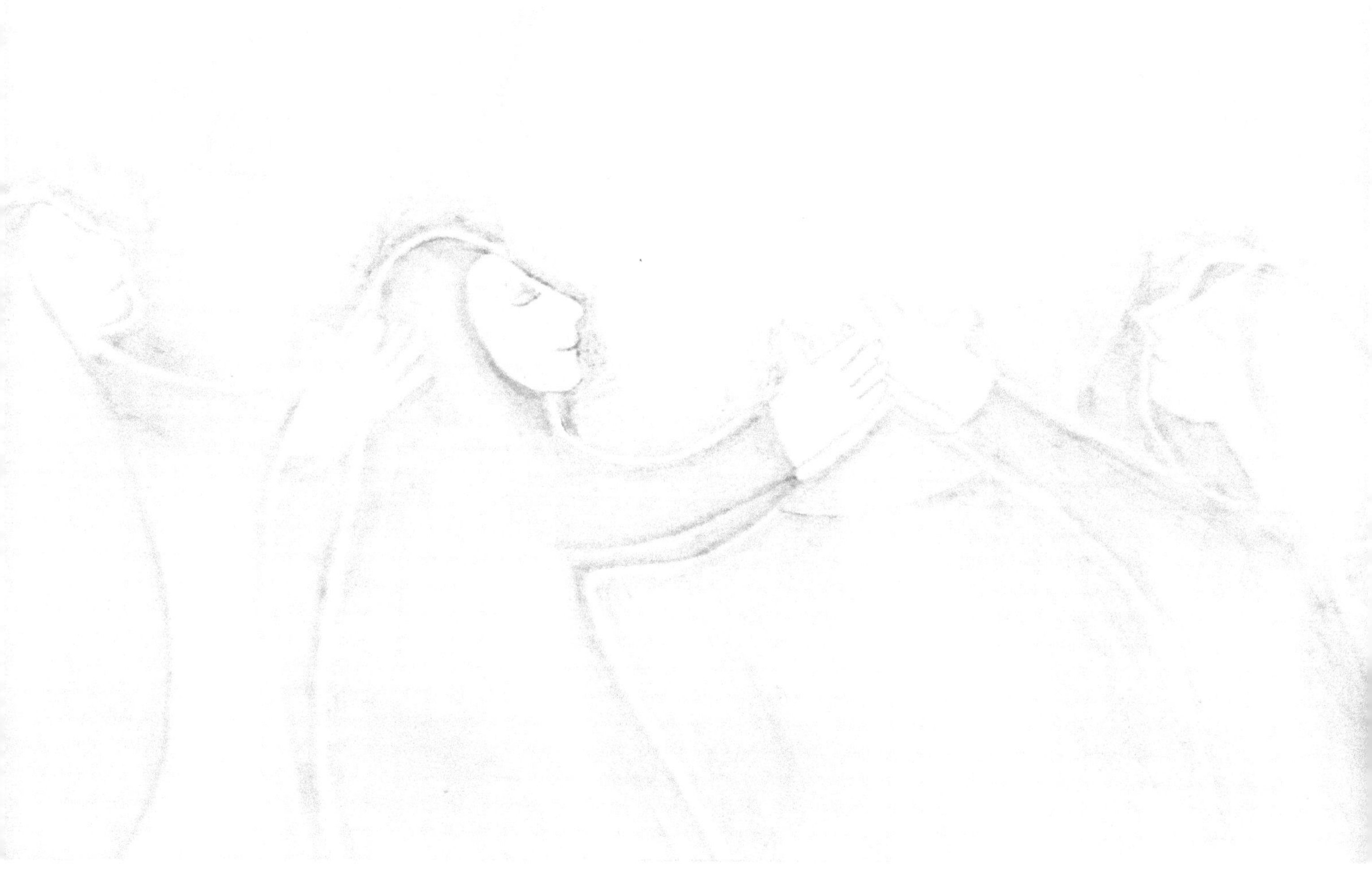

realm of purity

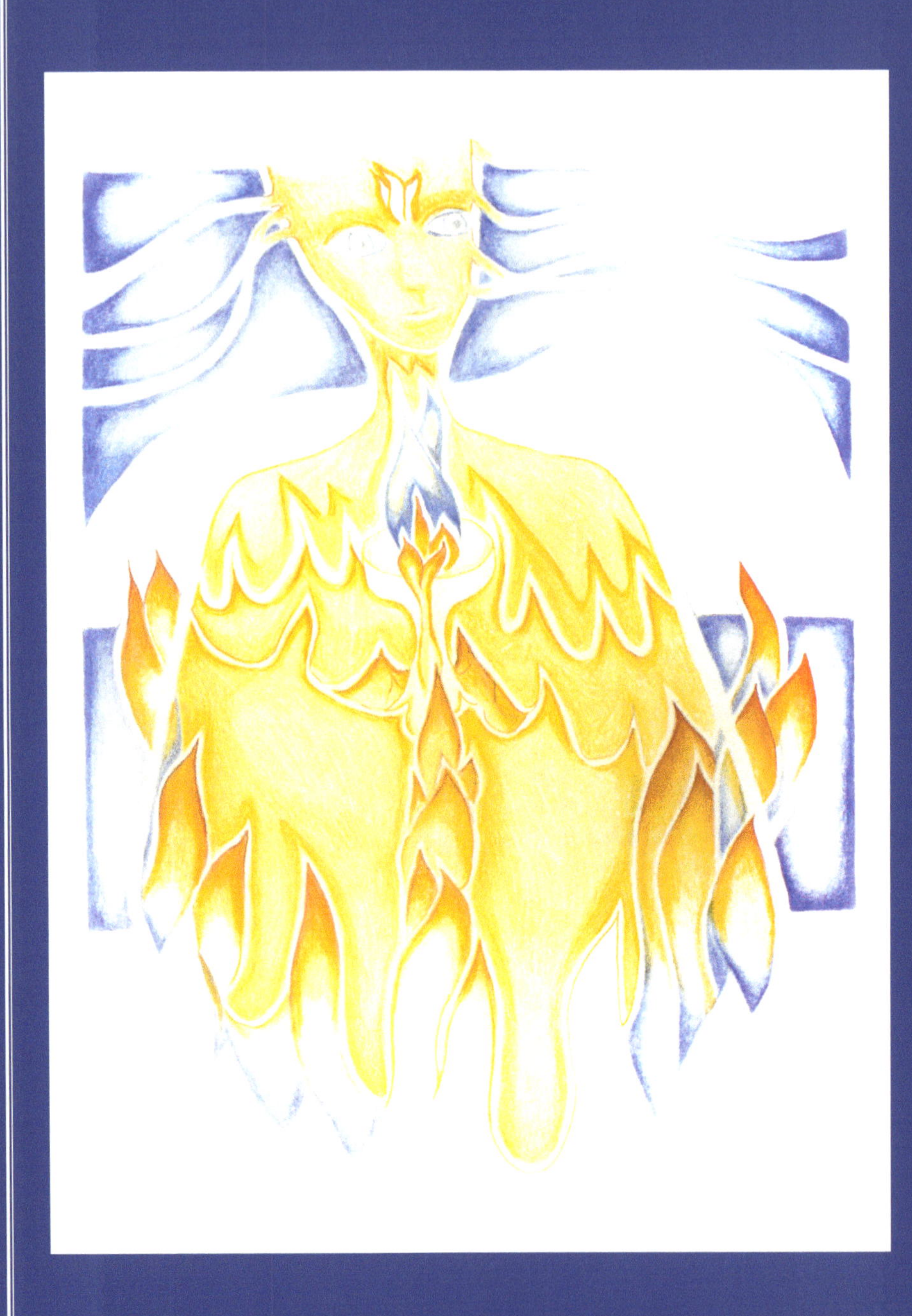

The Christ Child

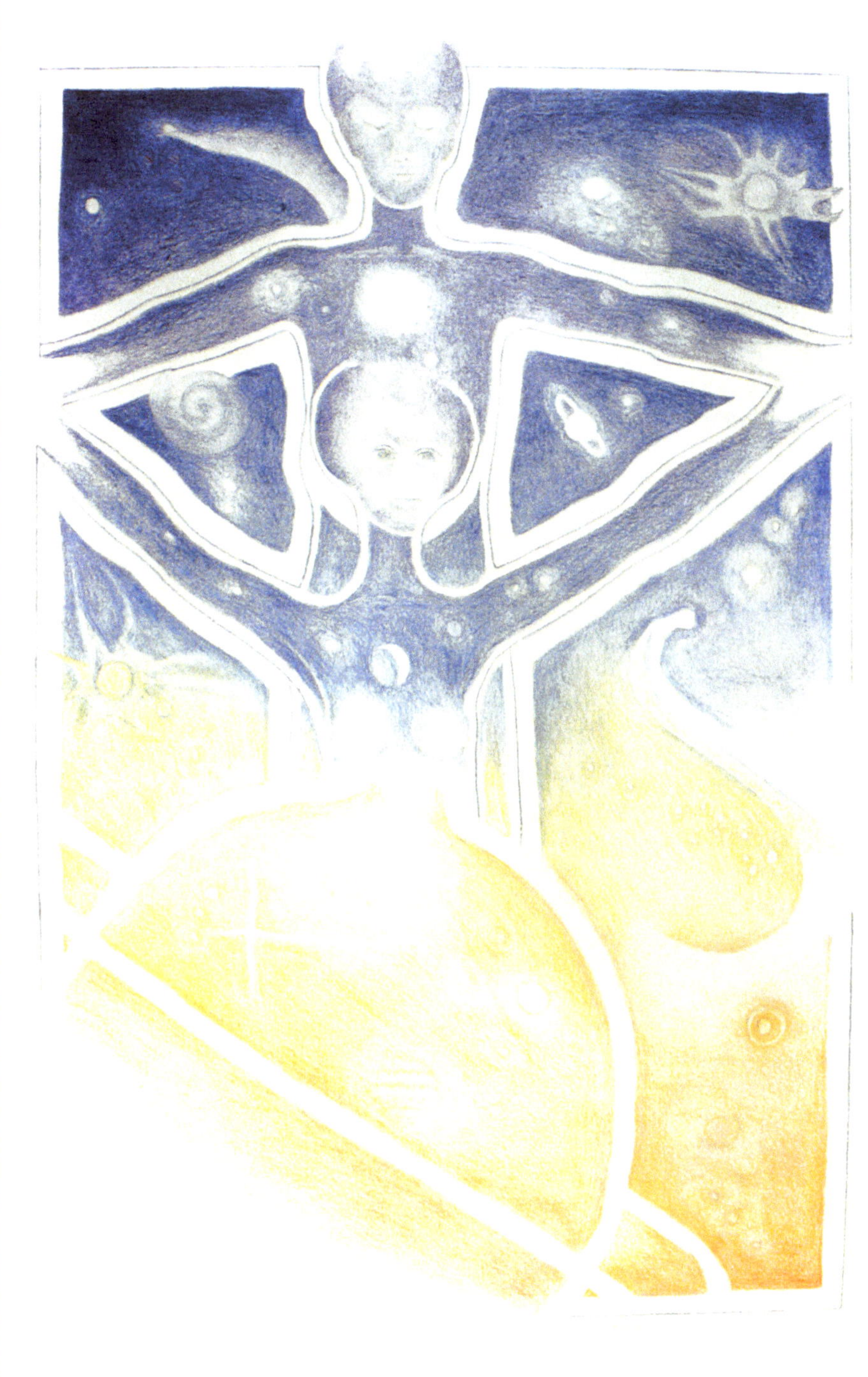

Union of Earth and Sky

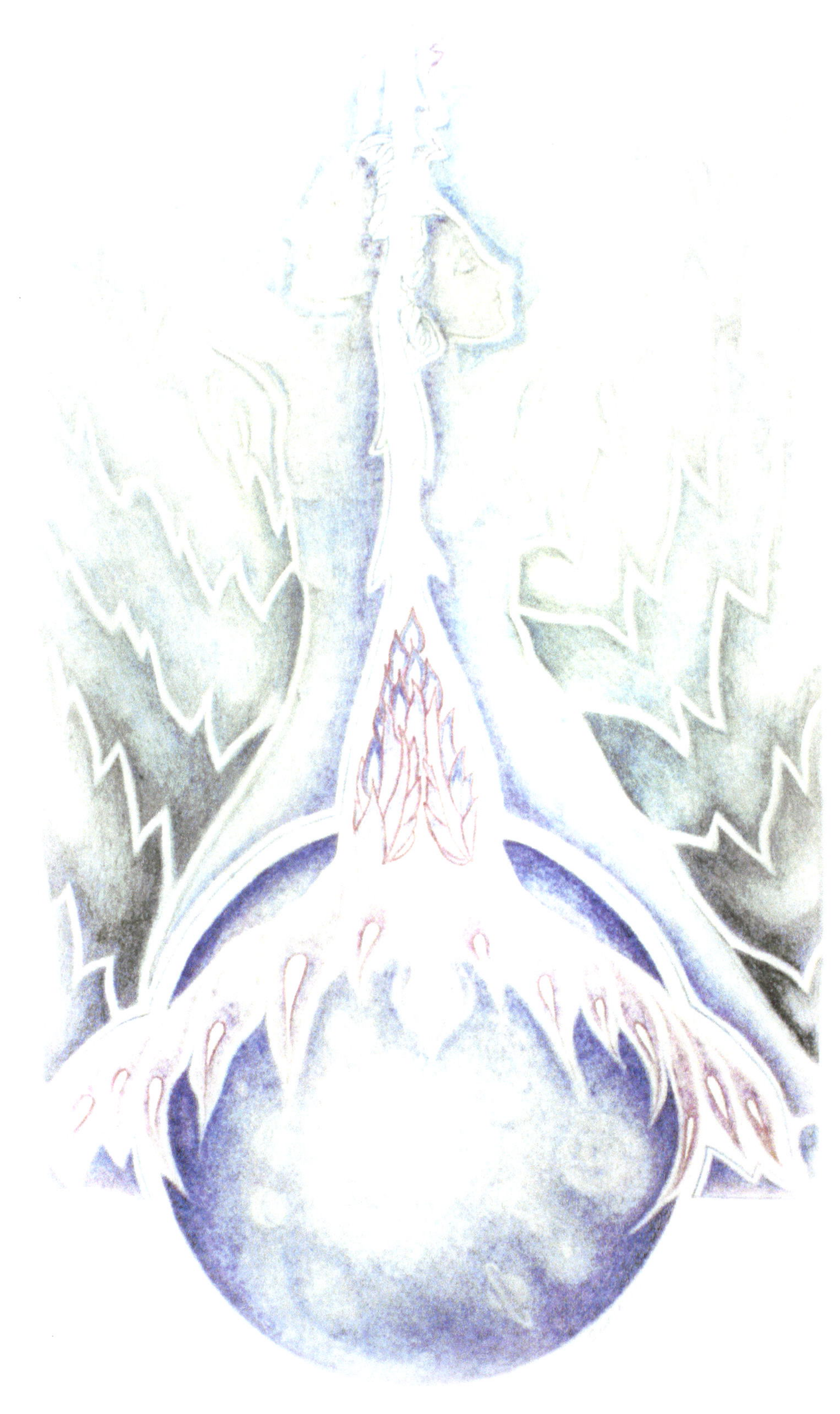

He and She...of the Earth and Sky

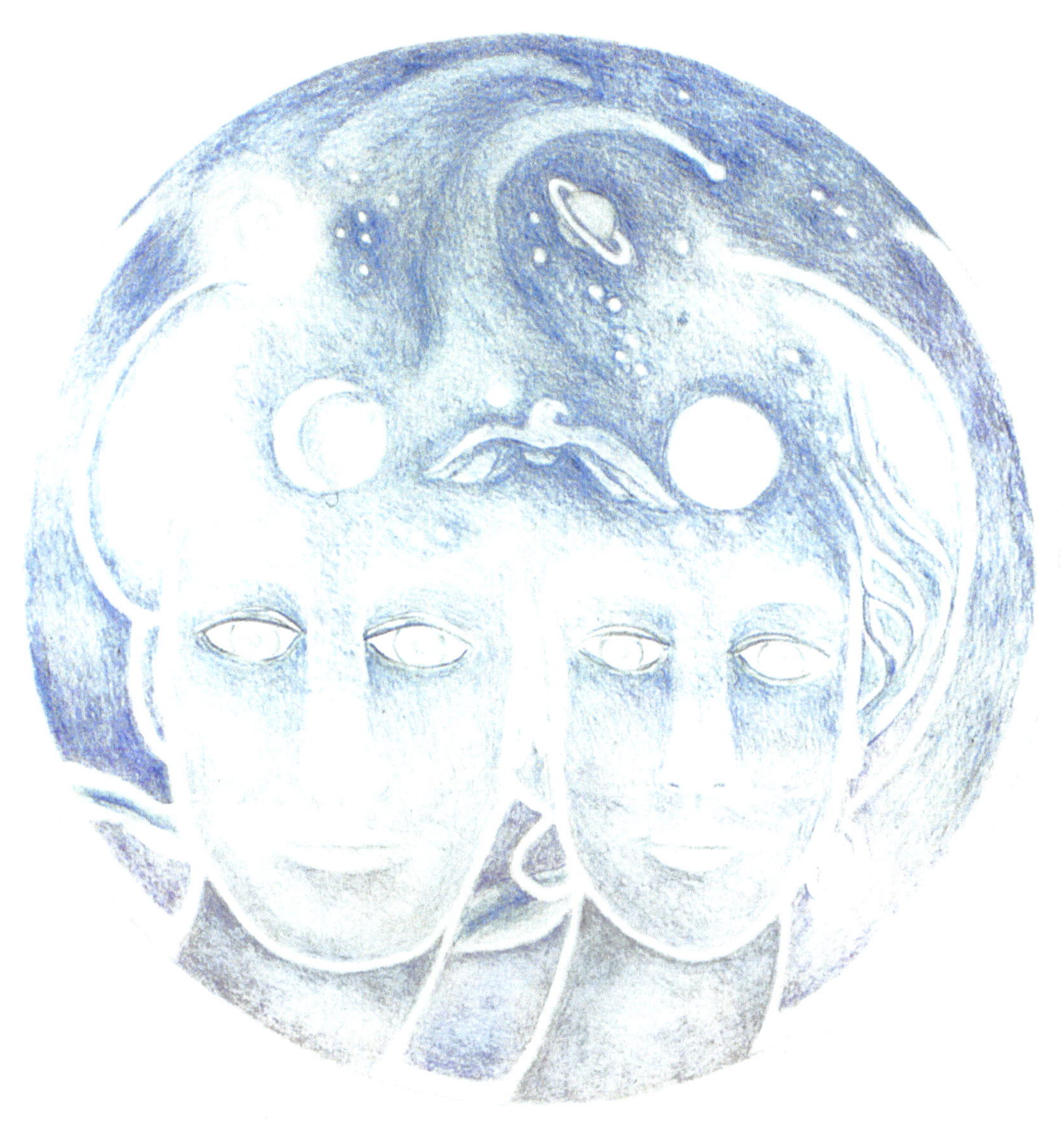

Unity Consciousness

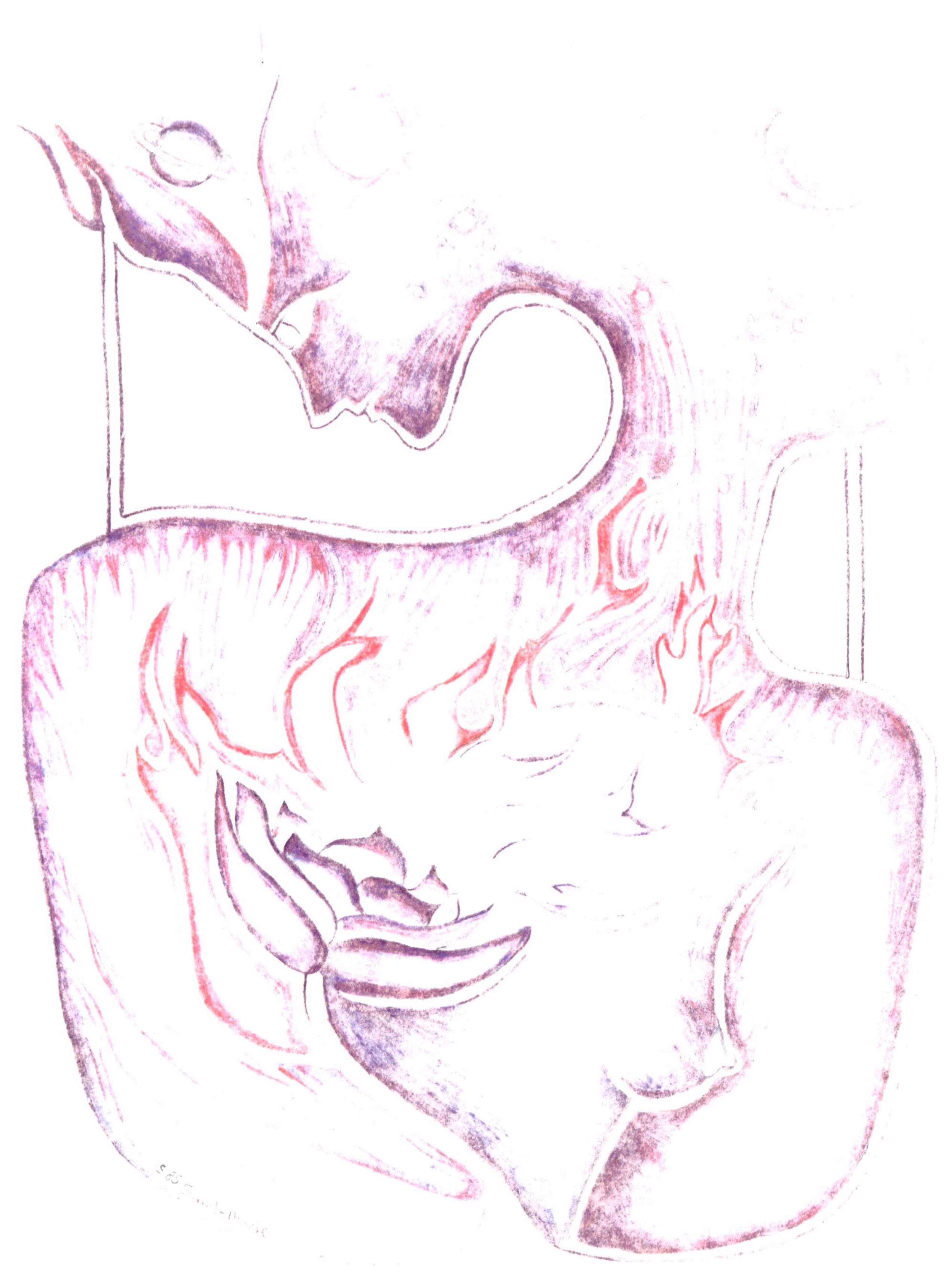

Cosmic Heart flame

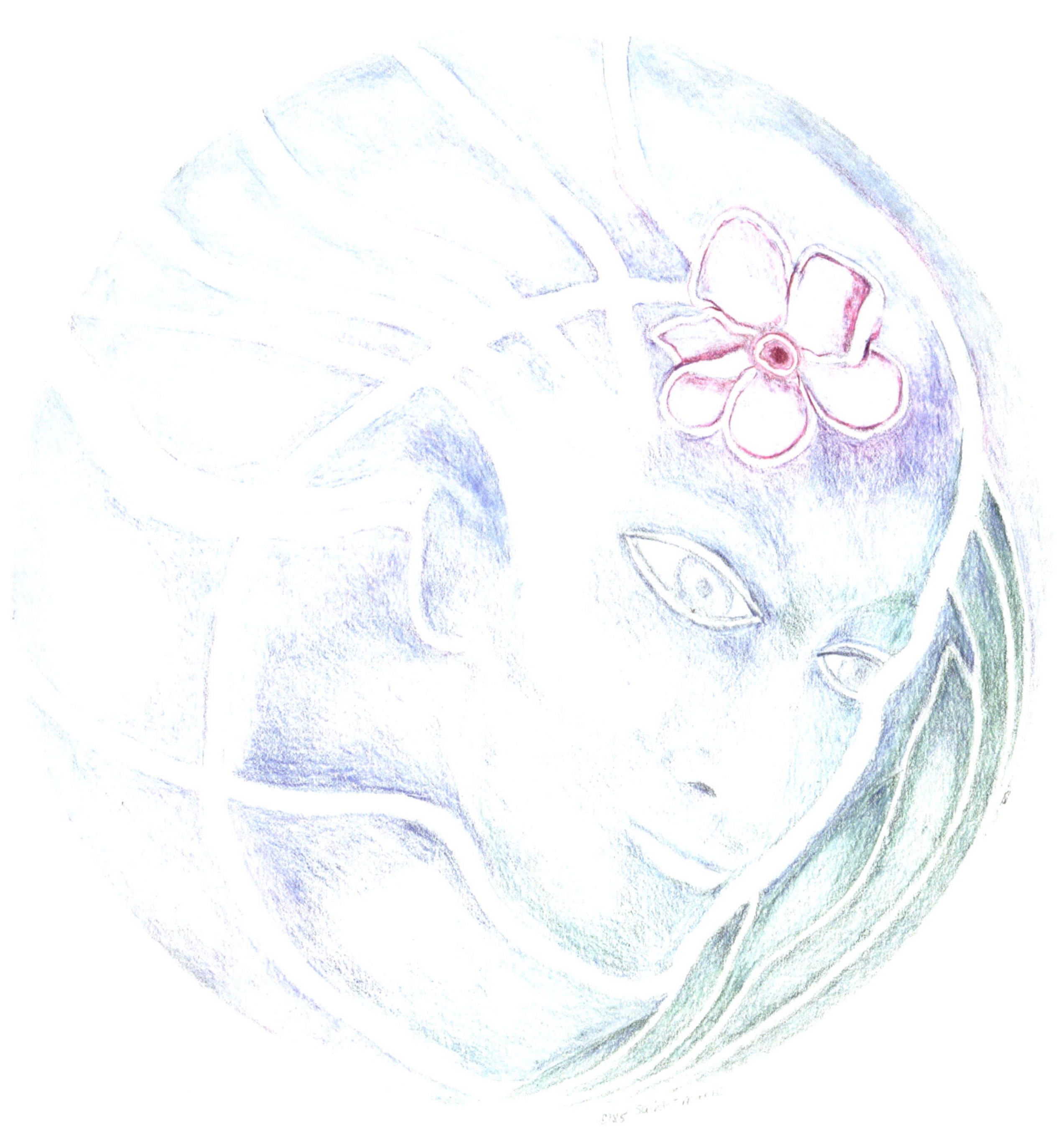

Armour of Beauty

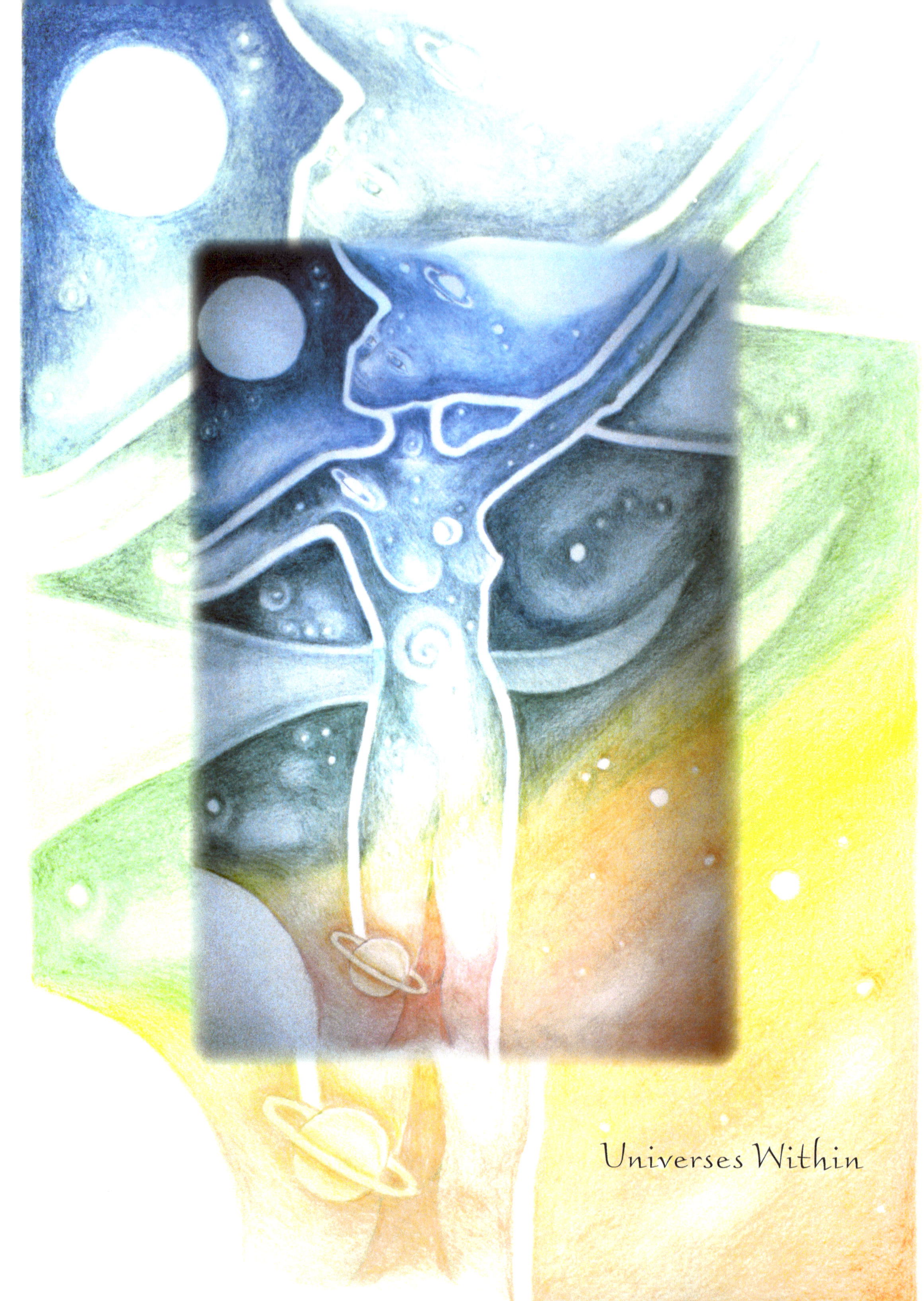
Universes Within

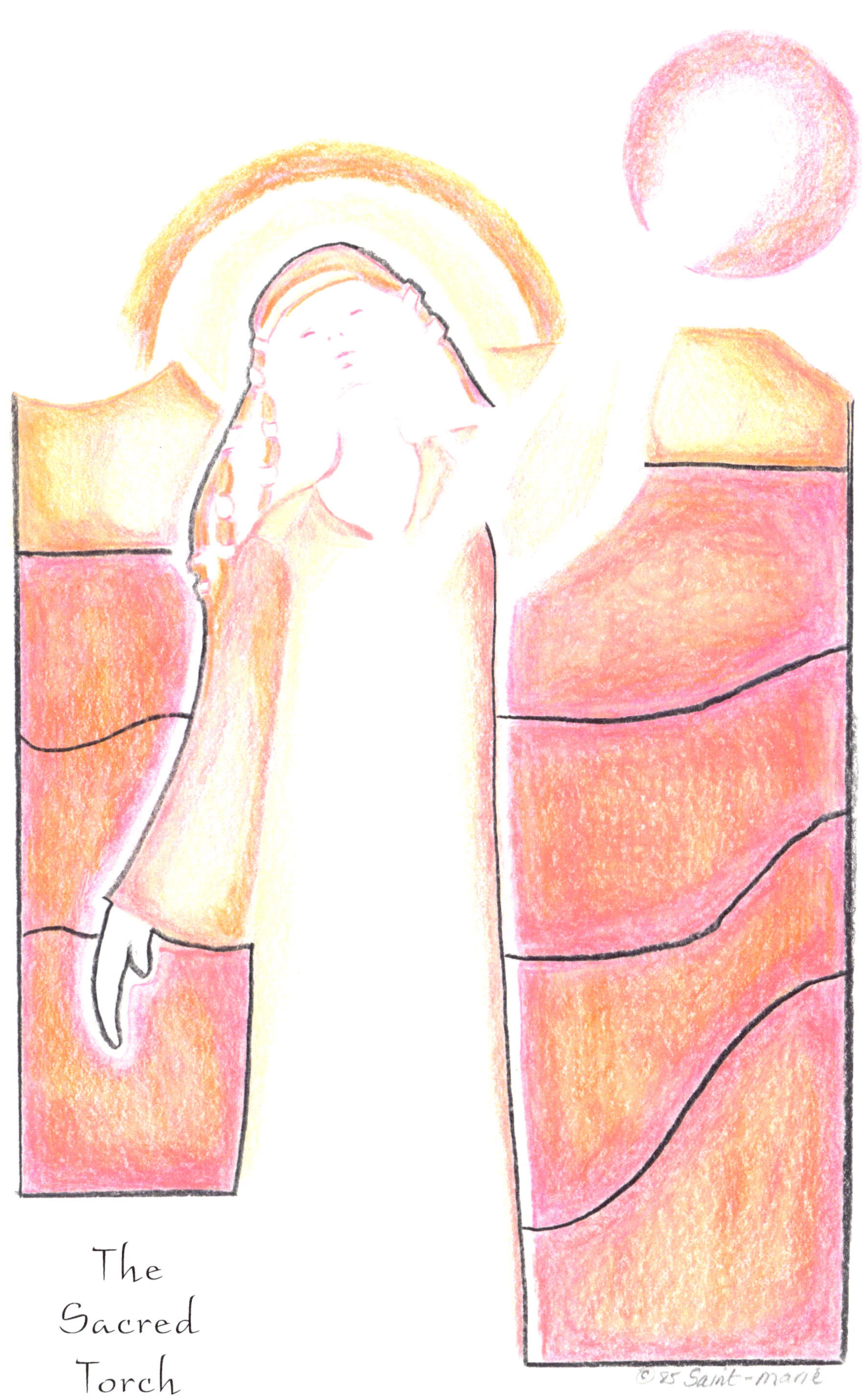

The Sacred Torch

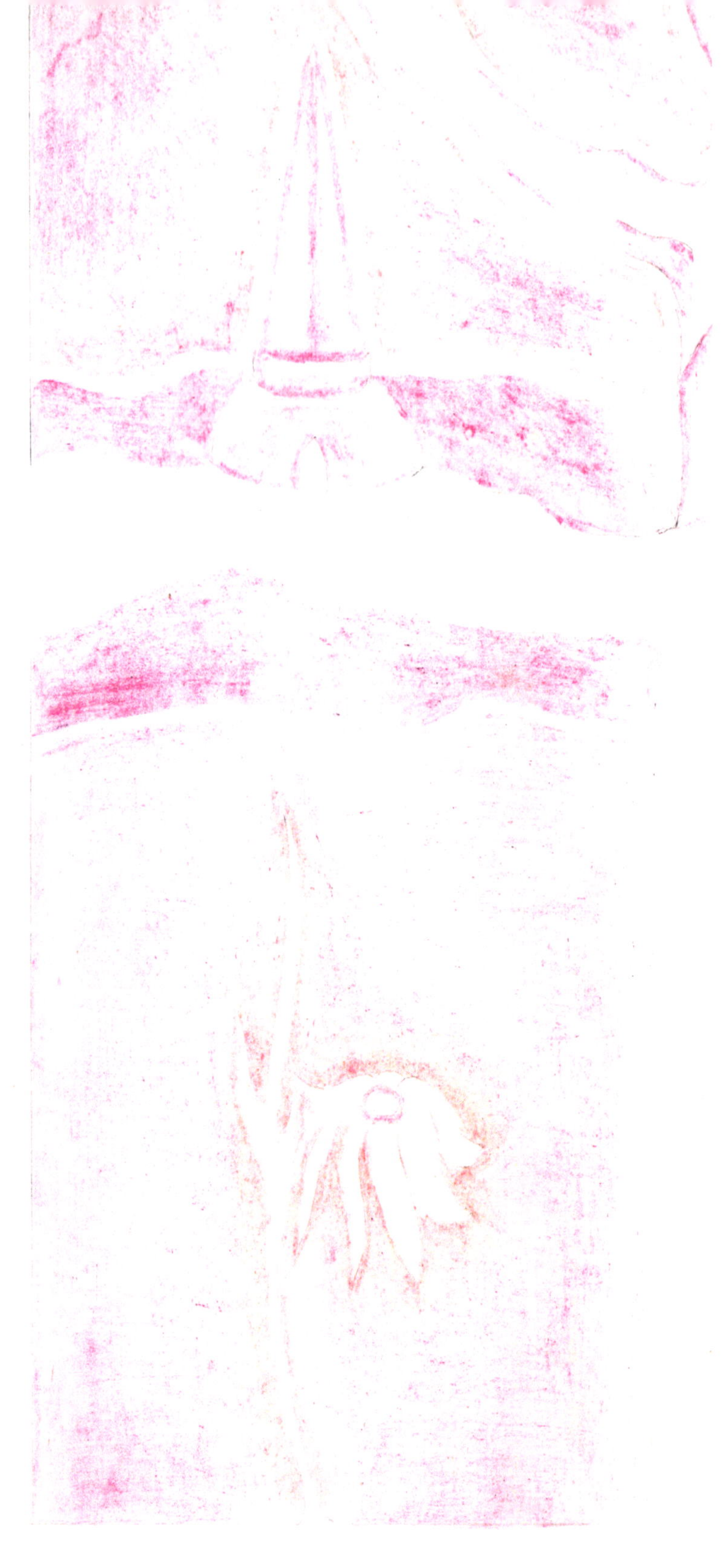

Temples of the Infinite

Presence Lights the Way

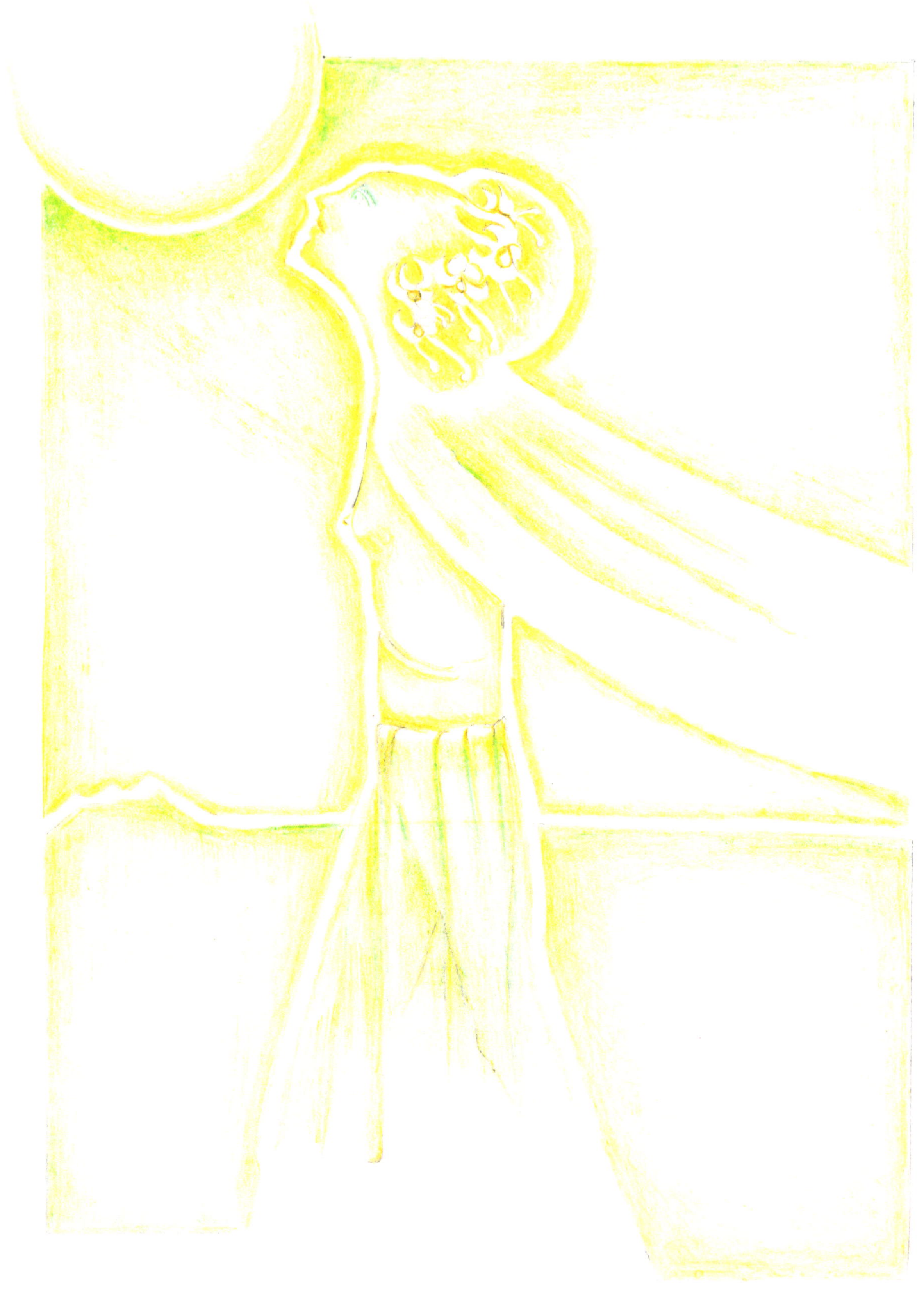

In You, I Am Free

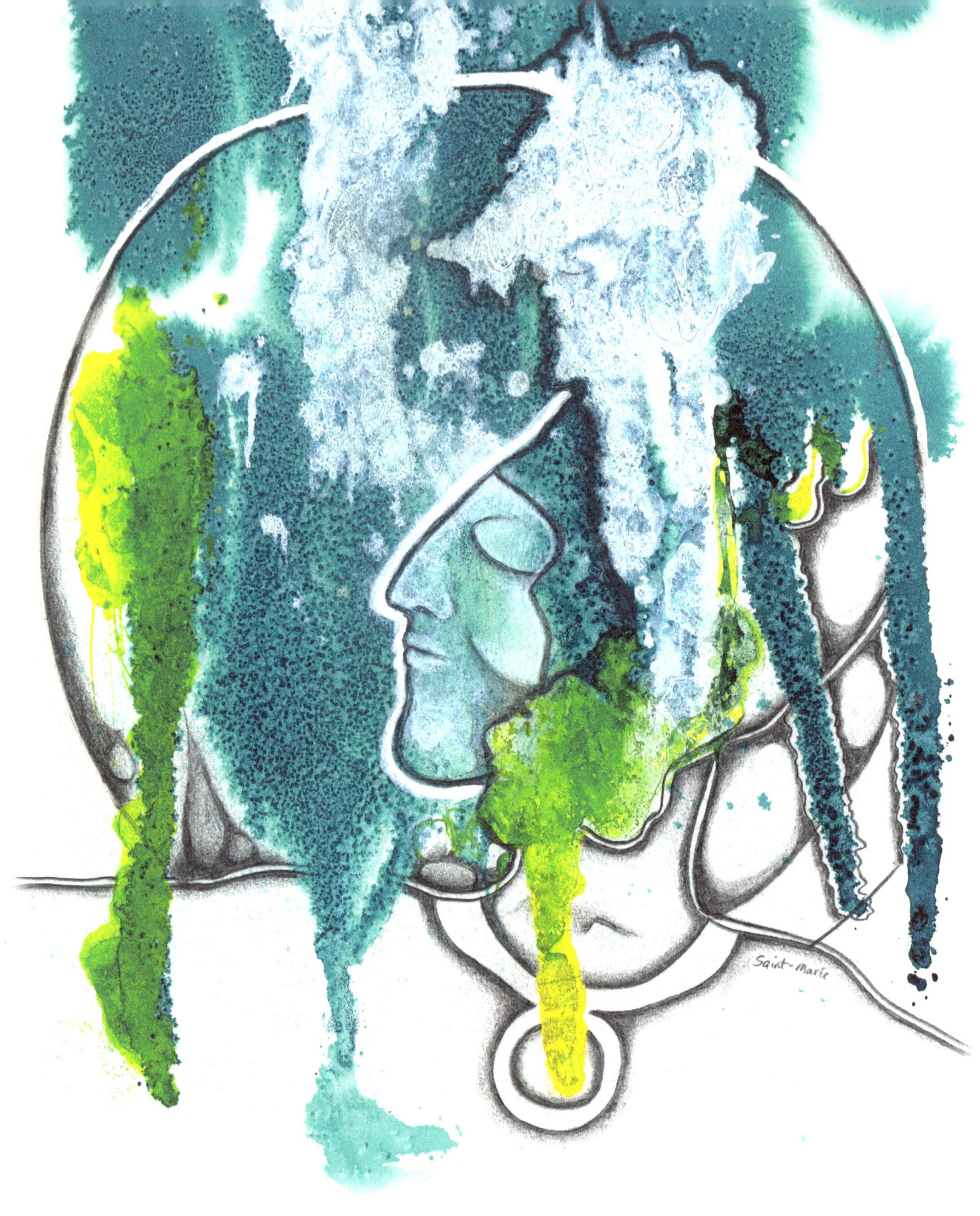

Ancient face

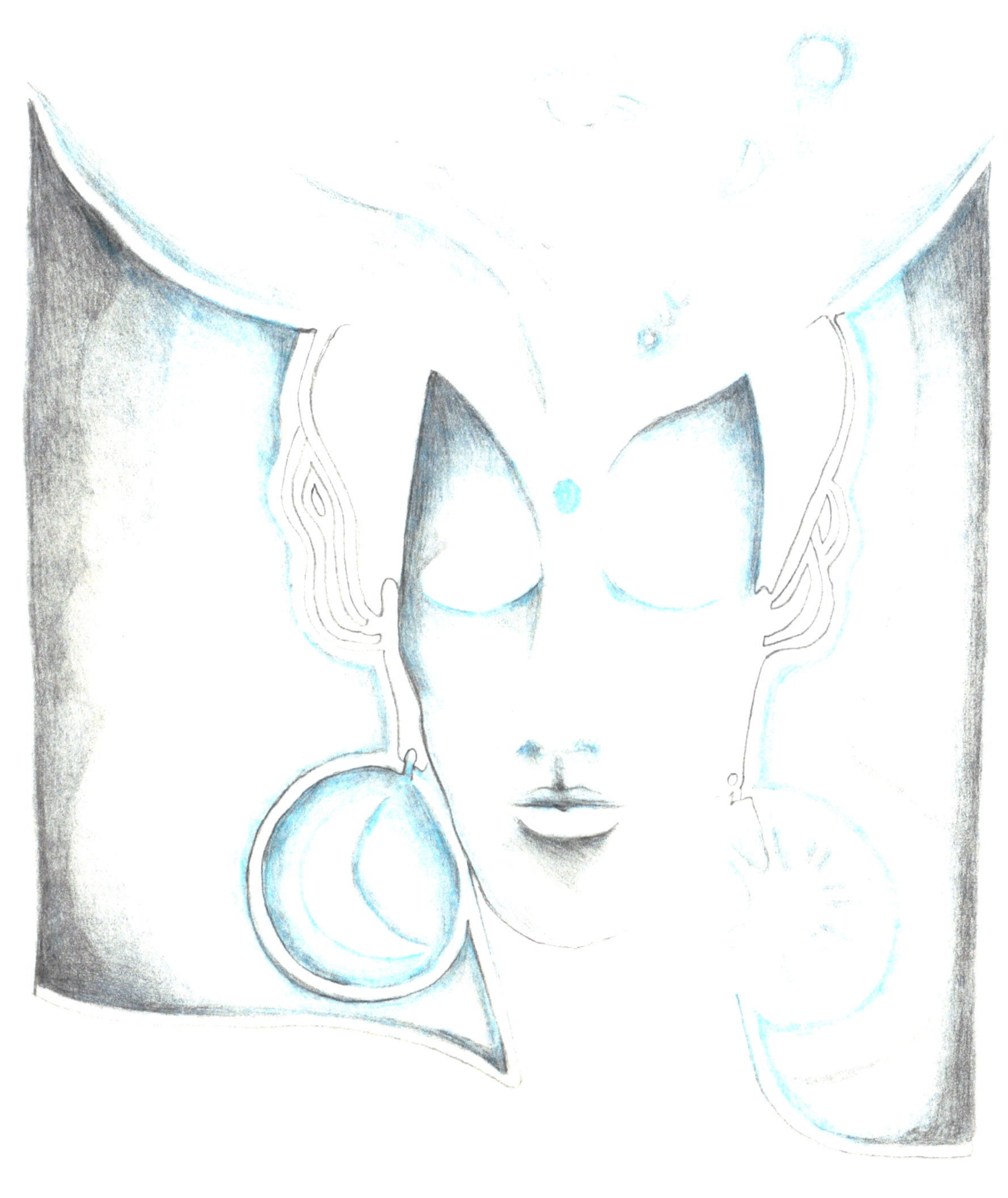

To Engage in YA-Land

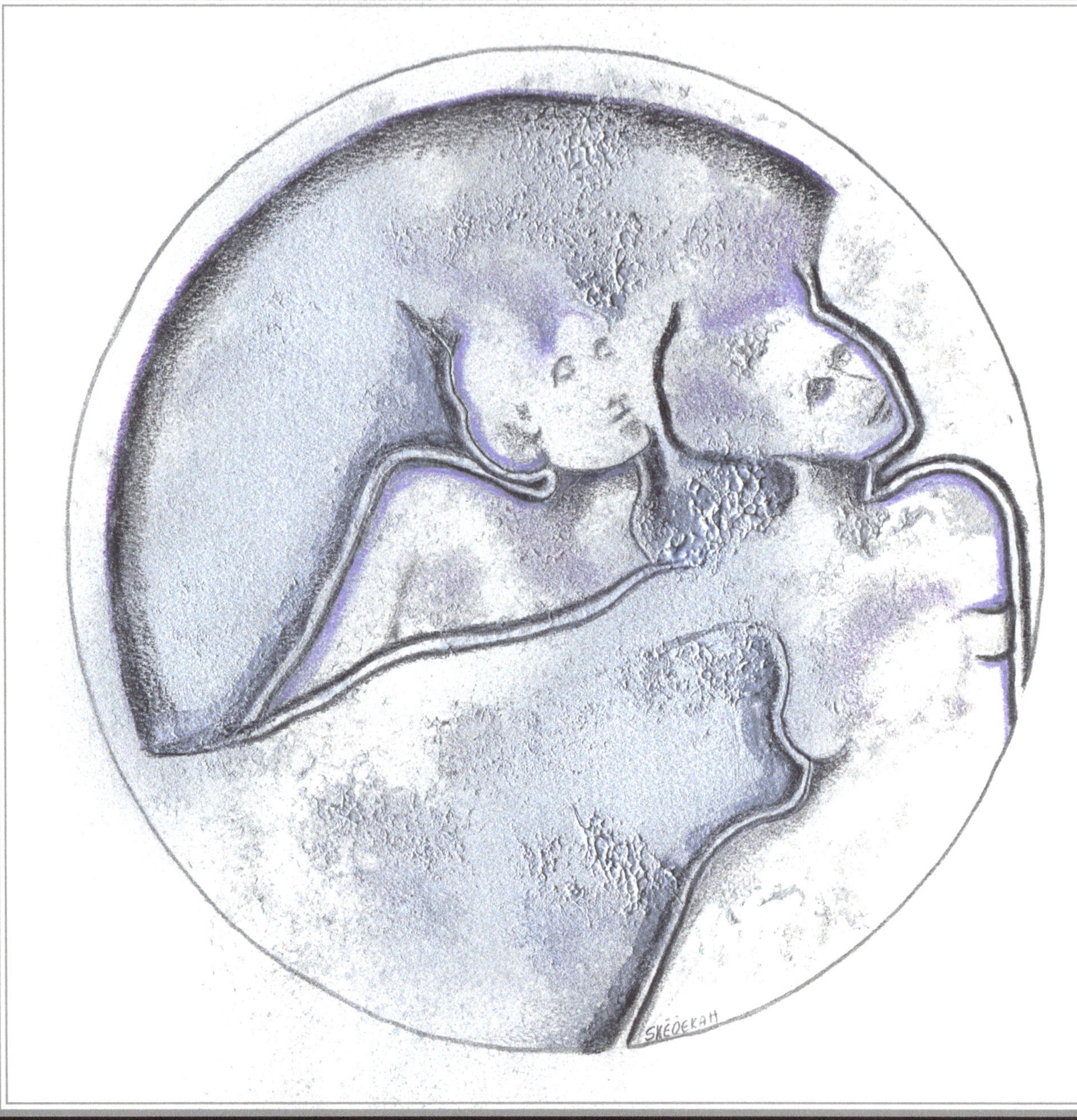

One Knowing

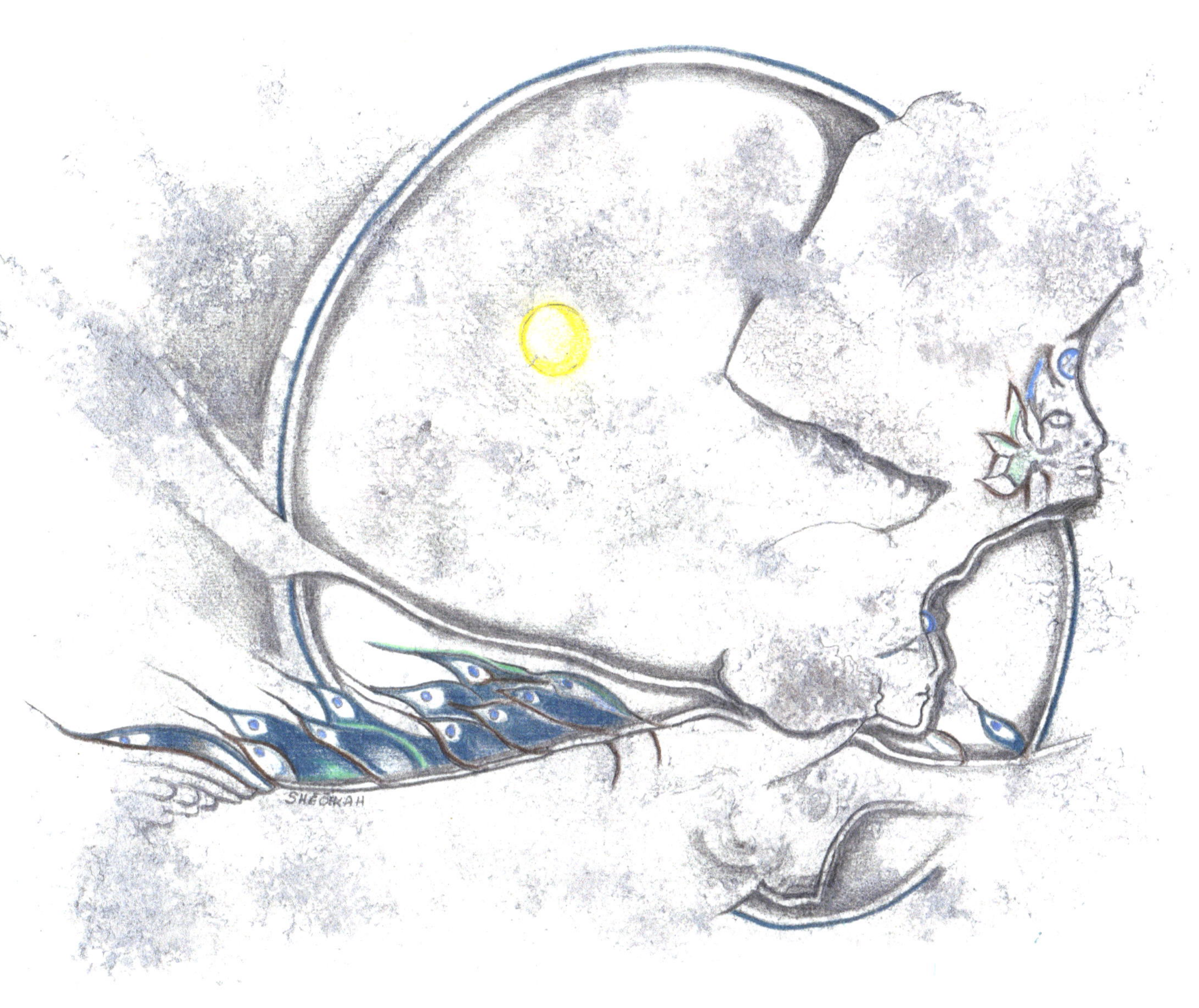

Beauty's Flight

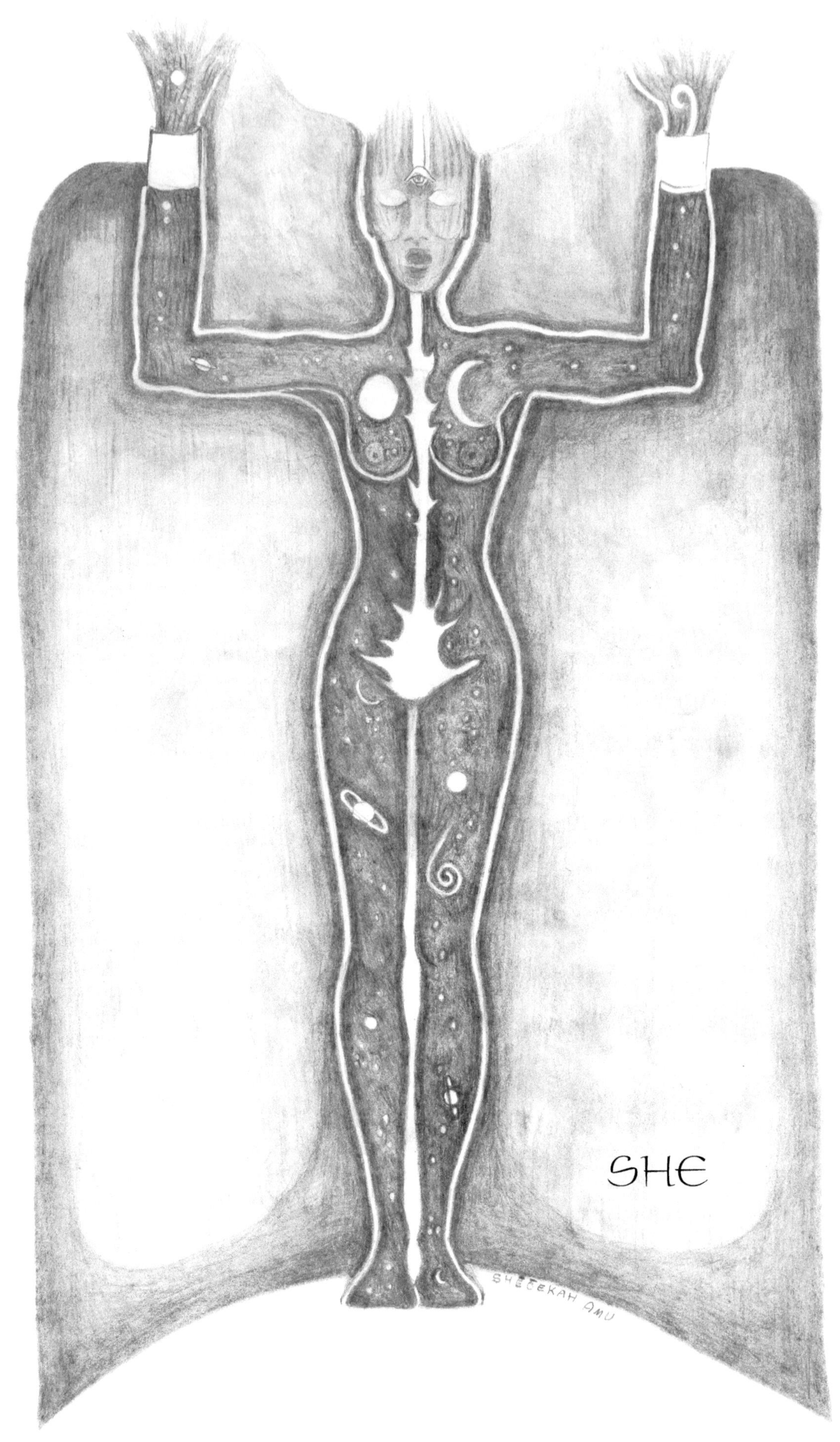
SHE

Warrior Woman

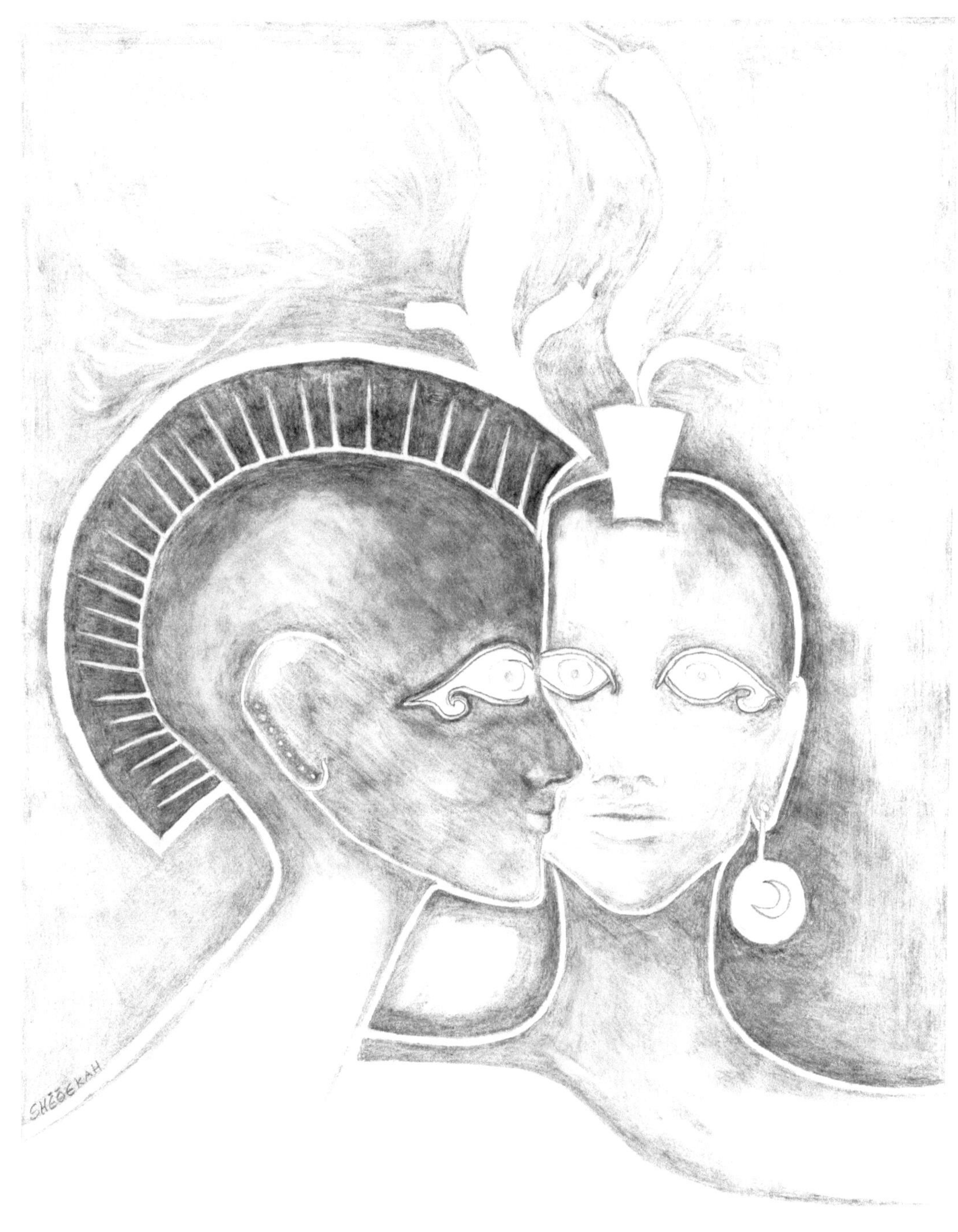

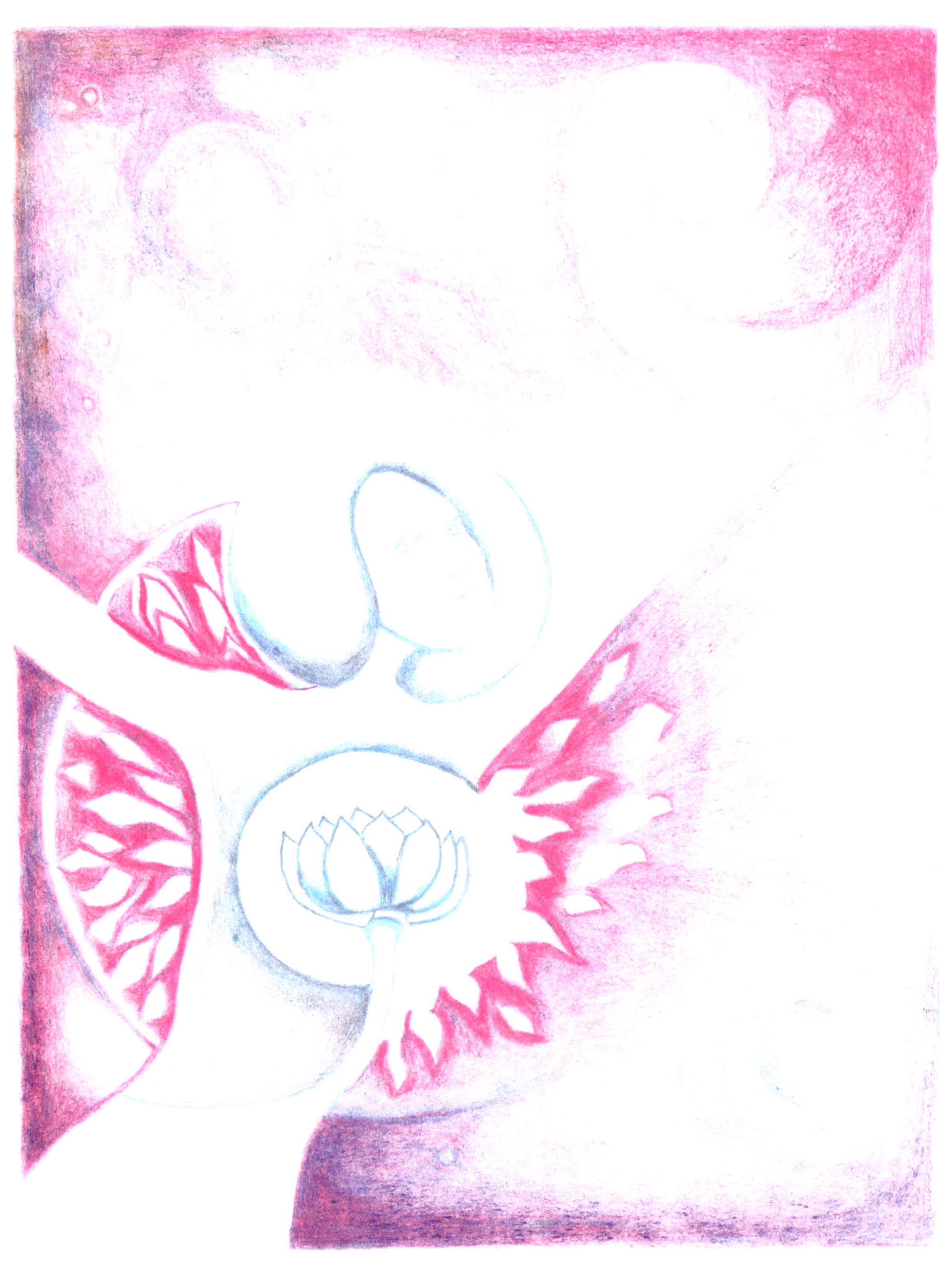

I Am Everywhere

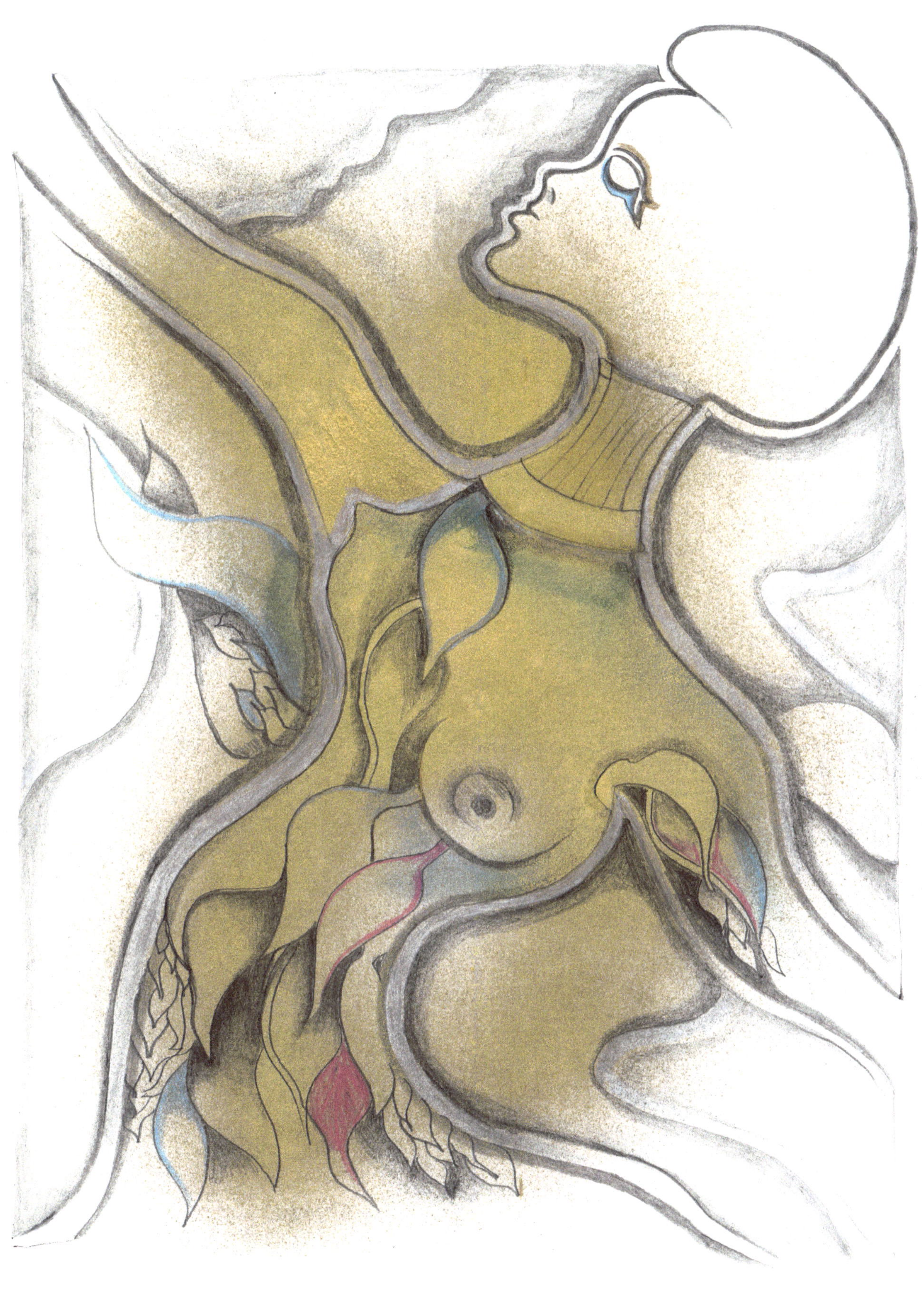

Africa frees Herself

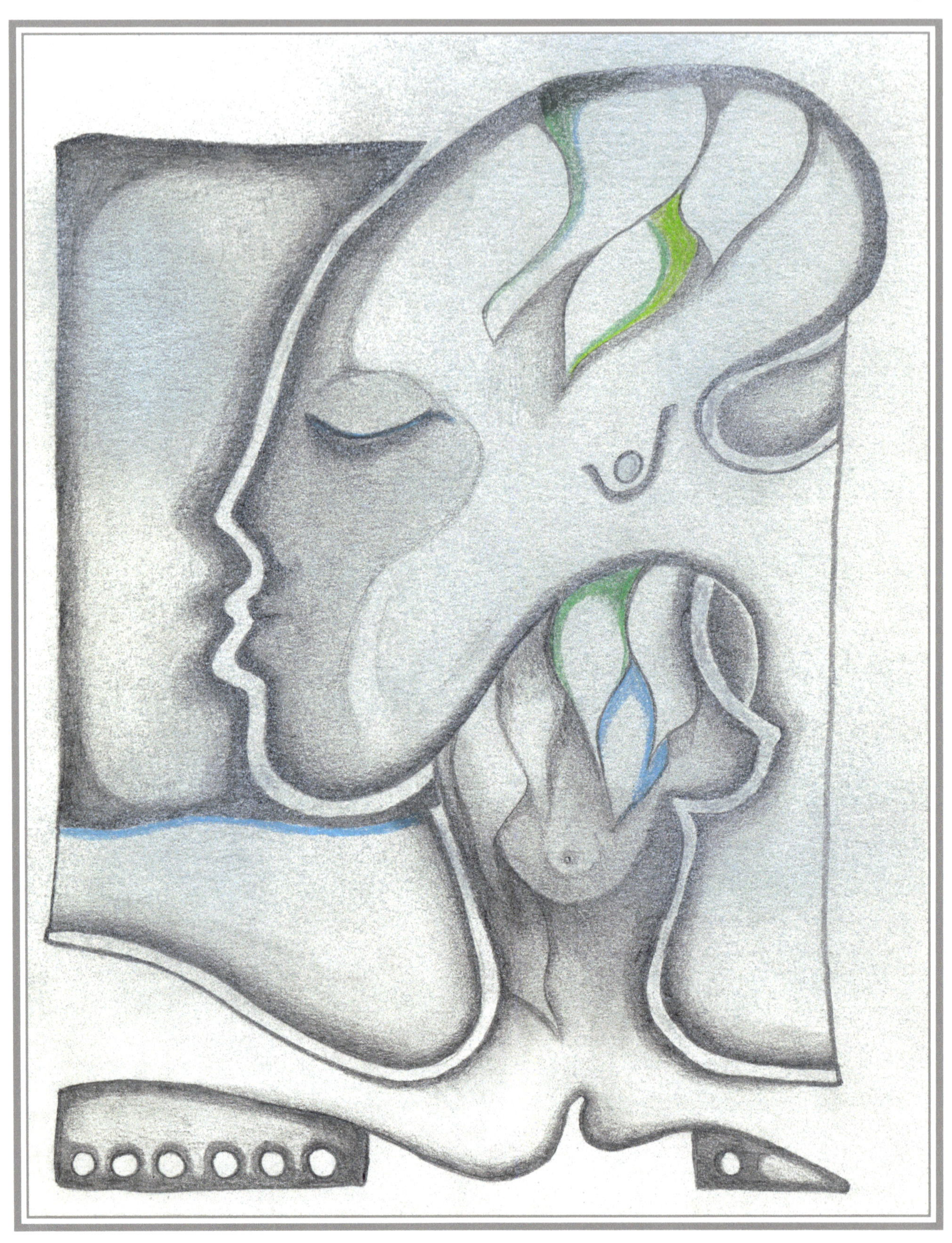

Native Knowing

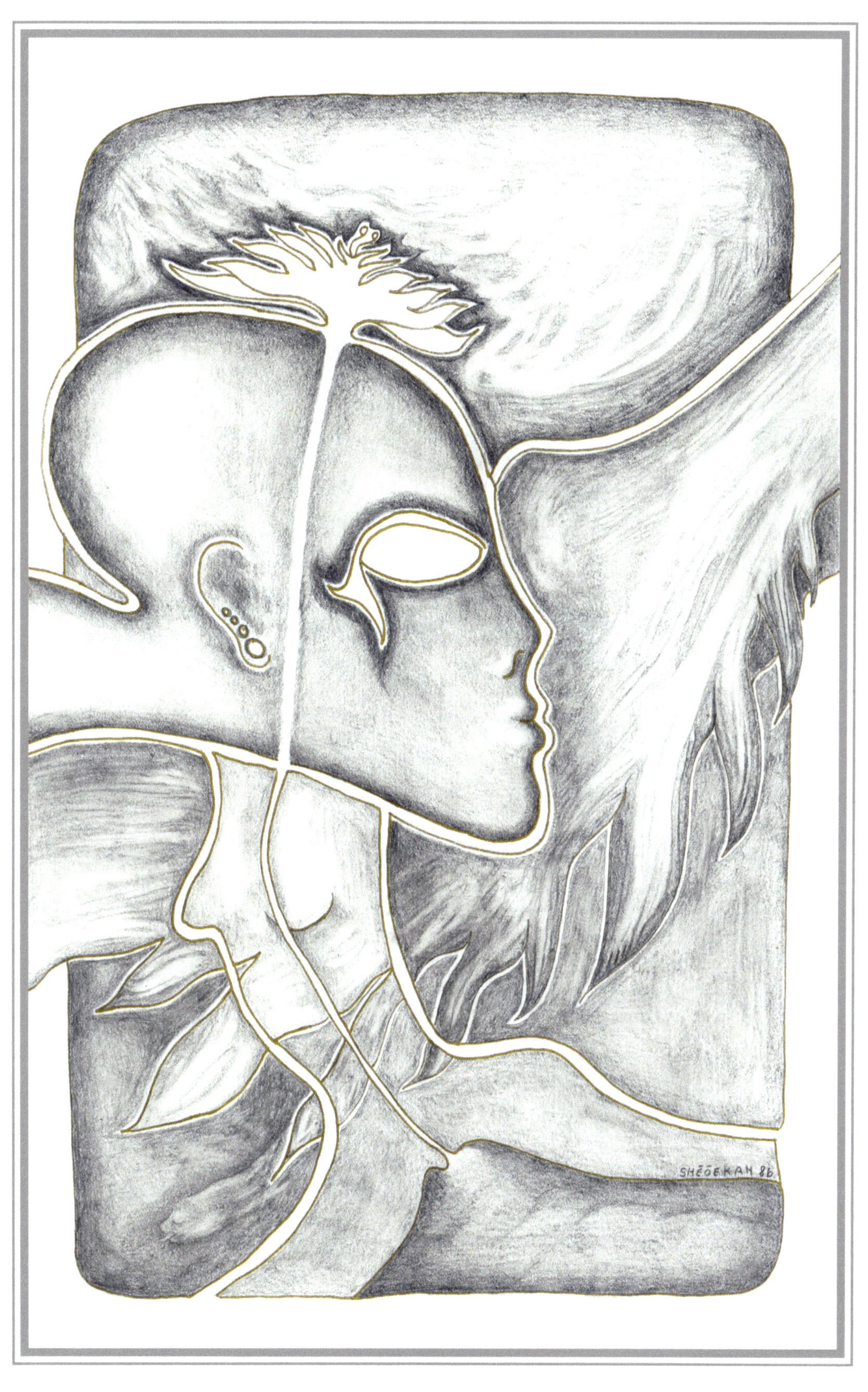

Golden Goddess

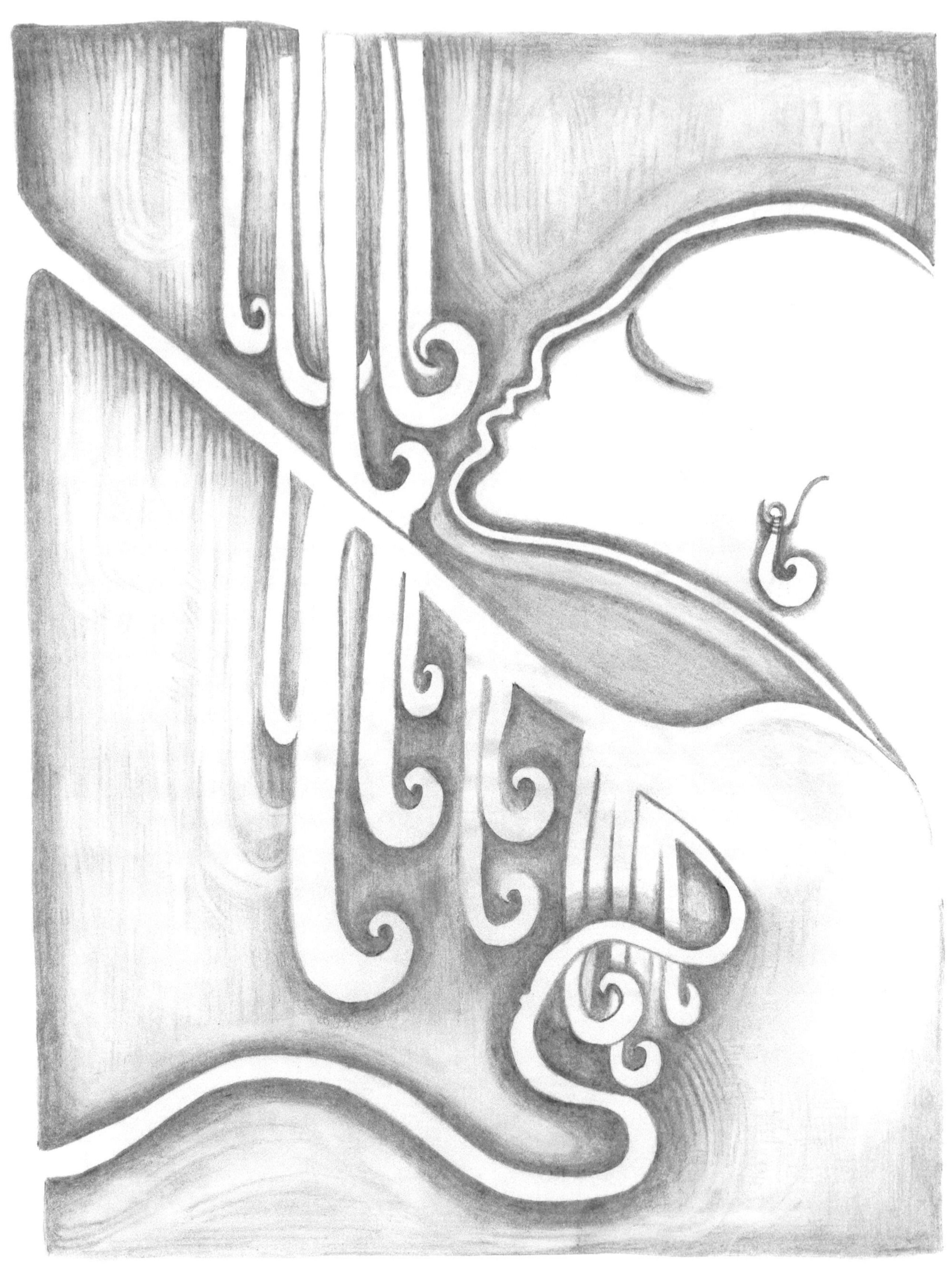

Woman of the Waterfall

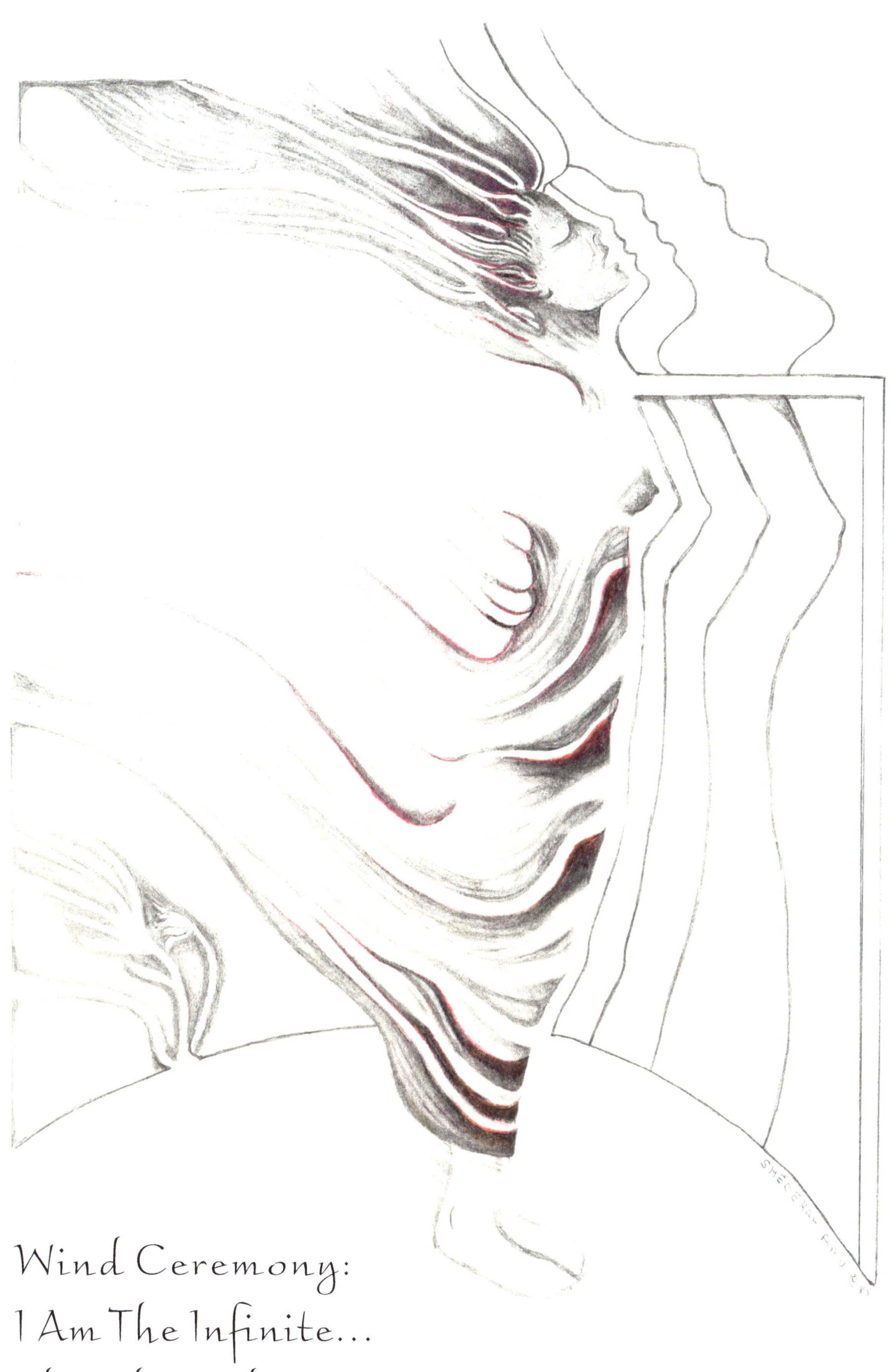

Wind Ceremony:
I Am The Infinite...
Play through Me...

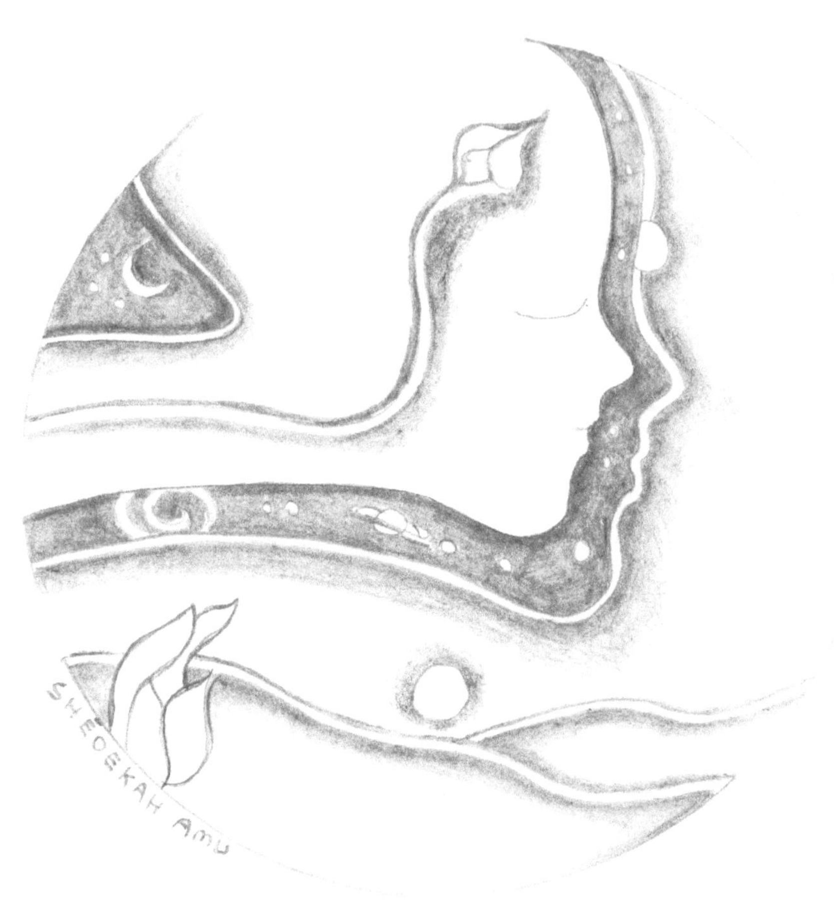

In form, I Am

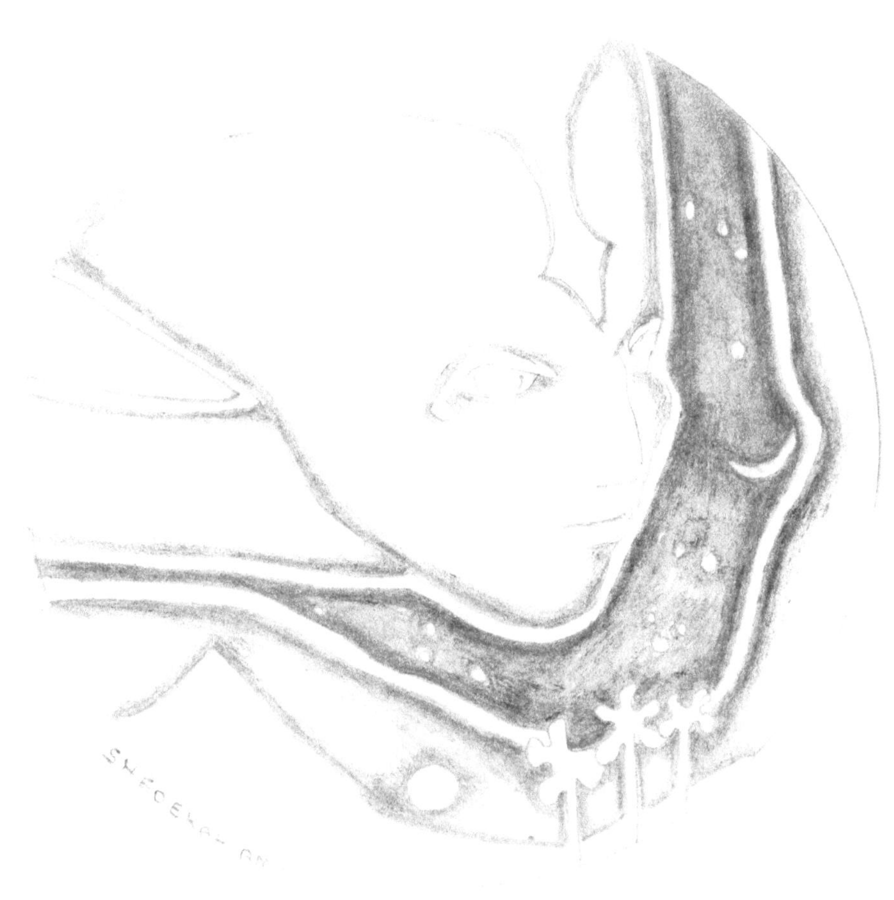

Come

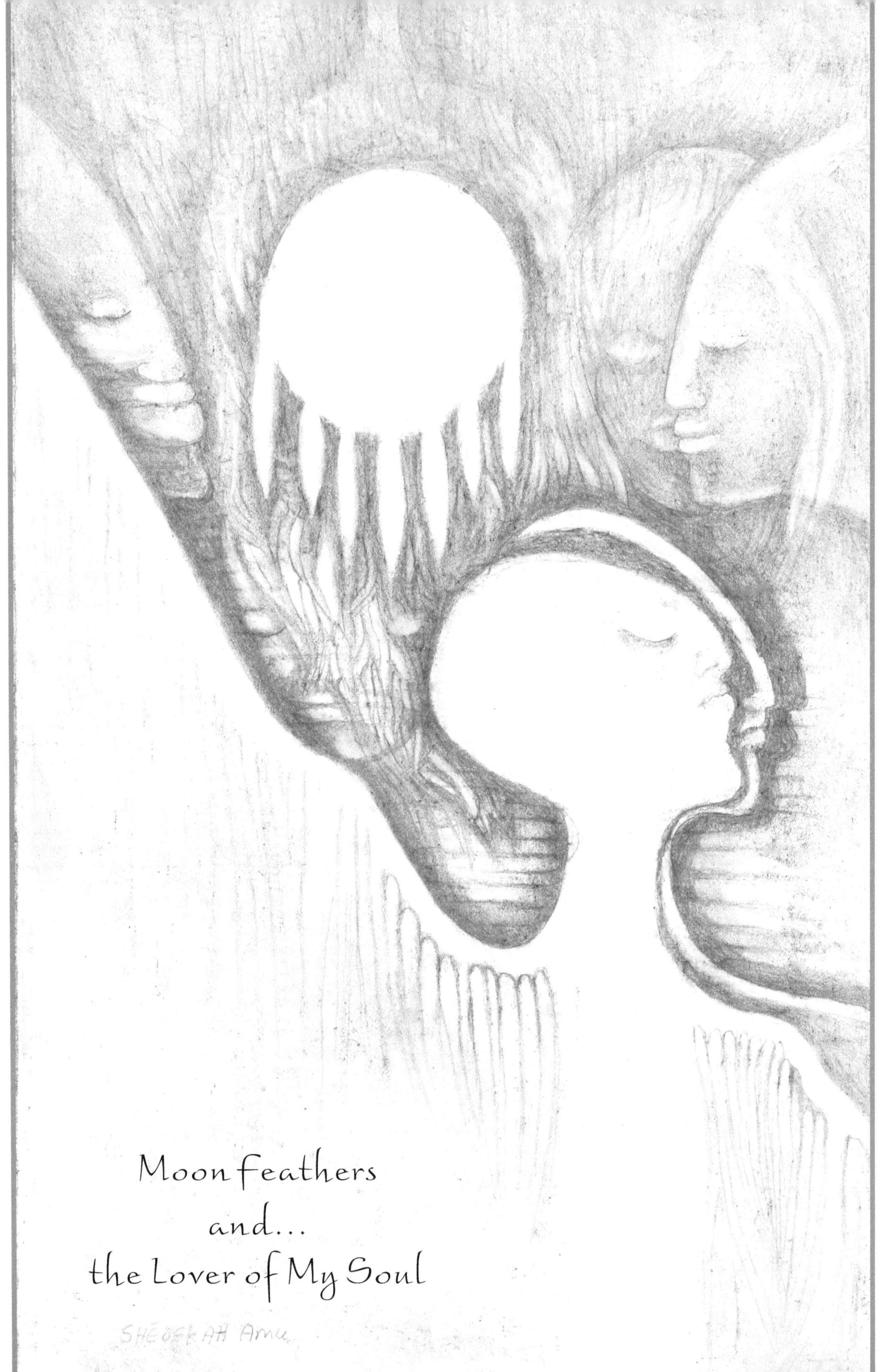
Moon feathers
and...
the Lover of My Soul

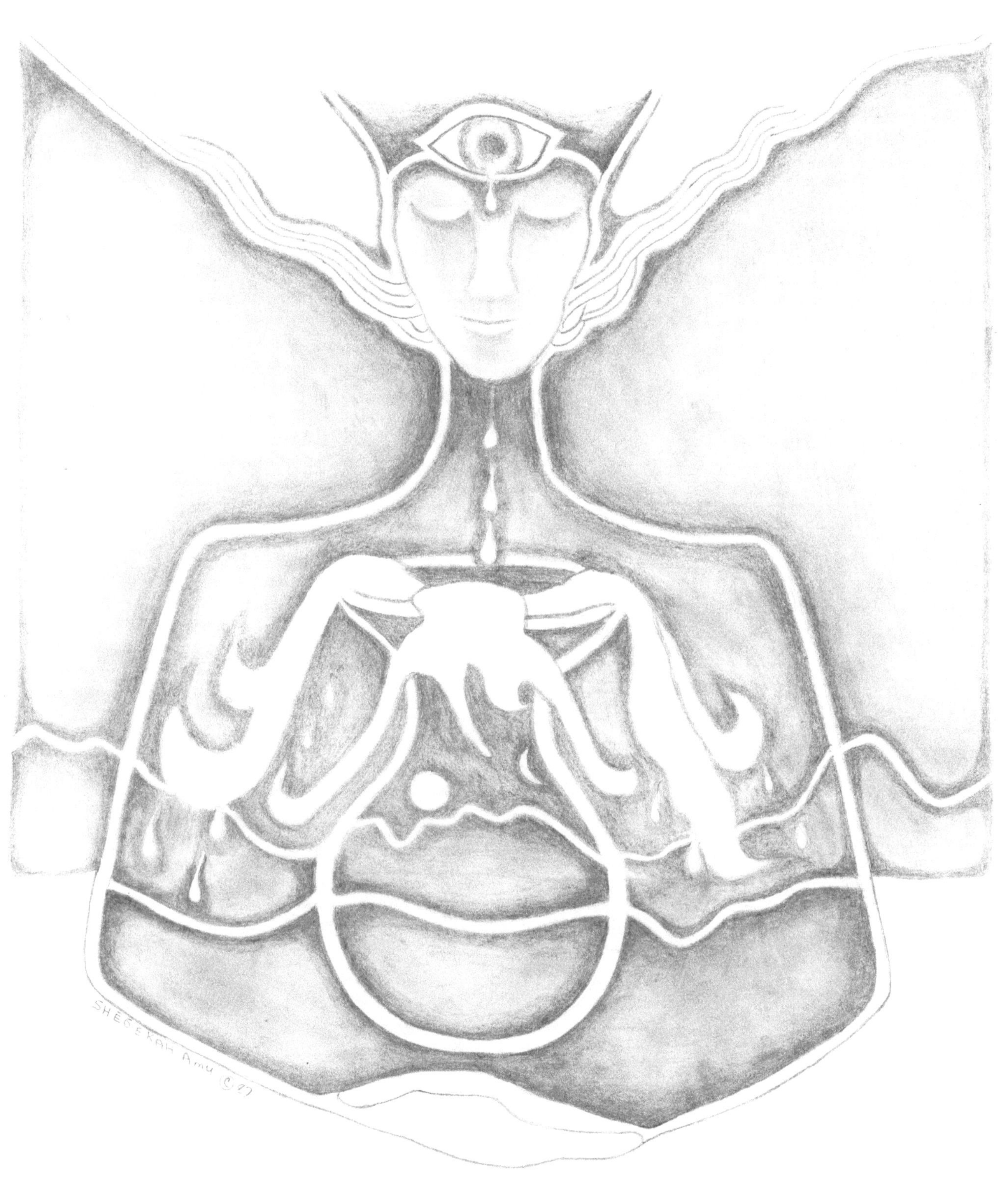

The Urn Ceremony

fire-
dancers

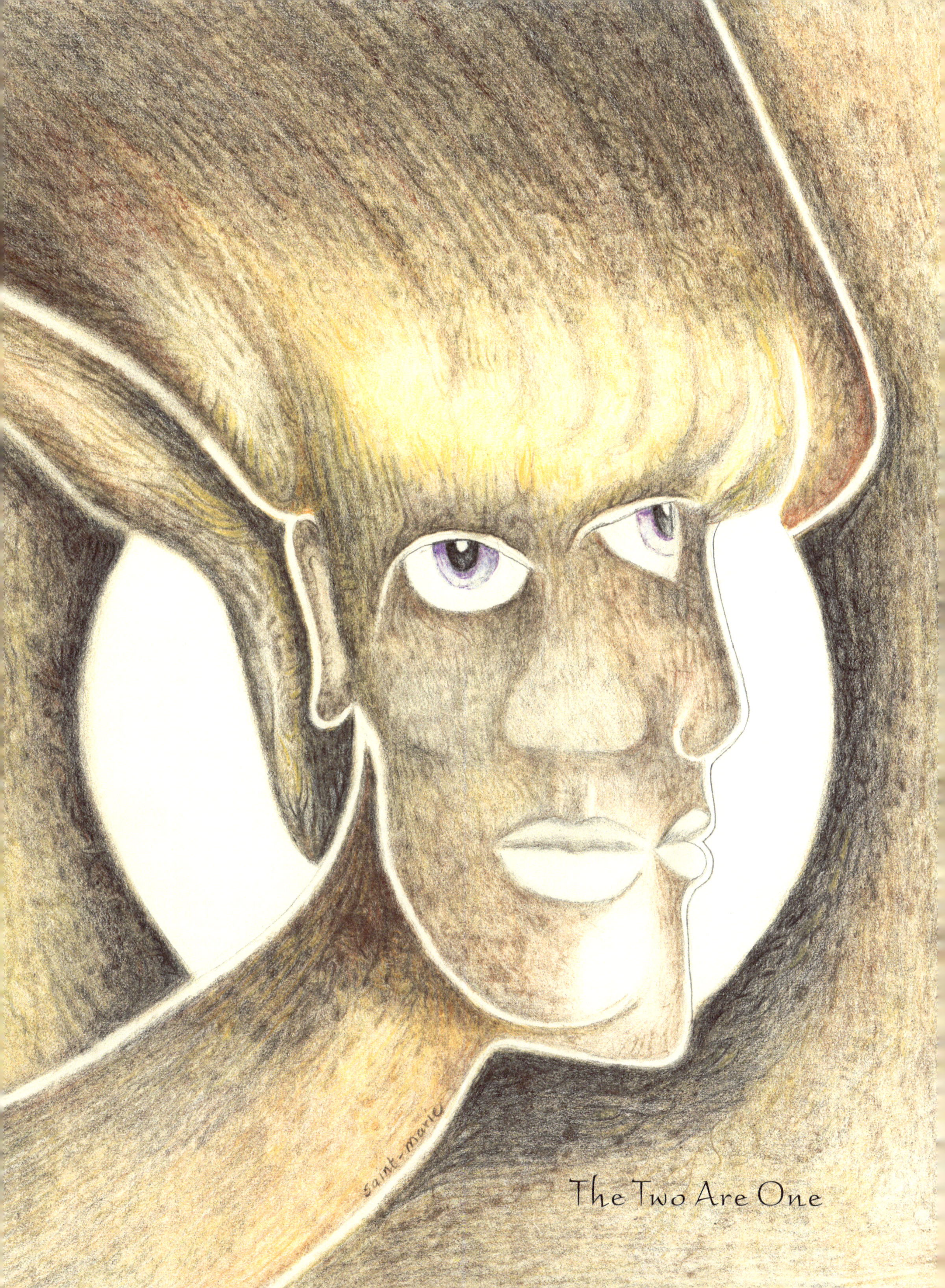

The Two Are One

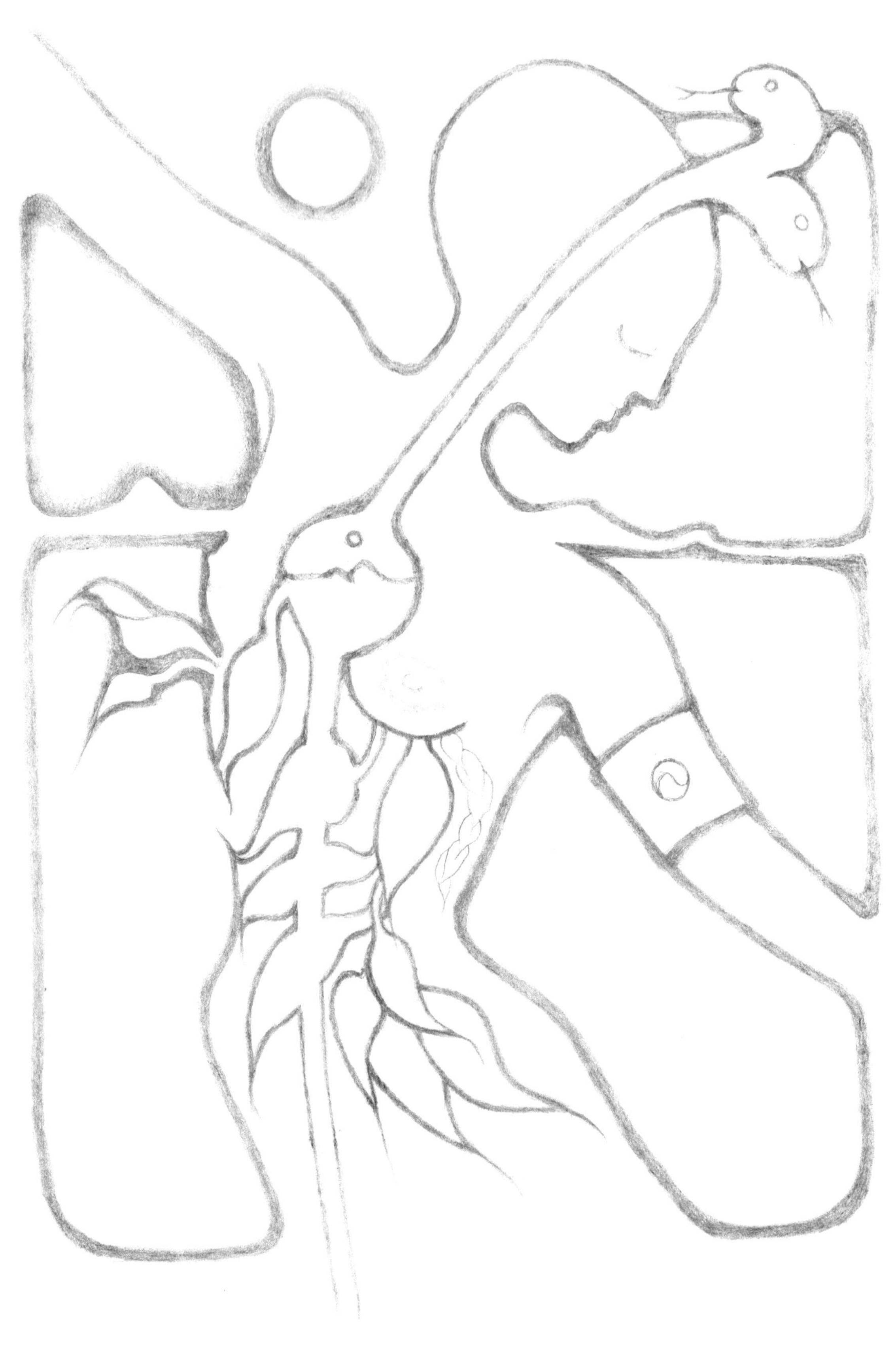

Creation-Dance of the New Way

The Image of Infinity

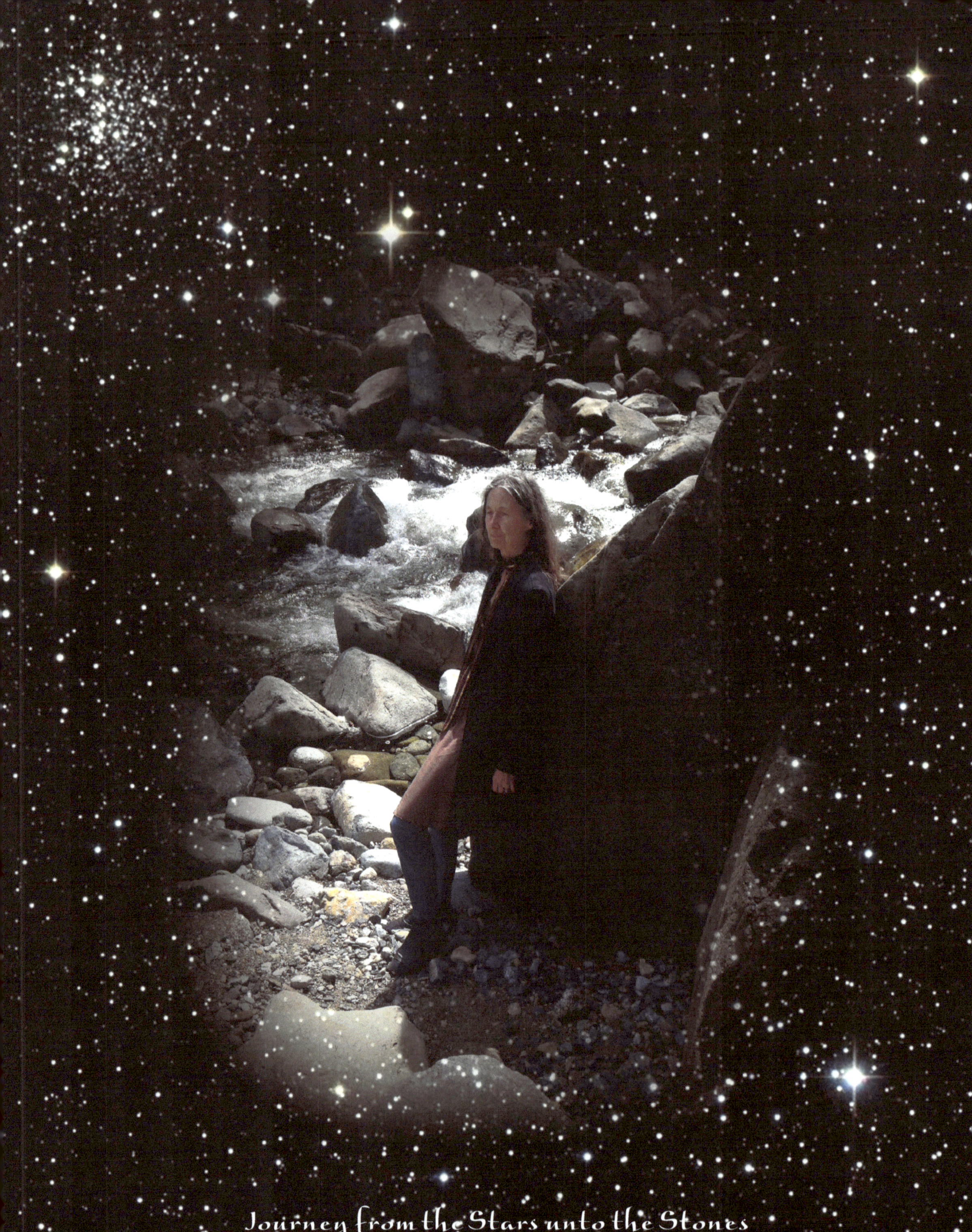

Journey from the Stars unto the Stones

Artist, Writer, and Spiritual Educator

Mary Saint-Marie, artist, writer and spiritual educator, has traveled extensively showing her art. She began to pioneer visionary art in 1972 in three Salem, Oregon art exhibits. Her body of spiritual Art of the Soul has been viewed and collected in the U.S., in over one hundred and fifty exhibits. Mary has exhibited in galleries, workshops, expositions, holistic faires, conferences, symposiums and spiritual centers. It has been shown and collected in Europe, as well.

The visionary and sacred art exhibits reveal the Invisible AS the visible. The Formless AS the formed. Mary reveals the delicate balance of earth and sky and the HE and SHE of Creation. The balance of the One. Mary expresses and reflects from both her experiences as well as from the Withinness.

A near death experience and numerous revelations and visions in meditation revealed the deeper Realm of the Real, the Soul Realm and life as pure I AM Awareness. All of this has become a part of the sacred art.

Mary's body of work houses the awareness of the sacred. Her intent is to reveal the inner Essence as Beauty. As the One Life.

This Art of the Soul has appeared on calendars, greeting cards, CD covers, books and magazines. Quest, Mystic Pop, Anemone, Dream Network Journal and Crone Chronicles have all featured Mary's art. Mary's art is also in the books, *One Source Sacred Journey*, a collection of 44 international visionary artists, as well as *Songs from the Edge of Everything* and *The Ways of Spirit*. The visionary art has appeared on numerous TV interviews, such as, Wisdom Channel and Channel 5 in San francisco. The art was also featured on television across Germany and at Bridging Heaven and Earth TV. Most recently, Mary's art was featured in the documentary *FEMME, Women Healing the World*. It is an award-winng film about Oneness and balance.

Art of the Soul also appears on Mary's books, *The Holy Sight*, *The Monitor and Laughter of the Gods*, *Messages from the Silence*, *Nectar of Woman*, *Galactic Shamanism*, as well as two previous art books, *The Sacred Two* and *The Star-Stone Ones*. The mystic art was also the main focus of her multi-media sacred enactment, *SHE...it is... who Remembers*, for 8 years. The art is seen on Mary's cds, *Journey of Consciousness* and *Soul Sounds for World Birth*.

Mary is continually inspired to create using new forms. After the pen and ink, airbrush, pencil, charcoal and Prismacolor phases of creating, Mary moved into multi-media on paper. She allowed the process to be revealed from within. Simultaneously she then began sculpting small pieces of altar art. These ceremonial and one of a kind sacred and infused figures remind ones of the sacred in everything. The Oneness. They reflect Life as Living Ceremony.

Mary also wrote a play, while on retreat for a weekend. It arose spontaneously from a dream, with no planning. She had no training in writing a play. It was a total surprise and a gift. While it is now available in book form, it began its life as a play. Sacred theatre.

The play, *The Monitor and Laughter of the Gods: Saraswati Comes Swingin' Her Hips*, was produced by Mary, in co-creation with many deeply inspired and gifted actors, dancers, directors, chanters and many other ones.

Mary's most recent creation is an Animation Meditation (video): *Holy Sight for the Earth and for the Sky*. In this one minute animation (see websites or YouTube), there is art, narration, soul sounding and a photo of the earth. An art designer put the art and photo together. A sound engineer recorded the narration and merged with soul sounding. The animator brought all the artistic elements together in one powerful transcendent minute to invite realization or remembrance of The One Illumined Self that we are. (credits on YouTube)

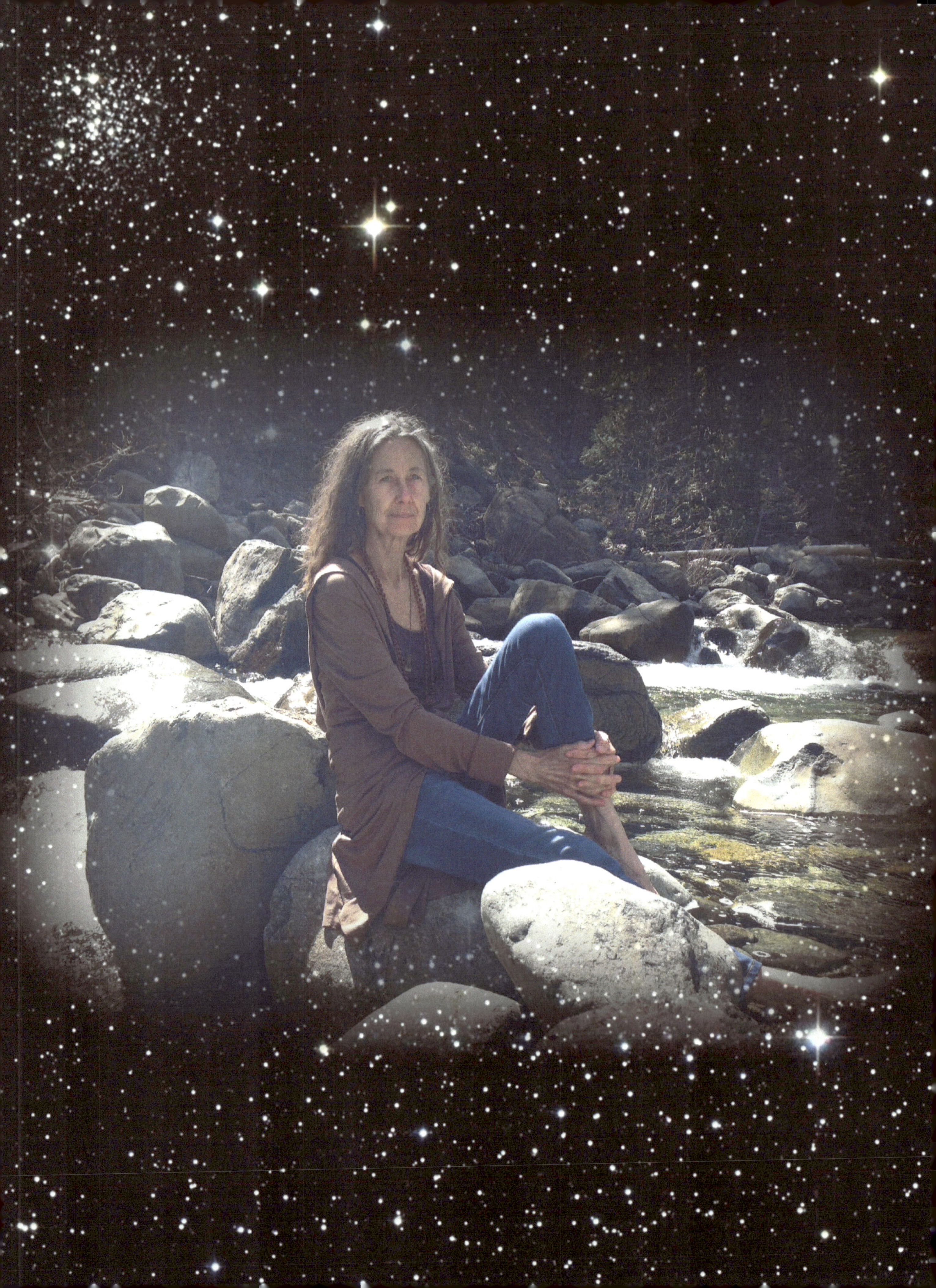

Biography and Education

Mary Saint-Marie lives close to rivers, lakes, high desert, waterfalls and a mountain of Northern California. She has mainly lived close to nature since 1974. Nature has been a teacher and companion since childhood. And both Nature and the Inner One have been her inspiration.

Formal education includes undergraduate degrees in Education and English. That was followed by eight years of teaching high school English, Mythology and Communications. Following that, Mary became an assistant coordinator in public educational television at the University of Wisconsin. There she began anew as a student in Fine Arts. Several years later, she was an instructor of English at a two year college in Oregon.

During her early adult life, Mary did not feel that she was in the right profession. She felt something more wanted expressing. There was a strong and unwavering impulse to leave teaching and begin to express through the arts.

This life in art was further catalyzed by the spontaneous soul experience/awakening during a head on collision that served as an opening to see her life via the luminous soul. Pure joy was experienced. And the experience was "more real" than the entire life lived up to that time. Following this opening, Mary was changed in many ways. She could see light (universal energy, aura) around living things. This collision provided and gifted an exalted and numinous experience. A new life was initiated.

Life as an artist began.

This led to the overland journey in Europe, the Middle East, India and Kashmir. Even Morocco. Drawing pad with Rapidograph were constant companions. Three exhibits were created on the return journey. The work sold.

That was a period before there was even a thought to make slides of the pen and ink drawings. There are no images available from this time period.

The simple drawings in this book were to follow. Drawing, as Soul Expression, became part of the spiritual path. Simple. Direct. Innocent. These expressions allowed a sense of dedication and devotion to the Christ Presence (by whatever name). They provided a way to contemplate the Infinite for long periods and to open to receive inspirations, revelations and illumined joy. Grace. For through this expression, Mary opened. And a flow began.

Mary did not turn to the commercial art world as a model for life as an artist. She continued opening to be a transparency through which to express sacred vision, awareness, joy.

The simple, almost childlike, and innocent drawings in this book became the foundation for this series of multi-media art and the altar art sculpture that began to come through in the mid-eighties. And the varied expressions that began when poems, books, two cds and a play began to flow through.

"We are all the One Self. As we attune to that, we need no mediums or intermediaries to listen for us. We are all potential transparencies for the One Divine Self. And in the art expressions, we may 'feel' that Self and we may allow it."

Mary Saint-Marie/Sheoekah

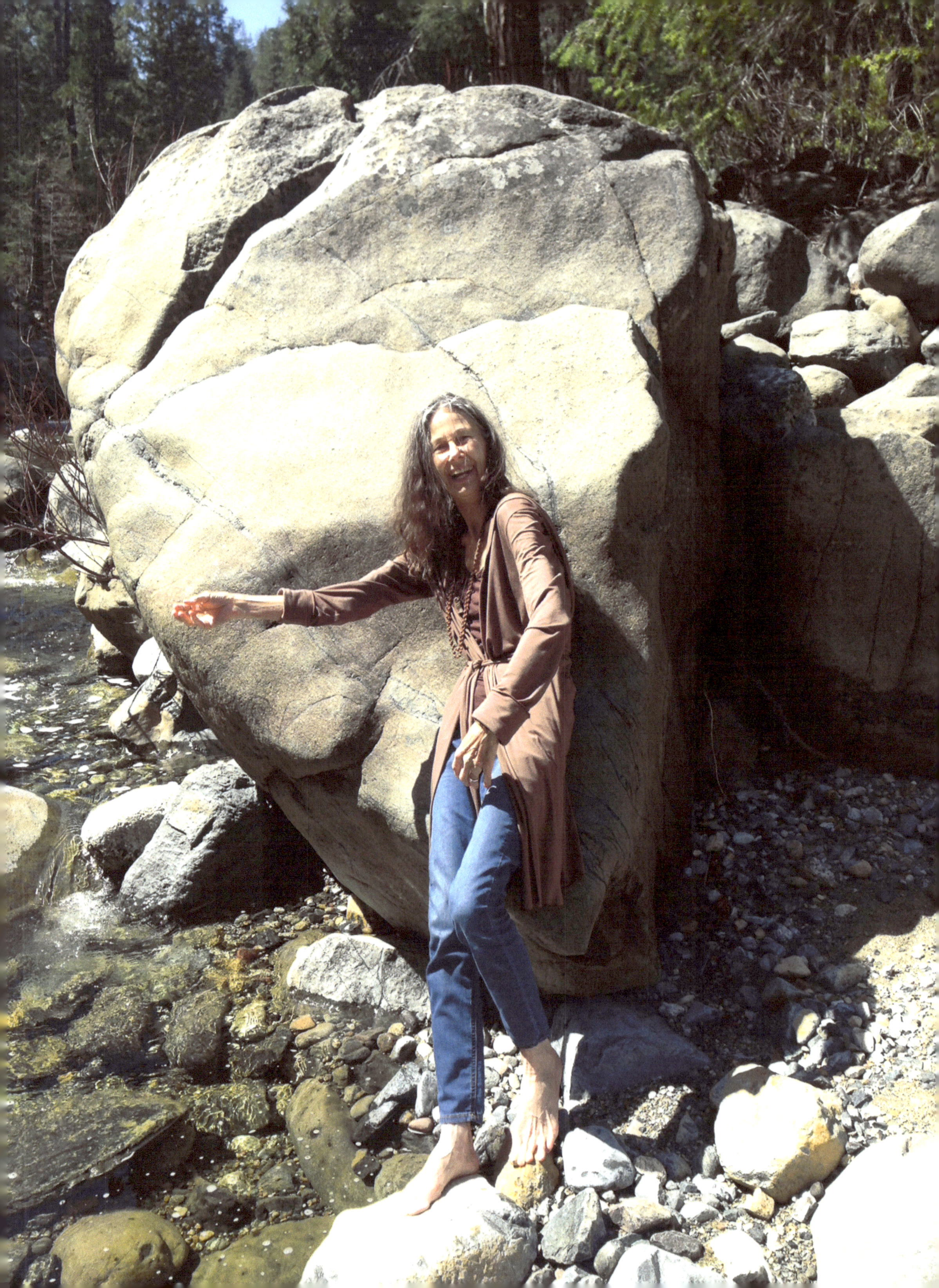

Art, Books, CDs, Soul Sessions and Soul Retreats

www.MarySaintMarie.com
www.EarthCareGlobalTV.com

Art:

All art in Art as Consciousness is available as giclee fine art reproductions.

Inquire to find out if pieces are available as originals.

Please email to find the names of current gallery showings.

*See the website to view videos/YouTubes with art.

Books:

The Holy Sight
The Sacred Two
The Star-Stone Ones
The Animating Presence
The Monitor and Laughter of the Gods, a play in book form
Messages from the Silence
Nectar of Woman
Galactic Shamanism

CDs:

Journey of Consciousness, a meditation
Soul Sounds of World Birth

Recording:

Return to Oneness, a recording giving Voice to the Animals and addressing Rights of Animals (will be made available as a cd)

Soul Sessions and Retreats:

*Please see the website to find out more about the spiritual education for individuals and groups. Mary works both in person and by phone.

EarthCare Global TV

Please see the website for the full vision of a profound unification of earth care.

EarthCare Global TV has as its purpose to freely educate and inspire people of the world about earth care. It serves to unify ones of like vision through communication and Vision in Action.

EarthCare Global TV sees the understanding of the Universal Law of Balance in all of nature being shared worldwide that the principle may be realized in daily life by all. The vision shares the practical understanding of the need of purity and sustainability.

*Please see the category, Internet TV, on the website, to see the listing of 220+ earth care documentaries. The documentaries are about being a Voice for the Earth. And they are education and inspiration for humanity to choose a new direction: Purity instead of pollution.

*See also the category, Videos, on website to view youtubes about the earth, created with the art of Mary Saint-Marie.

1. earth care, a short video created for The One Minute Shift, to expand awareness of the oneness of everyone, everything and everyplace.

2. *Holy Sight for the Earth and for the Sky*, an animation meditation

"Mystic art is an odyssey of vigilance."

"Mystic art is simply about
feeling the essence of life.
Feeling it unfettered of the never-ending beliefs
that arise from the belief in separation."

Mary Saint-Marie

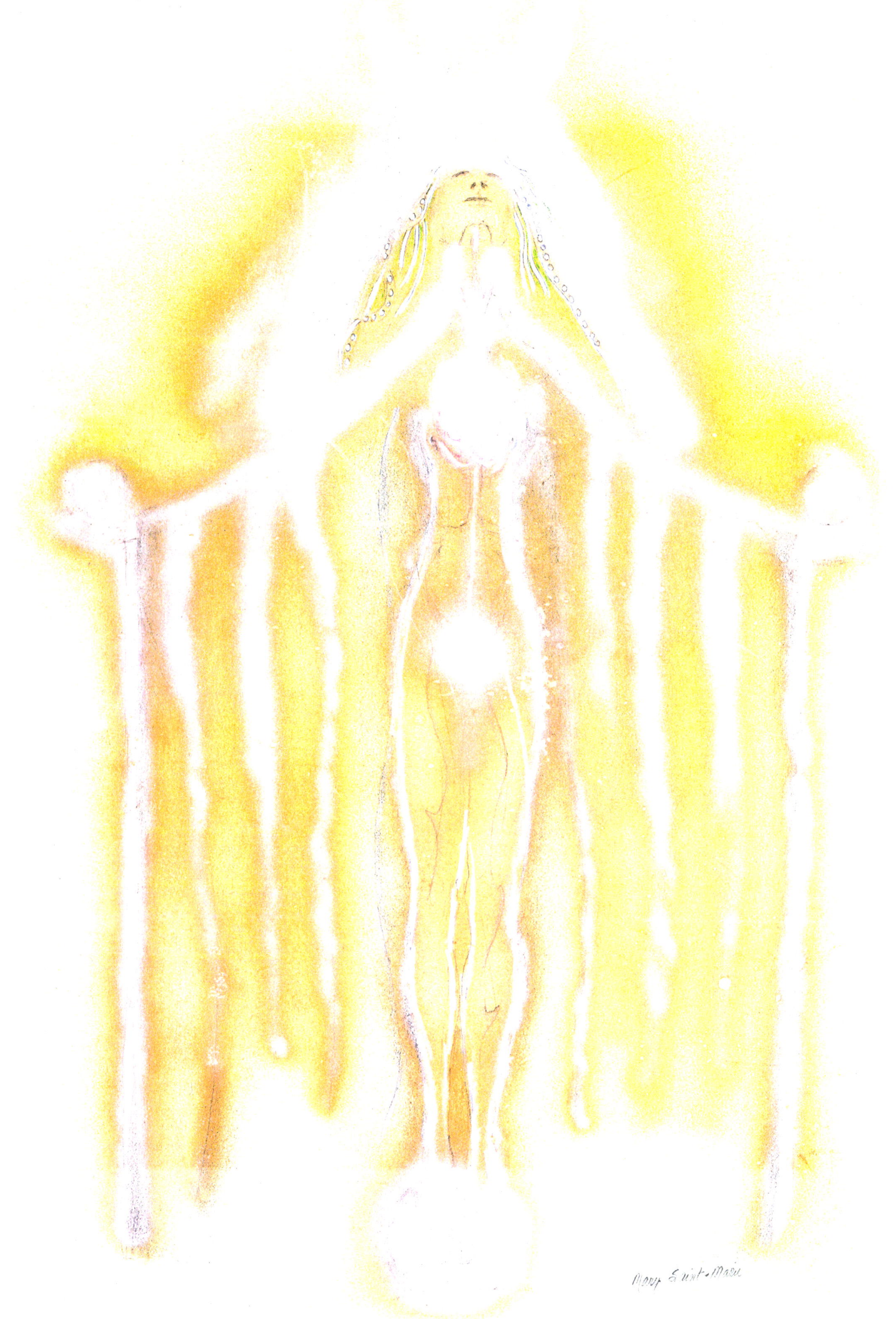

www.ingramcontent.com/pod-product-compliance
Lightning Source LLC
LaVergne TN
LVHW070118110826
845147LV00002B/152

* 9 7 8 0 9 6 4 6 5 7 2 2 9 *